African Americans by the Numbers

African Americans by the Numbers

Understanding and Interpreting Statistics on African American Life

Glenn L. Starks

 GREENWOOD™

An Imprint of ABC-CLIO, LLC
Santa Barbara, California • Denver, Colorado

Library of Congress Cataloging-in-Publication Data

Names: Starks, Glenn L., 1966– author.
Title: African Americans by the numbers : understanding and interpreting
    statistics on African American life / Glenn L. Starks.
Description: Santa Barbara, California : Greenwood, ABC-CLIO, LLC, 2017. |
    Includes bibliographical references and index.
Identifiers: LCCN 2017010831 (print) | LCCN 2017021279 (ebook) |
    ISBN 9781440845055 (ebook) | ISBN 9781440845048 (alk. paper)
Subjects: LCSH: African Americans—Population—Statistics. |
    African Americans—Statistics.
Classification: LCC E185.615 (ebook) | LCC E185.615 .S73 2017 (print) |
    DDC 305.896/073021—dc23
LC record available at https://lccn.loc.gov/2017010831

ISBN: 978-1-4408-4504-8
EISBN: 978-1-4408-4505-5

21 20 19 18 17   1 2 3 4 5

This book is also available as an eBook.

Greenwood
An Imprint of ABC-CLIO, LLC

ABC-CLIO, LLC
130 Cremona Drive, P.O. Box 1911
Santa Barbara, California 93116–1911
www.abc-clio.com

This book is printed on acid-free paper ∞

Manufactured in the United States of America

Contents

Tables   vii

Introduction   xi

    General Demographics   xii

    Fact Sheet on African Americans in the United States: 2016   xviii

    How to Navigate This Book   xxii

How to Find and Analyze Data   xxv
    Sources of Data   xxvi
    Using Data Sources   xxxi

1.   Education   1

    Education Achievement   2

    Segregated Schools   6

    Standardized Testing   12

    School-to-Prison Pipeline   13

    Disciplinary Actions   20

    Dropout Rates   23

    College Enrollment   24

2.   Health   35

    Primary Health Issues   36

    Health Insurance   37

	Obesity	42
	Diabetes	43
	Heart Disease	48
	Substance Abuse	50
3.	Crime and Criminal Justice	57
	U.S. Prison Population and Arrests	58
	Racial Profiling	61
	Violent Crimes	69
	Hate Crimes	72
	Police Shootings	74
4.	Employment	81
	Employment and Unemployment	82
	Homeownership	85
5.	Voting	91
	Voting Rates	92
	Political Party Identification	98
	Voter Disenfranchisement	99
6.	Family	109
	Traditional Family and Race	111
	Marriage	112
	Divorce	126
	Teen Pregnancy	131
	Teen Drug Use	137
	Teen Depression	138
	Teen Violence	145
7.	Religion	153
	Bibliography	159
	Index	175

Tables

I.1 Projections of the Population by Sex, Hispanic Origin, and Race
for the United States: 2015–2060 (NP2014-T10)   xiv

I.2 Annual Estimates of the Resident Population by Sex, Age,
and Race for the United States, as of July 1, 2014
(2014 Population Estimates)   xv

1.1 Detailed Years of School Completed by People 25 Years
and Older by Sex, Age Groups, Race, and Hispanic Origin, 2014   3

1.2 Educational Attainment of the Labor Force Aged 25
and Older by Race and Hispanic or Latino Ethnicity,
2014 Annual Averages (%)   5

1.3 Earning and Unemployment Rates by Educational
Attainment, 2014   5

1.4 Trend of Black and Latino Children (%) Attending
Segregated Schools   7

1.5 SAT Mean Scores of College-Bound Seniors, by
Race/Ethnicity, Selected Years, 1990–1991 through 2009–2010   14

1.6 Nationwide Suspension Rates (%) at U.S. Schools, 2011–2012   17

1.7 Students (%) Receiving Suspensions and Expulsions,
by Race/Ethnicity   21

1.8 Percentage of High School Dropouts among Persons
16 through 24-Years-Old (Status Dropout Rate), by
Sex and Race/Ethnicity, Selected Years, 1970–2013   25

1.9 Percentage Distribution of 6- to 18-Year-Olds, by
Parent's Highest Level of Educational Attainment,
Household Type, and Child's Race/Ethnicity, 2012   27

1.10 Number and Percentage of Students Enrolled at All Title IV
      Institutions, by Control of Institution, Student Level,
      Level of Institution, and Other Selected Characteristics,
      United States, Fall 2013   28
1.11 Population 14- to 24-Year-Olds by High School Graduate
      Status, College Enrollment, Attainment, Race, and
      Hispanic Origin, October 2007–2014   31
2.1   Leading Causes of Death for Whites and Blacks,
      United States, 2013 (Including Rates per 100,000
      Population in Specific Group)   38
2.2   Percentage of People by Type of Health Insurance
      Coverage and Selected Demographic Characteristics,
      2013 and 2014   40
2.3   Obesity Rates per State Based on Percentage of Obese
      (BMI > 30) in U.S. Adults, 2014   44
2.4   Prevalence of Self-Reported Obesity among Adults
      by Race/Ethnicity, by State, BRFSS, 2011–2013   45
2.5   Age-Adjusted Rates of Diagnosed Diabetes per 100
      Civilian, Noninstitutionalized Population, by Race
      and Sex, United States, Selected Years from 1980 to 2014   47
2.6   Past Month Illicit Drug Use among Persons Aged 12 or
      Older, by Race/Ethnicity, 2002–2013   51
2.7   Use of Selected Substances in the Past Month among
      Persons Aged 12 and over, by Age, Sex, Race, and
      Hispanic Origin, United States, Selected Years 2002–2013   52
3.1   Sentenced Prisoners under the Jurisdiction of State or
      Federal Correctional Authorities, by Age, Sex, Race,
      and Hispanic Origin, December 31, 2013   60
3.2   Arrests by Race, 2014   62
3.3   Prevalence of Violent Crime, by Victim Demographic
      Characteristics, 2005, 2013, and 2014   70
3.4   Race and Sex of Homicide Victims by Race and Sex of
      Offender, 2011 (Single Victim/Single Offender)   71
3.5   Incidents, Offenses, Victims, and Known Offenders by
      Bias Motivation, 2014   73
3.6   Hate Crime Incidents, Offenses, Victims, and Known
      Offenders by Offense Type, 2014   75
3.7   Number and Percentage of Law Enforcement Homicides
      Captured, by Source and Estimation Approach,
      2003–2009 and 2011   77
4.1   Selected Employment Statistics by Race, 2014   83
4.2   Percentage of the Unemployed Who Were Jobless for
      27 Weeks or Longer and 99 Weeks or Longer, by Gender, Race,
      and Hispanic and Latino Ethnicity, 2014 Annual Averages   84

4.3	Homeownership Rates by Race/Ethnicity of Householder, 2011–2015	87
5.1	Voter Turnout, by Race and Hispanic Origin, 2000, 2004, 2008, and 2012	93
5.2	Reported Voting and Registration by Race, Hispanic Origin, Sex, and Age Groups, November 1964–2014	96
5.3	Summary of Felony Disenfranchisement Restrictions in 2014	100
5.4	Estimates of Disenfranchised Felons, 2010	102
6.1	All Parent/Child Situations by Type, Race, and Hispanic Origin of the Householder or Reference Person, 1970–Present	113
6.2	Marital Status of the Population 15 Years Old and over by Sex, Race, and Hispanic Origin, 2008–2015	116
6.3	Percentage Ever Divorced for Ever-Married Women by Age, Race, and Hispanic Origin, for Selected Years, 1996–2009	121
6.4	Births and Birth Rates, by Race, United States, 2008–2014	123
6.5	Hispanic Origin and Race of Same-Sex Unmarried-Partner Households for the United States: 2010 Summary File Counts	125
6.6	Women's Age-Specific Rates of Divorce by Race, Ethnicity, and Nativity	127
6.7	Marriage Outcomes by Age 46 by Gender, Race/Ethnicity, and Educational Attainment: Based on the National Longitudinal Survey of Youth 1979 (NLSY79)	129
6.8	Birth Rates per 1,000 Females Ages 15–19, by Race/Ethnicity, 1990–2014	132
6.9	Adolescent Fertility Rates (Births per 1,000 Women Ages 15–19), Selected Years 1960–2014, for OECD High-Income Member Countries	133
6.10	Past Month Use of Selected Illicit Drugs among Youths Aged 12–17, 2002–2013	137
6.11	Poverty Status of People by Age, Race, and Hispanic Origin, 2007–2014	140
6.12	Juvenile Arrest Rates by Offense and Race, Selected Years 1980–2014	147

Introduction

African Americans have faced, and continue to face, unique challenges in the United States that have led to striking disparities as compared to other racial and ethnic groups. Beginning with slavery, they have faced legal, social, economic, and political challenges that supported discrimination and exclusion. This process began when blacks were denied rights under the U.S. Constitution, and continued to later laws forbidding any rights to blacks. Later, following Reconstruction, laws emerged establishing "separate but equal" facilities as upheld by *Plessy v. Ferguson* (1896). Finally, Jim Crow laws in much of the South stripped blacks the right to equal housing, transportation, voting, and education. It wasn't until Supreme Court case rulings and federal laws in favor of African Americans were issued in the 1950s and 1960s backed by legal enforcement that African Americans truly were given substantive equal rights. Today, centuries of civil rights struggles have resulted in legal equality and social advancements in basically every area. While African Americans enjoy basically the same legal freedoms as white Americans, they still fall short of having the same level of equality. Nick Wing (2015) has summed up the National Urban League's 2015 *State of Black America* study, indicating that black Americans lag far behind white Americans in terms of overall equality of life at 72.2%. The National Urban League explains such disparity as follows: "if you envisioned white America with a whole pie, at 100%, black America would be missing nearly 28% of that pie. This figure is up from the 71.5% equality report in the 2015 'State of Black America' report for 2014. It includes areas of economics, health, education, social justice and civic engagement."

With all the advancements that have been made, African Americans still face challenges due to disparities that are unique to its population. It can be argued that economic disparities are a primary contributor to many blacks still facing equality challenges. For example, on average, blacks in the United States have lower income levels, primarily due to lower levels of education but also a higher propensity for job discrimination. While they are generally supported by laws fostering equality, they continue to face marginalization in voting, employment, and other areas as some civil rights gains are being rescinded. Moreover, voting rights issues and crime laws have been blamed for having disparaging impacts on African Americans. In the former case, court rulings and voter identification laws are having a negative impact on African Americans being able to fully exercise voting in an equal manner. Crime laws that sometimes support rather than prohibit racial profiling are but one example of the need for equality in the justice system.

Other disparities are due to the vestiges of slavery, racism, and the resulting economic depression of blacks in the United States. Centuries of racism still impact housing, employment, and education opportunities. Racism and segregation have contributed to negative health issues that blacks suffer such as heart disease and diabetes. Still, other issues are due to continued economic segregation. Impoverished urban areas have the highest rates of violent crimes. Many of these areas developed due to failed federal and state attempts to actually revitalize urban housing centers. African Americans comprise the majority population of these areas. Crimes here have resulted in blacks comprising a vast majority of the U.S. prison population by racial percentage, and some argue this is also because blacks are targeted by police and the criminal justice system.

On the other hand, blacks have made tremendous accomplishments in the United States. Politically, the nation has seen its first African American president, and blacks hold prominent positions in Congress, gubernatorial and mayoral positions, as well as in the Supreme Court. Blacks are prominent in sports, entertainment, medicine, education, and science and technology. Blacks hold prominent positions in the public sector, but still lag somewhat in the private sector. In 2016, for example, only five chief executive officers of Fortune 500 companies were African American. However, the Census Bureau (2011) reports that "From 2002 to 2007, the number of black-owned businesses increased by 60.5% to 1.9 million, more than triple the national rate of 18.0%, according to the U.S. Census Bureau's Survey of Business Owners. Over the same period, receipts generated by black-owned businesses increased 55.1% to $137.5 billion." There were 2.6 million black or African American–owned firms nationally in 2012, up from 1.9 million or 34.5% from 2007. Further, reports show African American women are the fastest growing entrepreneurs in the United States, with the number of businesses owned growing 322% from 1997 through 2015 (Haimerl 2015; Workneh 2016).

GENERAL DEMOGRAPHICS

So what is the overall condition of African Americans in the United States? First, African Americans have become the third largest population in terms of both race and ethnicity due to the increase in the population of Hispanics (Hispanic is considered by the Census Bureau to be an ethnicity and not a race. It is defined by the heritage, nationality, lineage, or country of birth of the person or an individual's parents or ancestors before arriving in the United States). Blacks made up 13.2% of the U.S. population in 2015, and this percentage is expected to increase to 14.3% by 2060 (see Table I.1). In comparison, whites are expected to decrease from 77.3% to 68.5%, respectively. Hispanics are expected to significantly increase, from 17.4% in 2015 to 28.6% in 2060. For this reason, non-Hispanic whites will decrease from 62.2% to 43.6%, respectively. Another reason for the decrease in whites as a percentage of the population is the expected increase in Asians from 5.4% to 9.3%, respectively.

Table I.2 shows a host of data by sex, age, and race for the U.S. population in 2014 (note this data is by race only, so Hispanics are not included as that is again an ethnicity). First, whites comprise the overall majority of the U.S. population (77.4%), followed by blacks (13.2%), and Asians (5.4%). Notice, however, that the share of the population for whites decreases as the ages decrease. For example, whites comprise over 80% of those over 45 years of age, but 72.9% of those under 18 years old. Another interesting point is that whites are generally older than other races. The majority of whites (27.1%) are between 45 and 64 years. The majority of blacks (27.6%) are between 25 and 44 years, while the majority of all other races are also between 25 and 44 years (particularly Asians (33.3%) and Native Hawaiians and Other Pacific Islanders (32.5%)).

This can also be seen in looking at the median ages of each race. The median age for whites is 39.6, compared to 33 for blacks, 30.4 for American Indians and Alaskan Natives, 36.1 for Asians, and 30.1 for Native Hawaiians and Other Pacific Islanders. Whites are also the only race where the median age of females is over 40. For blacks, for example, the median age for females is 34.6. A particularly vital area in this chart is the data for those who identify as being from "Two or More Races." The average age for this population is only 19.8. Additionally, 46.5% of the population is under 18, signifying a continued growth in this population in the coming decades. As young people are more open to marrying those of other races and ethnicities, the population identifying themselves as being of "two or more races" will continue to grow.

The concern for African Americans as the nation's demographic changes is in public policies that are geared to improve their economic, social, and political well-being. Public policies are based on such factors as political influence, majority representation in executive and legislative bodies, and tax revenues obtained from different sectors of the population. Some minority populations find their concerns may not be a priority on the national agenda, as lawmakers and decision makers focus their attention on the needs of majority groups by number, income, interest group mobilization, and other factors. As such, if political support is based on the majority population, more public policies will be geared toward supporting the increasingly majority Hispanic population.

At issue is that African Americans are disparate in terms of education, health, social aspects, and many other areas that will be discussed later in this book. If these disparate trends continue over the coming decades, African Americans will find a reduction in political support, public policies, and funding targeted toward areas where they have the greatest need. A related factor is the expected reduction in tax revenues as the American population ages and the working population decreases. There will be less funding for federal, state, and local governments and

Table I.1   Projections of the Population by Sex, Hispanic Origin, and Race for the United States: 2015–2060 (NP2014-T10)

	2015	Percent	2020	Percent	2030	Percent	2040	Percent	2050	Percent	2060	Percent
Both sexes	321,369		334,503		359,402		380,219		398,328		416,795	
One race	313,114	97.4%	324,865	97.1%	346,571	96.4%	363,637	95.6%	377,357	94.7%	390,772	93.8%
White	248,369	77.3%	255,357	76.3%	267,459	74.4%	275,447	72.4%	280,503	70.4%	285,314	68.5%
Black[1]	42,456	13.2%	44,590	13.3%	48,768	13.6%	52,485	13.8%	56,007	14.1%	59,693	14.3%
AIAN	4,005	1.2%	4,242	1.3%	4,694	1.3%	5,074	1.3%	5,370	1.3%	5,607	1.3%
Asian	17,538	5.5%	19,869	5.9%	24,726	6.9%	29,603	7.8%	34,359	8.6%	38,965	9.3%
NHPI	746	0.2%	806	0.2%	923	0.3%	1,028	0.3%	1,118	0.3%	1,194	0.3%
Two or more races	8,255	2.6%	9,639	2.9%	12,831	3.6%	16,582	3.6%	20,971	5.3%	26,022	6.2%
Race alone or in combination[2]												
White	255,682	79.6%	263,969	78.9%	279,081	77.7%	290,635	76.4%	299,896	75.3%	309,567	74.3%
Black	46,126	14.4%	49,052	14.7%	55,121	15.3%	61,158	16.1%	67,499	16.9%	74,530	17.9%
AIAN	6,618	2.1%	7,071	2.1%	7,968	2.2%	8,777	2.3%	9,497	2.4%	10,169	2.4%
Asian	20,534	6.4%	23,380	7.0%	29,426	8.2%	35,709	9.4%	42,099	10.6%	48,575	11.7%
NHPI	1,486	0.5%	1,631	0.5%	1,940	0.5%	2,257	0.5%	2,586	0.6%	2,929	0.7%

Note: Resident population as of July 1. Numbers in thousands.

Hispanic origin is considered an ethnicity, not a race. Hispanics may be of any race. Responses of "Some Other Race" from the 2010 Census are modified. For more information, see http://www.census.gov/popest/data/historical/files/MRSF-01-US1.pdf.

[1] Black = Black or African American; AIAN = American Indian and Alaska Native; NHPI = Native Hawaiian and Other Pacific Islander.

[2] "In combination" means in combination with one or more other races. The sum of the five race groups adds to more than the total because individuals may report more than one race.

Source: U.S. Census Bureau, Population Division, Release Date: December 2014.

Table I.2 Annual Estimates of the Resident Population by Sex, Age, and Race for the United States, as of July 1, 2014 (2014 Population Estimates)

Age (in Years)	Total (or All)	White	% All	% Race	Black or African American	% All	% Race	American Indian and Alaska Native	% All	% Race	Asian	% All	% Race	Native Hawaiian/Other Pacific Islander	% All	% Race	Two or More Races	% All	% Race
Total	318,857,056	246,660,710	77.4		42,158,238	13.2		3,960,971	1.2		17,339,053	5.4		741,601	0.2		7,996,483	2.5	
Under 5	19,876,883	14,260,702	71.7	5.8	3,026,570	15.2	7.2	321,835	1.6	8.1	1,021,572	5.1	5.9	61,096	0.3	8.2	1,185,108	6.0	14.8
5–9	20,519,566	14,896,812	72.6	6.0	3,091,042	15.1	7.3	332,269	1.6	8.4	1,038,474	5.1	6.0	60,531	0.3	8.2	1,100,438	5.4	13.8
10–14	20,671,506	15,233,440	73.7	6.2	3,090,181	14.9	7.3	321,678	1.6	8.1	1,039,021	5.0	6.0	56,681	0.3	7.6	930,505	4.5	11.6
15–19	21,067,647	15,599,430	74.0	6.3	3,231,185	15.3	7.7	319,684	1.5	8.1	1,040,239	4.9	6.0	56,068	0.3	7.6	821,041	3.9	10.3
20–24	22,912,174	16,815,805	73.4	6.8	3,687,604	16.1	8.7	346,726	1.5	8.8	1,277,938	5.6	7.4	66,160	0.3	8.9	717,941	3.1	9.0
25–29	21,987,938	16,390,470	74.5	6.6	3,199,398	14.6	7.6	315,762	1.4	8.0	1,456,595	6.6	8.4	69,235	0.3	9.3	556,478	2.5	7.0
30–34	21,528,566	16,211,717	75.3	6.6	2,970,053	13.8	7.0	299,492	1.4	7.6	1,491,947	6.9	8.6	65,983	0.3	8.9	489,374	2.3	6.1
35–39	19,921,650	15,057,665	75.6	6.1	2,720,599	13.7	6.5	269,741	1.4	6.8	1,408,883	7.1	8.1	56,104	0.3	7.6	408,658	2.1	5.1
40–44	20,591,483	15,758,248	76.5	6.4	2,751,864	13.4	6.5	259,621	1.3	6.6	1,416,282	6.9	8.2	49,535	0.2	6.7	355,933	1.7	4.5
45–49	20,888,042	16,322,371	78.1	6.6	2,740,678	13.1	6.6	247,306	1.2	6.2	1,224,507	5.9	7.1	45,163	0.2	6.1	308,017	1.5	3.9
50–54	22,570,809	17,996,219	79.7	7.3	2,846,398	12.6	6.8	248,178	1.1	6.3	1,139,203	5.0	6.6	42,850	0.2	5.8	297,961	1.3	3.7
55–59	21,511,449	17,391,477	80.8	7.1	2,593,590	12.1	6.2	214,011	1.0	5.4	1,021,626	4.7	5.9	35,485	0.2	4.8	255,260	1.2	3.2
60–64	18,566,132	15,254,999	82.2	6.2	2,059,834	11.1	4.9	162,843	0.9	4.1	868,293	4.7	5.0	26,859	0.1	3.6	193,304	1.0	2.4
65–69	15,325,266	12,871,651	84.0	5.2	1,498,236	9.8	3.6	118,753	0.8	3.0	674,796	4.4	3.9	19,853	0.1	2.7	141,977	0.9	1.8
70–74	11,073,024	9,406,672	85.0	3.8	1,017,049	9.2	2.4	76,964	0.7	1.9	465,868	4.2	2.7	12,519	0.1	1.7	93,952	0.8	1.2
75–79	7,922,324	6,765,257	85.4	2.7	708,454	8.9	1.7	49,946	0.6	1.3	328,523	4.1	1.9	8,219	0.1	1.1	61,925	0.8	0.8
80–84	5,760,366	4,996,375	86.7	2.0	469,160	8.1	1.1	30,326	0.5	0.8	218,991	3.8	1.3	5,104	0.1	0.7	40,410	0.7	0.5
≥85	6,162,231	5,431,400	88.1	2.2	456,343	7.4	1.1	25,836	0.4	0.7	206,295	3.3	1.2	4,156	0.1	0.6	38,201	0.6	0.5
Under 18	73,583,618	53,660,157	72.9	21.8	11,120,298	15.1	26.4	1,167,010	1.6	29.5	3,703,735	5.0	21.4	211,377	0.3	28.5	3,721,041	5.1	46.5
Under 5	19,876,883	14,260,702	71.7	5.8	3,026,570	15.2	7.2	321,835	1.6	8.1	1,021,572	5.1	5.9	61,096	0.3	8.2	1,185,108	6.0	14.8
5–13	36,958,592	27,008,593	73.1	10.9	5,531,714	15.0	13.1	588,318	1.6	14.9	1,872,572	5.1	10.8	105,797	0.3	14.3	1,851,598	5.0	23.2
14–17	16,748,143	12,390,862	74.0	5.0	2,562,014	15.3	6.1	256,857	1.5	6.5	809,591	4.8	4.7	44,484	0.3	6.0	684,335	4.1	8.6
18–64	199,030,227	153,529,198	77.1	62.2	26,888,698	13.5	63.8	2,492,136	1.3	62.9	11,740,845	5.9	67.7	480,373	0.2	64.8	3,898,977	2.0	48.8
18–24	31,464,158	23,146,032	73.6	9.4	5,006,284	15.9	11.9	475,182	1.5	12.0	1,713,509	5.4	9.9	89,159	0.3	12.0	1,033,992	3.3	12.9

Columns under "White" through "Native Hawaiian/Other Pacific Islander" are grouped under **Race Alone**; final group is **Two or More Races**.

(Continued)

Table I.2 (Continued)

| Age (in Years) | Total (or All) | Race Alone ||||||||||||||||| Two or More Races |||
		White	% All	% Race	Black or African American	% All	% Race	American Indian and Alaska Native	% All	% Race	Asian	% All	% Race	Native Hawaiian/ Other Pacific Islander	% All	% Race	Two or More Races	% All	% Race
25–44	84,029,637	63,418,100	75.5	25.7	11,641,914	13.9	27.6	1,144,616	1.4	28.9	5,773,707	6.9	33.3	240,857	0.3	32.5	1,810,443	2.2	22.6
45–64	83,536,432	66,965,066	80.2	27.1	10,240,500	12.3	24.3	872,338	1.0	22.0	4,253,629	5.1	24.5	150,357	0.2	20.3	1,054,542	1.3	13.2
>65	46,243,211	39,471,355	85.4	16.0	4,149,242	9.0	9.8	301,825	0.7	7.6	1,894,473	4.1	10.9	49,851	0.1	6.7	376,465	0.8	4.7
≥85	6,162,231	5,431,400	88.1	2.2	456,343	7.4	1.1	25,836	0.4	0.7	206,295	3.3	1.2	4,156	0.1	0.6	38,201	0.6	0.5
Median age	37.7	39.6			33.0			30.4			36.1			30.1			19.8		
Total male	156,936,487	122,195,440	77.9	49.5	20,169,931	12.9	47.8	1,999,352	1.3	50.5	8,253,798	5.3	47.6	377,295	0.2	50.9	3,940,671	2.5	49.3
Median age	36.4	38.3			31.2			29.8			34.8			29.7			19.0		
Total female	161,920,569	124,465,270	76.9	50.5	21,988,307	13.6	52.2	1,961,619	1.2	49.5	9,085,255	5.6	52.4	364,306	0.2	49.1	4,055,812	2.5	50.7
Median age	39.0	41.0			34.6			31.0			37.2			30.5			20.5		

Note: The estimates are based on the 2010 Census and reflect changes to the April 1, 2010 population due to the Count Question Resolution program and geographic program revisions. Median age is calculated based on single year of age. Hispanic origin is considered an ethnicity, not a race. Hispanics may be of any race. Responses of "Some Other Race" from the 2010 Census are modified. This results in differences between the population for specific race categories shown for the 2010 Census population in this table versus those in the original 2010 Census data. For more information, see http://www.census.gov/popest/data/historical/files/MRSF-01-US1.pdf. For population estimates methodology statements, see http://www.census.gov/popest/methodology/index.html.

Source: U.S. Census Bureau, Population Division (2016). Annual Estimates of the Resident Population by Sex, Age, Race, and Hispanic Origin for the United States and States: April 1, 2010 to July 1, 2014 (Release Date: June 2015).

they will have to make choices on where cuts will be made, and those cuts will be based on the citizen demographics.

As continually stated, African Americans have many disparities as compared to other racial and ethnic groups. Primary among these, perhaps, is poverty, given the fact that it is a contributor to the long-term health conditions of any people and impacts areas such as mental and physical well-being. According the Census Bureau (DeNavas-Walt and Proctor 2015), in 2014 the poverty rate was 14.8%, which equated to 46.7 million people in poverty. While 10.1% of non-Hispanic whites lived below the poverty level, the rate was 26.2% for blacks. This is further compared to 12% of Asians and 23.6% of Hispanics of any race. Disparities due to poverty have a rippling effect, including increased drug and alcohol use, teenage pregnancies, and health issues ranging from depression to hypertension. Poverty also increases the propensity for committing crimes, having negative encounters with law enforcement, school truancy, and dropout rates.

There are several reasons for this continued disparity for African Americans. First is the result of centuries of institutionalized racism and discrimination. African Americans were denied equal access to housing, employment, education, and basically every other area that contributes to economic, political, and social well-being in comparison to their white counterparts. This has resulted in generations that have lagged in their ability to provide the same level of support to their children, creating generational disparities that are still apparent today. Second, public policies (even those well intended) have actually supported segregationist results. Federal and state programs geared to create housing opportunities have resulted in segregated communities across the country. For example, some cities have established zoned housing areas that prevent low-income housing and restrict development projects that would benefit those in poverty. They have used the justification that low-income housing communities lead to lower tax revenues for these areas, leading to schools with far less resources, poor police and fire protection, and a lack of access to quality health care.

Even changes to welfare programs have created negative outcomes, due to lifetime limitations, family support caps, and strict sanctions for noncompliance, without accompanying support in the areas of job training and placement. A third contributing factor is the greater propensity for blacks to be charged for committing crimes than their white counterparts, even for the same or similar offences. As a result, the majority of prisoners in federal and state correctional facilities are young black males. This is not a recent issue, but one that has persisted for decades. With felony convictions, those who have served their sentences are unable to vote, qualify for some jobs, have access to federal college loans and grants, or even live in certain housing communities. The War on Crime, War on Drugs, and introduction of privatized prisons have led to more and stricter laws for less severe offenses. These efforts have significantly contributed to black males being targeted by police and the criminal justice system.

To outline the condition of African Americans, the following Fact Sheet provides specific statistics in the most prominent areas of analysis and reporting.

(Some of this data was obtained from the U.S. Bureau of Census annual com-memoration of Black History Month found at https://www.census.gov/newsroom/facts-for-features/2016/cb16-ff01.html.)

FACT SHEET ON AFRICAN AMERICANS IN THE UNITED STATES: 2016

Population (in 2015)

In 2015 there were 321,369,000 people in the United States. The following are the percentage of Americans by race (and the expected percentage by 2060):

- White alone: 77.3% (68.5%)
- Black or African American alone: 13.2% (14.3%)
- American Indian and Alaska Native alone: 1.2% (1.3%)
- Asian alone: 5.5% (9.3%)
- Native Hawaiian and Other Pacific Islander alone: 0.2% (0.3%)
- Two or More Races: 2.6% (6.2%)
- Hispanic or Latino (may be of any race): 17.4% (28.6%)

By state, New York leads the nation with the largest African American population by number (3.7 million). Mississippi leads the nation with the largest African American population by percent (38%). If this included the District of Columbia, it would have the largest percentage of African Americans (51%).

By county, Cook County, Illinois (Chicago), leads all counties in the size of the black population with 1.3 million. Holmes County, Mississippi, has the largest percentage of blacks (82.5%).

By 2060, the African American population is expected to reach 74.5 million, or 17.9% of the U.S. population (including blacks alone or in combination with another ethnicity). Blacks alone are expected to reach 59.6 million or 14.3% of the U.S. population.

Education (in 2014)

- Percentage with a high school diploma or higher (25 years or older)—84.4
- Percentage with a bachelor's degree or higher (25 years or older)—19.7
- Number with an advanced degree (25 years or older)—1.8 million
- Number enrolled in undergraduate college—2.8 million (5.3% increase since 2009)

Health

- Number of live births in 2013: 583,834
- Births per 1,000 women 15–44 years: 65.4 in 2011, 64.6 in 2013

- Percentage of births with low birth weight in 2013: 13.1%
- Number of deaths in 2013: 299,227
- Deaths per 100,000 population in 2013: 733.4
- Leading causes of deaths for African American in 2013: heart disease, cancer, and stroke
- Infant deaths per 1,000 live births in 2016: 11.11
- Percentage of African Americans in fair or poor health in 2013: 14.6%
- Percentage of non-Hispanic black or African American adults 18 years and over who smoked cigarettes in 2013: 25.5%
- Percentage of African American men over 20 years old in 2012 who were obese: 37.9%
- Percentage of African American women over 20 years old in 2012 who were obese: 57.6%
- Percentage of non-Hispanic black or African American men 20 years and over with hypertension (measured high blood pressure and/or taking antihypertensive medication): 39.9% (2009–2012)
- Percentage of non-Hispanic black or African American women 20 years and over with hypertension (measured high blood pressure and/or taking antihypertensive medication): 44.5% (2009–2012)
- Percentage of persons under 65 years without health insurance coverage: 17.8%

Crime and Criminal Justice

- Percentage of black males sentenced to more than 1 year in state or federal prison in 2014: 2.7%
- Percentage of male prison population that was African American in 2014: 37% (516,900)
- Percentage of male prison population that was white in 2014: 32% (453,500)
- Percentage of male prison population that was Hispanic in 2014: 22% (308,700)

White females (53,100 prisoners, or 49% of the female prison population) in state or federal prison at year-end 2014 outnumbered both black (22,600, or 22%) and Hispanic (17,800, or 17%) females (Carson 2015).

Employment

Type of Occupation for Blacks in 2014 (by Percentage)

- Management, professional, and related occupations: 29.5%
- Service jobs: 25%
- Sales or office jobs: 23.9%
- Professional and related jobs: 19.1%

- Production, transportation, or material-moving jobs: 15.7%
- Natural resources, construction, and maintenance jobs: 5.9%

Type of Occupation for Whites in 2014 (by Percentage)

- Management or professional jobs: 39%
- Service jobs: 16.5%
- Sales or office jobs: 22.9%
- Professional or related jobs: 22.3%
- Production, transportation, or material-moving jobs: 11.5%
- Natural resources, construction, and maintenance jobs: 10.1%

Unemployment (by Percentage)

- African Americans unemployed in 2014: 11.3%
- Latinos unemployed in 2014: 7.4%
- Whites unemployed in 2014: 5.3%
- Asians unemployed in 2014: 5%
- American Indians/Alaska Natives unemployed in 2014: 11.3%
- Native Hawaiians and Pacific Islanders unemployed in 2014: 6.1%
- National average unemployment rate in 2014: 6.2%

The unemployment rate in 2014 for black men was 12.2%, compared to 10.5% for black women. Among the major race and Hispanic ethnicity groups in 2014, 39.6% of unemployed blacks or African Americans and 37.7% of unemployed Asians had been looking for work for 27 weeks or longer. In contrast, whites and Hispanics were less likely to be unemployed long term (31.5% and 29.9%, respectively). Read more from Bureau of Labor Statistics at http://www.bls.gov/spotlight/2015/long-term-unemployment/pdf/long-term-unemployment.pdf.

The unemployment rate for blacks 25 years and older with less than a high school diploma in 2014 was 17.2%, compared to 10.7% of black high school graduates with no college degree, 6.8% for those with an associate's degree, and 5.2% for those with a bachelor's degree and higher. This is compared to 9% of the total population with less than a high school diploma, 6% with high school but no college, 4.5% with an associate degree, and 3.2% of those with a bachelor's degree and higher.

Income

- Annual median income of black households in 2014: $35,398
- Annual median income of non-Hispanic white households in 2014: $60,256
- National annual median income in 2014: $53,657

The official poverty rate in 2014 was 14.8%, representing 46.7 million people in poverty. The poverty rate for blacks was 26.2%, compared to 10.1% for non-Hispanic whites, 12% for Asians, and 23.6% for Hispanics of any race.

Home Ownership (by Percentage)

- African Americans owning homes in 2015: 41.9%
- Whites owning homes in 2015: 72.2%
- Hispanics owning homes in 2015: 46.7%
- National average in 2015: 63.8%

Businesses

(Source: U.S. Bureau of Census at https://www.census.gov/newsroom/press-releases/2015/cb15-209.html)

- There were 2.6 million black- or African American–owned firms nationally in 2012, up from 1.9 million, or 34.5%, from 2007.
- All except for 109,137, or 4.2%, of black- or African American–owned firms were nonemployers.
- While 9.4% of all U.S. firms were black or African American owned, the largest percentage was 19.2% in the health care and social assistance sector. For comparison, blacks or African Americans accounted for 13.1% of the 18 and older population in 2012.
- The Atlanta metro area had more black- or African American–owned firms (176,245) in 2012 than any other metro area besides New York (250,890).
- Georgia had more black- or African American–owned firms in 2012 than any other state (256,848), followed by Florida (251,216).
- Cook County, Illinois, led all counties in the number of black- or African American–owned firms, with 110,155.
- The District of Columbia, Mississippi, and Georgia were the only states where more than one-quarter of all firms were black or African American owned (34.8%, 27.7% and 27.6%, respectively).
- Among the nation's 50 most populous cities, black- or African American–owned firms as a percentage of all firms were highest in Detroit and Memphis, Tennessee, in 2012 (77% and 56.2%, respectively).

Voting

- Percentage of African Americans who voted in the 2012 presidential election: 66.2% (17.8 million)

- Percentage of non-Hispanic whites who voted in the 2012 presidential election: 64.1% (98 million)
- Percentage of African American voters who identified as Democrats in the 2012 presidential election: 64%
- Percentage of African American voters who identified as Independents or were unsure of party affiliation in the 2012 presidential election: 29%
- Percentage of African American voters who identified as Republicans in the 2012 presidential election: 5%

Family

- Percentage of black households that contained a family in 2014: 61.3%
- Number of black family households in 2014: 9.9 million
- Number of black grandparents who lived with grandchildren in 2014: 1.2 million
- Percentage of grandparents responsible for grandchildren's care: 44%

HOW TO NAVIGATE THIS BOOK

This book explores data for primary subjects used to gauge the demographic, economic, social, political, and health condition of blacks in the United States. The data provided is predominantly for African Americans (those who are citizens of the United States), but some data will include all blacks (those who are actual citizens plus those in the country but not a citizen such as those attending a U.S. college or university on a student visa). By examining a wide range of socioeconomic topics and providing necessary background and contextual information, this book offers readers a multidimensional view of African American life.

The topics discussed in this book are divided into the following categories as individual chapters: Education, Health, Crime and Criminal Justice, Employment, Voting, Family, and Religion. Each chapter then includes specific sections discussing issues with the greatest impact on African Americans. For example, areas African Americans face the greatest adverse risks under the category of Crime and Criminal Justice include being the victims of murder, hate crimes, rape and robberies, and having higher rates of incarceration.

The chapters of this book are organized by major areas to analyze Africans Americans in relation to other races and ethnicities in the United States. Each chapter begins with a brief discussion on considerations for researching and using data related to that topic. For example, there are general areas of interest in analyzing education data such as how educational achievement is defined at each level of government. The remainder of each chapter then discusses different aspects of the topic of the chapter, presenting relevant data tables and discussion on the information contained in each table as well as additional statistics in discussion form. Each chapter also includes discussion to exemplify the condition of African

Americans based on the most recent data from various sources. Academic discussion is also provided to further support the data provided. In addition, discussion questions listed under Further Investigations are provided at the end of each chapter section to spur discussion and debate on each issue. Lastly, "Further Readings" provide additional scholarly resources on each topic. Both of these are provided with the goal of the reader fostering research on each topic for themselves.

To support the information in this book, the first section covers how to find and analyze data. This includes pointers on using secondary data, major sources of data and related information, and recommendations for improving the use of data. When analyzing the data in this book, the reader should look at the table title to be clear on what is being presented, the source of data, notes on how the data is being presented (e.g., in thousands or millions, by race or ethnicity), and any notes elaborating on the data or methodology used. The reader should also visit the data sources to gain additional insights on the data and the methodology used to obtain it.

How to Find and Analyze Data

There is an abundance of data available to analyze the American population and specifically African Americans in basically every area of study. Multidisciplinary research by public, private, and nonprofit agencies has produced scores of sources for both quantitative and qualitative data, but the focus of this book is on quantitative (or numerical) data. This data has been segmented by race, ethnicity, sex, and a host of other demographic factors. However, with this abundance of data comes the need to understand its sources and scope and also the meaning of the variables used to present findings. For example, some sources of data are very unreliable due to the entity that developed the data and methods of research used. Some sources present information that is purposely presented with a bias to purport a position or stance on an issue. Other data is questionable by using such research fallacies as only analyzing a very small sample and then producing results that imply the data applies to the entire population. For example, a researcher may only analyze voting in a couple of states and then report the results apply to all African Americans in the United States.

The primary focus of this book is providing information based on secondary data (i.e., data and information already produced from websites, books, journals, magazines, or newspapers) specific to African Americans. This is distinguished from primary data, where a researcher conducts their own study and produces data results themselves. Secondary data sources are usable as they were developed in a neutral manner based on reliable and valid statistical methods. In statistical terminology, validity means the researcher was able to obtain data results to measure what was intended by the research methodology. For example, the researcher determined political ideology by asking questions directly tied to voting habits rather than perceptions about a particular candidate. Reliability means the results can be applied to the entire population of study. For example, the researcher can conclude that in general, blacks support Democrats because a large enough sample was obtained over a period of time to suggest continuing support for Democratic candidates. So the questions this section answers are: where do you find good data on the status of African Americans, and how do you interpret the data once it was obtained?

SOURCES OF DATA

There are many sources of data, some more reliable than the others. The most reliable data to analyze demographic groups comes from federal agencies. However, states and localities also maintain specific data for their individual populations, which are great resources. Data can be obtained, for example, from state departments and agencies, city mayors' offices, local chambers of commerce, local colleges and universities, state and local police departments, state and local boards and commissions, clerks and registrars (in towns, cities, or counties), public health departments and offices, offices of tourism, and school boards and superintendent offices. There are also many private and nonprofit organizations that produce data and related information. Again, care should be given to fully research these organizations to determine their missions, affiliations, and methodologies for obtaining the data.

The following are sources of online data per categories or types of information discussed for each. The reader will find these sites useful to conduct their own research of data and statistics related to African Americans, particularly since data on this topic is dynamic and continuously being updated. Please note these websites are current as of 2016. Website addresses may change and organizations may change what data is made available:

- Data.gov (www.data.gov or https://www.data.gov/open-gov/) is a central government source for open data. It provides a host of data, tools, and resources for conducting research, developing web mobile applications, designing data visualizations, and more. The site allows users to pull datasets by specific topic or by conducting a search, and includes domestic federal, state, and local data, as well as international data.

- USA.gov (https://www.usa.gov/statistics#item-37157) is a central repository of data on a host of topics including health, housing and community, jobs and employment, money and shopping, travel and immigration, and others. The site also provides links to many government sources of data. There are also links for state and territorial, local, and quick facts about the country.

- The Library of Congress (https://www.loc.gov/) is the nation's first established cultural institution and the largest library in the world, with millions of items including books, recordings, photographs, maps, and manuscripts in its collections.

- Department of Labor (http://www.dol.gov/) produces a wide range of U.S. economic and labor data. Data categories include current and projected employment, inflation and prices, pay and benefits, workforce injuries, productivity, and regional resources of information (e.g., by national region, state, or county).

- Bureau of Labor Statistics (BLS) (http://www.bls.gov/) is part of the U.S. Department of Labor. It measures labor market activity (e.g., employment and unemployment), working conditions, employee productivity, pay and benefits, and inflation and price changes in the economy. The site provides data, publications, and series reports. There are databases, tables, and calculators that can be used to retrieve data.

- Centers for Disease Control and Prevention (CDC) (www.cdc.gov) and its National Center for Health Statistics (www.cdc.gov/nchs/), part of the Department of Health and Human Services, provide data on health issues affecting individuals and demographic groups, as well as global health issues. Both current and trend data are presented in multiple formats.

- The U.S. Department of Health and Human Services Office of Minority Health (http://minorityhealth.hhs.gov/) provides a wide range of data on each major American minority group, to include selection pages for each group. This includes sourcing and maintaining a body of expert knowledge on minority health status initiatives, and demographic statistics and analyses on minority populations, compiled by the National Center for Health Statistics, the Census Bureau, private foundations, clinical practitioners, private data sources, and public agencies.

- Global Health Observatory Data Repository (http://www.who.int/gho/en/ or http://apps.who.int/gho/data/?theme=main), provided by the World Health Organization, provides a wide range of health statistics for countries around the world, as well as information on global health issues by category.

- U.S. Bureau of Census (www.census.gov) is part of the U.S. Department of Commerce and is the leading source of data about the nation's people and economy. Data is provided in a variety of formats from the decennial census, economic census, census of governments, the American Community Survey, and the bureau's surveys and programs. It is also a repository of data from multiple federal agencies. Additionally, http://www.census.gov/data.html provides access to data through products and tools including data visualizations, mobile apps, interactive web apps, and other software.

- The U.S. Department of Housing and Urban Development has data sets, reports, survey results, and a host of other data available at http://data.hud.gov/data_sets.html and https://www.huduser.gov/portal/datasets/pdrdatas.html. This latter source is produced and maintained by the U.S. Department of Housing and Urban Development's (HUD's) Office of Policy Development and Research (PD&R) that supports the Department's efforts to help create cohesive, economically healthy communities.

- HealthData.gov (www.healthdata.gov) provides health data for researchers. It provides datasets on a host of topics that can be downloaded in several formats (e.g., CSV, Excel, and RDF). This federal government website is managed by the U.S. Department of Health and Human Services.

- The Institute for Health Metrics and Evaluation (IHME; http://www.healthdata. org/) is an independent global health research center at the University of Washington that provides rigorous and comparable measurement of the world's most important health problems and evaluates the strategies used to address them. IHME makes this information freely available so that policy makers have the evidence they need to make informed decisions about how to allocate resources to best improve population health.

- Bureau of Economic Analysis (BEA) (www.bea.gov) is part of the Department of Commerce. It provides information on economic indicators such as Gross Domestic Product and personal income, national and international trade in goods and services, and data on different industries. One great feature it provides is interactive data that can be modified, downloaded, and converted into charts.

- The Economics and Statistics Administration (ESA) releases 12-monthly and quarterly Principal Federal Economic Indicators collected by its constituent bureaus: the U.S. Census Bureau and the BEA (http://www.esa.doc.gov/).

- The International Trade Administration (ITA) strengthens the competitiveness of U.S. industry, promotes trade and investment, and ensures fair trade through the rigorous enforcement of trade laws and agreements. Trade Policy & Analysis (TP&A) publishes a variety of data series and reports for both public and government use (http://trade.gov/mas/ian/tradestatistics/index.asp).

- The Small Business Administration (SBA) provides Open Data Sources (https://www.sba.gov/about-sba/sba-performance/open-government/digital-sba/open-data/open-data-sources), which is available to the public. A host of data related to small businesses is available in various formats (e.g., html, Excel, pdf).

- The Inter-university Consortium for Political and Social Research (ICPSR) (http://www.icpsr.umich.edu/icpsrweb/landing.jsps) is a data source for social science researchers located at the University of Michigan. This source provided 65,000 data sets from over 8,000 discrete studies or surveys, online analysis tools to generate simple descriptive statistics including frequencies and cross-tabulations, and several options for downloading data in formats that are compatible with popular statistical software packages. In order to download data, users need to register with the system.

- Bureau of Justice Statistics (http://www.bjs.gov/) is part of the Department of Justice. It collects and publishes vast amounts of information and data on crime, including types, victim information, and information on crime perpetrators. The data covers crimes at the federal, state, and local levels. In supporting crime reporting, data is also provided on the courts and law enforcement. In addition to raw data provided, there are also a wide range of related publications.

- The National Institute of Corrections (www.nicic.gov) is an agency within the U.S. Department of Justice, Federal Bureau of Prisons. The institute is headed by a director appointed by the U.S. Attorney General. A 16-member advisory board, also appointed by the Attorney General, was established by the enabling legislation (Public Law 93-415) to provide policy direction to the institute. It provides corrections-related resources including training plans, research reports, and program evaluations.

- Bureau of Transportation Statistics (http://www.rita.dot.gov/bts/) is part of the U.S. Department of Transportation. The bureau collects and reports transportation statistics that can be analyzed by mode (e.g., highway, maritime, or airlines), region (national, international, or state and local), or subject (e.g., safety, vehicles, freight, and infrastructure). Like the other government sites listed here, there is a data dictionary that explains the variables used. There are also many resources and tools to assist users, such as research tools and prepared statistics.

- The National Center for Statistics and Analysis (NCSA) is an office of the National Highway Traffic Safety Administration. This organization is responsible for providing a wide range of analytical and statistical support to the NHTSA and the highway safety community at large (http://www.nhtsa.gov/NCSA).

- Economic Research Service (http://www.ers.usda.gov/) is part of the U.S. Department of Agriculture. Most of the data focuses on agriculture and farming, but the site also includes data on rural development, poverty, the environment, trade, and health issues. Information is provided in an array of methods, including charts, applications, and actual data files. There are publications on an array of topics that go back for decades.

- National Agricultural Statistical Service (http://www.nass.usda.gov/) is also part of the U.S. Department of Agriculture. Data and statistics are provided on agriculture in the United States, as well as publications, surveys, and series reports. The site provides specific agricultural data by race and ethnicity. The geospatial and interactive maps provide a great way to access information is a very unique extrapolation method. The site provides a direct link to the Census of Agriculture (http://agcensus.usda.gov/), which provides a detailed picture of U.S. farms and ranches and the people who operate them.

- The National Weather Service is a component of the National Oceanic and Atmospheric Administration (NOAA). NOAA is an operating unit of the U.S. Department of Commerce. It provides weather, water, and climate data, forecasts and warnings for the protection of life and property, and enhancement of the national economy (http://www.weather.gov/).

- U.S. Energy Information Administration (http://www.eia.gov/) provides a wide range of information and data products covering energy production, stocks, demand, imports, exports, and prices domestically and internationally. It also provides analyses and special reports on topics of current interest, as data and reports are provided in the form of daily, weekly, monthly, quarterly, and annual products. The site includes information by race and ethnicity such as energy consumption data.

- The Environmental Protection Agency (EPA) has many data sources available. These cover topics including but not limited to air, climate change, health risks, pollutants and contaminants, waste, and water. The data are downloadable and available through the Environmental Dataset Gateway (EDG) (https://edg.epa.gov/metadata/catalog/main/home.page).

- National Center for Education Statistics (NCES) (https://nces.ed.gov/), under the U.S. Department of Education, is the primary federal entity for collecting and analyzing data related to all levels of education, including extensive U.S. data at the federal, state, and local levels, and also some international information. There are search tools for aggregate data, as well as by individual schools, colleges and universities, and areas. The data tools allow users to conduct searches on a wide range of topics, and publications and reports can also be obtained from the interactive search tool.

- The National Center for Science and Engineering Statistics (NCSES) is the nation's leading provider of statistical data on the U.S. science and engineering enterprise (http://www.nsf.gov/statistics/index.cfm). The NCSES statistical data are available in a variety of formats: preformatted and interactive tables, data tools to help you generate your own tables, and microdata files.

- Social Security Administration's Office of Research and Statistics (http://www.ssa.gov/policy/about/ORES.html) collects, analyzes, and disseminates information on social security in the form of statistic, reports, figures, and briefs.

- Statistics of Income (SOI) (http://www.irs.gov/uac/SOI-Tax-Stats-Statistics-of-Income) is provided by the Internal Revenue Service and publishes an annual publication of statistics related to the operations of the internal revenue laws as well as provides related data. It provides papers, several data products, and periodic publications, and supporting information on the IRS's tax statistics site (http://www.irs.gov/uac/Tax-Stats-2).

- The Substance Abuse and Mental Health Services Administration's (SAMHSA) data (http://www.samhsa.gov/data/) measures and reports changes to U.S. health care that assists in addressing behavioral health disparities. Data can be accessed through a variety of methods.

- U.S. Government Accountability Office (http://www.gao.gov/), which is an independent, nonpartisan agency that works for Congress, provides a host of reports and testimonies that include data and study results from a host of topics of interest to the U.S. government.

- The United Nations Children's Fund (UNICEF) maintains data on children and women around the world. It has one site, for example, dedicated to statistics (http://www.unicef.org/statistics/).

- The World Health Organization (WHO) is a great source of global data, particularly to compare data and other information on African Americans to blacks in other countries. It maintains a data repository, reports, country statistics, map galleries, and standards (http://www.who.int/en/).
- The United Nations Statistics Division, in its mission to promote the development of national statistical systems, has developed a central repository of country profiles of statistical systems. The country profiles include, among others, a brief history of the country's statistical system, legal basis, the statistical program, and much more (http://unstats.un.org/unsd/methods/inter-natlinks/sd_natstat.asp).

USING DATA SOURCES

When using existing data sources, it is very important to carefully review the methodology that was used. This can be found in indicated sections and also in footnotes to tables and other data presented. Some sources that provide recurring data will have a specific section on a website dedicated solely to explaining their methodologies and variable definitions. The key information that should be provided are the method(s) used to collect the data, the time frame of data collection, size of the sample or population analyzed, any assumptions made as part of data collection, discussions on the limitations of the study and data findings, and at least some summary discussion on missing data or other concerns about the data. There should also be a description of all variables presented in the data findings. Many websites, for example, will provide a data dictionary that defines variables in terms of what they stand for and what they mean. Finding and using this dictionary is particularly important when using raw data from a source versus their prepared tables or reports. As shown in the list of sources earlier, many sites allow the researcher to extract raw data from provided databases.

Be very mindful to look for noted errors or cautions in using the data. This will normally be outlined in footnotes of reported tables, or directions may be given to a specific appendix or website. For example, time series data may have had changes in the methodology used over the period the data is being reported. For that reason, older data may not be comparable to the results of newer data. Other concerns are being able to ascertain if all the data collected is being reported, how missing data elements were handled, and what the response rate was from the sampled or studied population. If all else fails, call or e-mail the department, agency, or office that produced the data in order to gain greater insights and to ask questions. Most sites will provide specific contact information of an office or even the person who prepared the data results.

There are many other sources of data from private and nonprofit sources. Some notable online sources include the Pew Research Center, the Henry J. Kaiser Family Foundation, and Gallup, Inc. Some sources are dedicated to single topics and provide a wealth of data on specific issues. For example, the Sentencing Project focuses on crime and justice. It reports a wealth of data on such issues as incarceration, felony disenfranchisement, and drug policies. BlackDemographics.

com provides extensive data on blacks in the United States from various sources on a single website. Data on African Americans includes population, household, economics, education, health, culture, geography, and statistics. The Joint Center for Political and Economic Studies is a nonprofit public policy organization that produces research and policy solutions targeting minorities.

Scholars and other researchers also publish data as part of books, journals, and reports. However, ensure the books were published by reputable publishing companies. For example, data in books that have been self-published have most likely not been reviewed for accuracy. Often writers pay a fee to have their books bound and the books haven't even been checked for spelling errors or the validity of sources used. One has to research the author and the publishing company before relying on data provided. The most reliable sources of published data are from refereed journal articles and books published by renowned publishing companies. These journals normally publish articles that have resulted from rigorous research using established academic methods such as proper survey techniques. The articles were reviewed and approved by "peers" in the writers' field of study. This means experts in the field have reviewed the articles to ensure that they meet standards of academic and research quality. They also ensure the results of research are valid and that the research methods used were reliable. Reputable publishing companies will thoroughly edit books before publication and conduct a fact check of information and verification of data sources.

Be wary of websites that do not verify the accuracy of information posted. For example, many sites containing "pedia" in their title are not reliable sources of data. These sites may be used as a starting point for pointing you in the right direction to find data, but the information provided should be validated by the researcher using reputable sources. Another issue is websites that use data to support an ideological position. The owners or supporters of these sites often slant data results, such as only showing certain facts, purposely omitting information, overexaggerating certain results, or reporting information based upon their personal knowledge without validating accuracy and the information being current. This is true of many private and nonprofit managed websites. It also applies to data provided by news organizations, as many take a more liberal or conservative stance on a wide range of issues.

Whether using government sources, published works, or data from websites, data should be verified using multiple sources. Cross-checking information helps the user validate the accuracy and meaning of data. For example, two government sources may report similar information, but the meaning of the data may vary based upon the purpose of the research. This cross-checking process includes determining what variables actually mean in the data presented. The user must also carefully read the methodology that outlines why and how the data was obtained. Different studies have different purposes, often described in the explicit or implicit research question of the study. The research questions and hypotheses will be the foundation for how and why the study was conducted. If these elements are not present, the user can often contact the organization that completed the study for more information.

1

Education

Education data is divided by levels. These include the following:

- Early childhood (or prekindergarten) education
- Primary (or elementary) school
- Middle (or junior high) school
- Secondary (or high) school
- Postsecondary (college, career, or technical schools) education

Some studies may aggregate data into more discrete categories, such as primary education representing grades kindergarten through 12 (notice this does not include preschool or day care); college education, including those with an associate and bachelor's degree; and graduate education, including those with a master's degree and PhD. Care must be taken to understand how "education level" is defined for each study used. There is a difference between the classification of students who actually completed each level (e.g., "some high school" means a person attended but did not actually graduate from high school, and "some college" means some courses were taken but a degree was not obtained).

Education data generally outlines those who have completed high school or obtained a high school equivalency, for example, passed the General Educational Development (GED) test. Data also outlines those who are enrolled in college, completed some college courses, or have actually obtained at least a bachelor's degree. For students in college, data may be distinguished by those with or pursuing an associate degree (e.g., in community college), bachelor's degree, or an advanced degree. Data that shows the number or percentage of those with a bachelor's or higher means those that have a bachelor's, master's, or doctoral degree or hold a professional degree required for their profession, for example, juris doctor (JD) for lawyers or doctor of medicine (MD) for doctors.

Search for data dictionaries used to arrive at education statistics. For example, the National Center for Education Statistics provides a comprehensive glossary of terms used in its survey materials (National Center for Education Statistics 2016). They also provide data definitions as an appendix to many of their major reports.

EDUCATION ACHIEVEMENT

Educational achievement is a primary indicator of economic and social well-being, as well as health disparities. For example, those with lower levels of education have less knowledge of the value of healthful living habits as well as regular medical care. They thus suffer health disparities in comparison to those with more formal education. It is not only an indicator of one's ability to obtain stable employment at a competitive wage, but it also influences one's propensity to commit crimes, vote, and generally be able to successfully advance in most facets of society. African Americans have made tremendous strides in educational achievement, particularly since the end of segregation. The education gap between blacks and whites has narrowed, particularly at the high school and undergraduate levels. Historically, black colleges and universities continue to play a primary role; 33% of all blacks who have bachelor's degrees, 75% of blacks who have PhDs, 46% of black business executives, 50% of black engineers, 80% of black federal judges, and 50% of black doctors and lawyers in the United States have graduated from these schools. However, challenges still exist, such as black students scoring lower than their peers on standardized tests, disparities in discipline, the existence of the school-to-prison pipeline, and the continued existence of segregated schools.

Table 1.1 shows the educational achievement of persons over 25 years of age in 2014 by race and Hispanic origin. The rates of high school completion are comparable across all races, with African Americans actually having the highest rate of completion at 30% (compared to the national average of 26.7%). However, the disparity for African Americans is apparent as the level of educational achievement increases. At the bachelor's degree level, only 10.3% of blacks hold a degree, compared to 16.4% of non-Hispanic whites and 24.3% of Asians. Hispanics have the lowest rate at 8.1%. African Africans fall behind whites and Asians for master's degrees, and for PhDs, only 0.8% hold a degree compared to 2% of non-Hispanic whites and 4.1% of Asians. This data is a primary indicator of why African Americans earn less than their white and Asian counterparts and lag in other related areas such as home ownership.

It is very important to point out that there is a disparity also between black males and black females, as the latter have the higher rate of educational achievement. For example, McDaniel et al. (2011) analyzed 60 years of education data by race and sex to conclude, "At no point did a larger proportion of black men complete college than black women. Less than 1% of black men earned a college

Table 1.1 Detailed Years of School Completed by People 25 Years and Older by Sex, Age Groups, Race, and Hispanic Origin, 2014

Detailed Years of School	All Races		White		Non-Hispanic White		Black		Asian		Hispanic (of Any Race)	
	Number	Percent	Number	Percent	Number	Percent	Number	Percent	Number	Percent	Number	Percent
Total	**209,287**	**100**	**166,962**	**100**	**140,124**	**100**	**24,864**	**100**	**11,801**	**100**	**29,919**	**100**
High school diploma	55,845	26.7	44,641	26.7	37,424	26.7	7,460	30.0	2,313	19.6	7,980	26.7
Bachelor's degree only	31,123	14.9	25,051	15.0	22,919	16.4	2,558	10.3	2,865	24.3	2,408	8.1
Master's degree programs												
Master's degree 1-year program	1,360	0.7	1,203	0.7	1,148	0.8	65	0.3	78	0.7	60	0.2
Master's degree 2-year program	11,443	5.5	9,076	5.4	8,465	6.0	1,014	4.1	1,171	9.9	684	2.3
Master's degree 3 or more years program	4,969	2.4	4,038	2.4	3,771	2.7	427	1.7	450	3.8	294	1.0
Professional degree	3,148	1.5	2,601	1.6	2,471	1.8	179	0.7	312	2.6	141	0.5
Doctorate degree	3,703	1.8	2,970	1.8	2,785	2.0	206	0.8	478	4.0	193	0.7

Note: Numbers in thousands. Civilian noninstitutionalized population. Excluding members of the Armed Forces living in barracks.
Source: U.S. Census Bureau, Current Population Survey, 2014 Annual Social and Economic Supplement.

degree in 1940, compared with less than 2% of black women. By 2000, approximately 10% of black men and 15% of black women completed college. Blacks'
rates of college completion have steadily risen over time, but more rapidly for
women than for men. For blacks, women have held a consistent advantage in
college completion over men for more than 70 years; for whites, women's advantage in college completion emerged in recent decades." Karl Reid (2013) reported
the same conclusions in *The Journal of Negro Education*, pointing out that black
males only comprise 4% of the total college enrollment. As far as actual degrees
attained, black women earned 55% of all bachelor's degrees conferred to African
Americans in 2008–2009, as well as the majority of all master's and nonprofes-
sional doctoral degrees. This education gap was supported by only 33% of black
men graduating within six years, compared to 44% of black women and 57% of
white males.

Analysis

There is a direct correlation between educational attainment and job participation. For example, Table 1.2 shows the educational attainment of those in the
labor force in 2014 by race. The table shows that the majority of whites in the
labor force (38%) have a bachelor's degree or higher, compared to Asians at 6%.
However, the majority of working African Americans (31%) held a high school
diploma only. This rate was comparable to that of Hispanics, where the majority
of those working were also only high school graduates (30%). This lack of educational attainment in comparison to whites and Asians negatively impacts the
ability of many to find jobs, even for those that are the most persistent in seeking
employment opportunities. Johnson (2000, p. 59) points out the need to refute
false perceptions about the poor, particularly those centered around race, such as
those in poverty being unwilling to work. He referenced a study of unemployed
black youth that found the majority were persistent to find work. Specifically,
"Among those youth considered to be chronically unemployed, about half viewed
jobs as impossible to find; even so, more than 85% continued to be hopeful about
finding another job. Even more contradictory to the prevailing myths, among
Black men who had experienced multiple episodes of chronic unemployment
(6 months with no job), 70% remained hopeful. Myths about lack of responsi-
bility, feigned attempts at job searches, and the hopelessness of our youth are
dissolved in the face of such studies."

The level of educational achievement is directly related to unemployment and
earnings. Data in Table 1.3 shows the unemployment rates and median weekly
earnings by level of education attainment. Note that this data is for persons aged
25 and over, and earnings are for full-time wage and salary workers. Notice the
employment rate ranges from a high of 9% for those with less than a high school
diploma down to 1.9% for those with a professional degree, and 2.1% for those
with a doctorate. Median weekly earnings follow the same trend but in reverse,
ranging from $488 for those with less than a high school diploma to $1,639

Table 1.2   Educational Attainment of the Labor Force Aged 25 and Older by Race and Hispanic or Latino Ethnicity, 2014 Annual Averages (%)

	White	Black or African American	Asian	Hispanic or Latino
Less than a high school diploma	8	8	6	28
High school graduates, no college	27	31	17	30
Some college, no degree	16	22	10	15
Associate degree	11	11	7	8
Bachelor's degree or higher	38	27	60	19

Note: People whose ethnicity is identified as Hispanic or Latino may be of any race. Data may not sum to 100% due to rounding.
Source: Bureau of Labor Statistics (2015). Current Population Survey. Labor Force Characteristics by Race and Ethnicity, 2014 (Report 1057). November.

Table 1.3   Earning and Unemployment Rates by Educational Attainment, 2014

Education Attained	Unemployment Rate in 2014 (%)	Median Weekly Earnings in 2014 ($)
Less than a high school diploma	9.0	488
High school diploma	6.0	668
Some college, no degree	6.0	741
Associate's degree	4.5	792
Bachelor's degree	3.5	1,101
Master's degree	2.8	1,326
Professional degree	1.9	1,639
Doctoral degree	2.1	1,591
All workers	5.0	839

Note: Data are for persons aged 25 and over. Earnings are for full-time wage and salary workers.
Source: Bureau of Labor Statistics (2015). *Current Population Survey*. U.S. Department of Labor, U.S. Bureau of Labor Statistics. Retrieved from http://www.bls.gov/emp/ep_table_001.htm on December 28, 2015.

for those holding a professional degree and $1,591 for those with a doctorate. Holding constant for any other factors, the majority of African Americans and Hispanics would be at the lower end of the earning scale and face the highest unemployment levels. Data from the Bureau of Labor Statistics (2015) reveals that African Americans had an unemployment rate of 11.3% in 2014, compared to a national average (among people of working age) of 6.2%, 5.3% for whites, 5.0% for Asians and 7.4% for Hispanics.

Having less education exacerbates other challenges blacks have in finding equal employment opportunities. As pointed out by Stephen Zanskas, Daniel C. Lustig, and Terry T. Ishitani (2011, p. 127), "The labor market participation of African Americans and Hispanics is affected by many factors, including employment in occupations with higher levels of unemployment, lower average levels of educational attainment, residing in urban areas with limited employment opportunities, and discrimination." However, studies have shown that education breaks down at least some of these barriers, particularly discrimination. For example, Geoffrey T. Wodtke (2012) outlined how this is consistent with the findings of the enlightenment theory in that those with more education are more likely to reject racial stereotypes, support residential and school integration, and support policies fostering democratic equality. The author attributes these more progressive racial attitudes to such mechanisms in postsecondary institutions as enrollment in multicultural classes and contact with minority students and faculty.

SEGREGATED SCHOOLS

Many Americans are surprised to hear that some parts of the country still have segregated schools. While no longer supported by laws, segregation exists due to practices within certain communities due to the policies supported by some in official positions. The Supreme Court's *Brown v. Board of Education of Topeka, Kansas* decision in 1954 legally ended education segregation in the United States, even though it took decades for some schools to fully comply with the court's ruling. The ruling was further supported by the passage of the Civil Rights Act of 1964, which allowed the Attorney General to file lawsuits against states with segregated school systems. However, this problem still persists, mostly along a combination of racial and economic lines. For example, Table 1.4 shows the trend of black and Latino children attending segregated schools for select school years from 1968–1969 through 2009–2010 from an article in the *Huffington Post* (Goyette and Scheller 2014). Notice that the rates for blacks are much lower than their peak in the 1968–1969 year, when 64.3% of black children in the country attended intensely segregated schools (meaning 90–100% of the student population was nonwhite). Another 12.3% attended schools that were segregated (meaning 50–100% of students were nonwhite). Still, the rate has been on a gradual increase since the 1980–1981 year. The same is true as far as an upward trend for Latino children. Per the article, in the 2009–2010 year, 80% of Latino students attended segregated schools and 43% attended intensely segregated schools (% schools in which white students accounted for 10% or less of the student population). The same year, 74% of black students attended segregated schools, and 38% attended intensely segregated schools.

This increase in segregated schools indicates a lack of policies to address reversing these trends, and also an increase in segregation among economic lines where those who are poor are most likely to attend segregated schools. This includes discriminatory housing practices in which blacks and Latinos are purposely segregated from predominantly white and/or wealthy neighborhoods. Busing is the practice of physically transporting students from poor schools to more affluent schools with better educational resources. Busing minority students to

Table 1.4   Trend of Black and Latino Children (%) Attending Segregated Schools

	School Year				
	1968–1969	1980–1981	1991–1992	2001–2002	2009–2010
Black children in segregated (50–100% nonwhite) schools	12.3	29.7	32.7	33.7	36.0
Black children in intensely segregated (90–100% nonwhite) schools	64.3	33.2	32.7	38.0	38.1
Latino children in segregate (50–100% nonwhite) schools	31.7	39.3	39.1	36.1	36.4
Latino children in intensely segregated (90–100% nonwhite) schools	23.1	28.8	33.9	42.0	43.1

Source: Goyette, Braden and Alissa Scheller (2014). "15 Charts that Prove We're Far from Post-Racial." *Huffington Post*, July 2. Retrieved from http://www.huffingtonpost.com/2014/07/02/civil-rights-act-anniversary-racism-charts_n_5521104.html on May 20, 2016.

more prominent schools in other districts has never been truly successful. When used in the 1960s and 1970s, it created a hardship on schools and families. As the middle and upper class left urban areas in the 1970s and 1980s, busing became impractical, and those with the financial means enrolled their children in private schools where busing was not permitted. Rulings up to the Supreme Court also reduced the use of busing. For example, the high court ruled in *Milliken v. Bradley*, 418 U.S. 717 (1974) that school systems did have to employ such desegregation strategies as busing unless there was evidence that those systems had deliberately engaged in segregationist policies.

Additionally, a report in *USA Today* (Lee 2014) lists the following states as being the most segregated for black students during the 2011–2012 school year, with the percentage of black students attending predominantly white schools. Those states with highest numbers also have very large minority populations, some of which are most concentrated in urban areas, such as in Michigan, and others are dispersed more evenly in the entire state, such as North Carolina:

California, 8%

Connecticut, 18.5%

Florida, 20.9%

Georgia, 19.5%

Illinois, 14.8%

Indiana, 28%

Louisiana, 28.6%

Maryland, 14%

Michigan, 25.1%

Mississippi, 22.9%

Nevada, 14.6%

New Jersey, 20.8%

New York, 13.3%

North Carolina, 26.6%

Ohio, 28.1%

Pennsylvania, 28.1%

Tennessee, 25.3%

Texas, 13.1%

Virginia, 28.9%

Wisconsin, 28.2%

The report further outlines that the percentage of black students attending majority white schools increased from 9% in 1954 to over 30% in 1970, and to a high of 43.5% in 1988. Since 1988, the percentage has consistently gone down each year, to a point of 23.2% in 2011.

The above percentages are supported by studies conducted on this topic, such as one by The Civil Rights Project (Orfield et al. 2014). It released a profound report in 2014 entitled *Brown at 60: Great Progress, a Long Retreat and an Uncertain Future* detailing the results of their study of segregation in the United States. The following are some key findings outlined in the press release for the report (Epperly 2014):

- Black and Latino students are an increasingly large percentage of suburban enrollments, particularly in larger metropolitan areas, and they are moving to schools with relatively few white students.

- Latinos are now significantly more segregated than blacks in suburban America.

- Black and Latino students tend to be in schools with a substantial majority of poor children, while white and Asian students typically attend middle-class schools.

- Segregation for blacks is the highest in the Northeast, a region with extremely high district fragmentation.

- Segregation is by far the most common in the central cities of the largest metropolitan areas; the states of New York, Illinois, and California are the worst in terms of isolating black students.

- California is the state in which Latino students are most segregated.

Analysis

A study conducted by the Economic Policy Institute (Rothstein 2013) extensively outlined the achievement gaps between African American and white students, as well as the issue of school segregation. The study found that poverty among blacks is a significant contributing factor to the gap because far fewer white students face the effects of generational poverty. Additionally, the study outlines how political agendas and court systems have basically ceased to take action to integrate schools, even when black and white students have similar poverty levels and family characteristics. This is due to black children being more concentrated in neighborhoods with high poverty levels, fewer job opportunities for their parents, and frequent violence. Additionally, "Neighborhood desegregation has disappeared from mainstream policy agendas partly because of beliefs that little can be done about it and that residential isolation has no constitutionally compelled remedy. In 2007, the Supreme Court prohibited districts from taking explicit steps to increase racial diversity because, according to the plurality opinion, racial isolation in schools resulted only from 'de facto' neighborhood segregation—accidents of economic differences, demographic trends, and personal choices" (p. 19).

As mentioned earlier, one of the primary reasons for an increase in segregated schools has been the courts' decisions to release states from abiding by segregation laws. Federal courts, in particular, are taking stances that racial discrimination in education has been reduced to such a low level that federal oversight is no longer needed to remedy disparities as had been before and immediately after school integration. According to a report on the rise in school segregation by Jason Breslow, Evan Wexler, and Robert Collins (2014), court rulings released 45% of school districts from judicial oversight between 1990 and 2009. The Stanford University Center for Education Policy Analysis found that the number of districts that were released rose from approximately 7 per year in the 1990s to approximately 15 per year in the 2000s. Researchers measure integration by using a "dissimilarity index," in which the scale runs from 0 to 1. A score of 0 shows a school with balanced integration and 1 represents complete segregation. The authors found that "When the Stanford researchers looked at what happens when districts leave court oversight, they found schools typically climb back toward 1, or more segregation. Schools released from integration plans saw the gulf between whites and blacks grow by 24% after 10 years as compared to schools still under court order. The split between white students and Latinos grew by 10% after a decade."

One of the formative cases that ended federal segregation oversight was *Board of Education of Oklahoma City Public Schools v. Dowell*, 498 U.S. 237 (1991). The case focused on a 1972 federal district court injunction that ordered the Board of Education of Oklahoma to implement a "Finger Plan" that bused black students to predominantly white schools in order to end segregation. The district court withdrew the plan in 1977 because it felt the plan had reached unitary racial composition, and in 1984 the busing plan was reversed. When the case reached the

Supreme Court, the court ruled "federal supervision of local school systems [has] been intended as a temporary measure to remedy past discrimination." Further, the district court could remove the injunction if it found "that the school system was being operated in compliance with the Equal Protection Clause, and that it was unlikely that the Board would return to its former ways." In other words, lower courts were given the authority to enjoin school districts if they felt that a remedy of past discrimination has been practically achieved, and if a school district has made a good faith attempt to remedy past segregated situations.

A related issue is that even when black students attend majority white schools, they may still be segregated by classes and curriculums. For example, Katrina Walsenmann and Bethany Bell (2010) found that black students are more likely to be given less rigorous academic coursework—even if they have equal academic abilities as other students—as part of a process known as "tracking." The authors explain that, "in theory, the process of tracking should be based on student ability, previous academic achievement, and course availability. In reality, however, other factors often influence track assignments, including pressure placed on school decision-makers by parents, as well as students' race/ethnicity, socioeconomic status (SES), and gender."

Addressing the pros and cons of "tracking," Sonali Kohli (2014) points out that the arguments for and against this practice are based on both economics and racial equality. Addressing the use of tracking in gifted and talented programs, advanced placement courses, and upper-level classes, the author outlines that those who support tracking see it as a means for students with similar educational needs to be placed in the same classroom. This allows the teacher to provide more focused instruction based on the students' learning needs, whether the students are grouped as remedial or gifted. However, opponents argue those in lower-skilled classes are not afforded the educational advantages of those in advanced classes. This leads to a permanent learning gap between many minority students, who are the majority in low-skilled classes, compared to white and Asian students who predominantly make up advanced classes.

Ending or even reducing segregated schools is complicated by factors beyond the courts reversing their stance on the issue. First, busing programs are being reduced due to their costs to school systems and even the costs to parents. Second, school systems either will not or cannot by law use race as a factor in determining strategies to support students in their districts. Third, more affluent families are not supportive of efforts to integrate schools, and these families move to areas where racial discrimination is inherent based on residents' income levels. They also resist efforts to support bringing children from poorer areas to their schools out of concern for their own children. In other words, the "NIMBY (not-in-my-backyard) syndrome" is used to justify efforts to stop school integration and supporting programs such as low-income housing in upper-income neighborhoods. Finally, political ideology regarding segregation versus integration is based on support from those who predominantly vote and contribute to political candidates and their parties. This, of course, means the poor are politically disenfranchised.

Rose Mary Wentling and Consuelo Luisa Waight (1999) conducted a survey about barriers that hinder the successful transition of minority youth into the workplace, and found segregated schools to be a contributing factor. From their survey of a panel of school-to-work partnership directors located throughout the United States, they found almost three-fourths identified lack of an integrated or relevant curriculum as a barrier. Wentling and Waight pointed to black students being placed in prevocational curriculums and the lowest academic tracks, with teachers actively segregating academic and vocational student curriculums based on race.

Finally, a blog in the *Huffington Post* (2013) outlines the same findings. Pointing to schools being more segregated due to a reversal of the progress made in integrating schools as a result of the ruling in *Brown v. Board of Education of Topeka, Kansas* (1954) and subsequent court decisions, the article outlines that "while more recent Supreme Court decisions from Oklahoma City, Louisville, KY, and Seattle, WA, and policy-level failures such as No Child Left Behind (NCLB) are rightfully viewed among myriad protagonists of these trends, often overlooked by integration advocates is the reality of 'dual school systems' operating at the curricular level, not just at the facility level."

The U.S. Department of Education continues to investigate segregated curriculums in integrated schools. For example, it outlined how it resolved this condition in Orange-Maplewood, New Jersey, in a press release issued by the U.S. Department of Education's Office of Civil Rights in 2014 (Press Office 2014):

> The U.S. Department of Education's Office for Civil Rights (OCR) announced today that it has entered into an agreement with the School District of South Orange & Maplewood, New Jersey, to resolve a compliance review that examined whether black students are provided an equal opportunity to access and participate in advanced and higher-level learning opportunities. OCR's investigation revealed that the school district's nearly 2,500 black students are significantly underrepresented in advanced and higher-level learning opportunities at the district's elementary, middle and high school levels For example, in the 2012–13 school year, black students had only 148 of the nearly 800 spots (18.7%) in the district's Advanced Placement (AP) courses, while they represented more than half (51.5%) of the district's high school enrollment Black students were also underrepresented in elementary and middle school math enrichment programs and advanced courses.

Educational disparities facing blacks are discussed in an Executive Order signed by President Barack Obama on July 25, 2012, entitled *White House Initiative on Educational Excellence for African Americans*. The initiative was launched to help accelerate national efforts to support African American students. As outlined in the order:

> Substantial obstacles to equal educational opportunity still remain in America's educational system. African Americans lack equal access

to highly effective teachers and principals, safe schools, and challenging college-preparatory classes, and they disproportionately experience school discipline and referrals to special education. African American student achievement not only lags behind that of their domestic peers by an average of two grade levels, but also behind students in almost every other developed nation. Over a third of African American students do not graduate from high school on time with a regular high school diploma, and only four% of African American high school graduates interested in college are college-ready across a range of subjects. An even greater number of African American males do not graduate with a regular high school diploma, and African American males also experience disparate rates of incarceration.

STANDARDIZED TESTING

Standardized testing has become a requirement for determining the preparedness of students to advance in secondary and higher levels of education. These tests are used to measure what students have learned, and also predict future academic success. In secondary schools, students are required to obtain minimum levels of academic achievement in mathematics, reading, and writing in order to pass standards of learning tests. These tests are also used to gauge the academic adequacy of teachers and school systems in student instruction. Admission into any college or university's undergraduate, graduate, or professional program requires the institutions' approval of each student's standardized test scores. These exams include the Scholastic Aptitude Test (SAT), American College Testing Program (ACT), Graduate Management Aptitude Test (GMAT), Graduate Record Examination (GRE), or Law School Admission Test (LSAT), to name a few.

Standardized tests (also referred to as readiness tests) are developed by testing experts as part of a national, state, or local program. The basic intended purpose of these tests is to provide an objective measure of student preparedness, sometimes coupled with subjective measures such as written essays. These tests measure a student's score against the average, or mean, of all scores. All student scores are divided according to the standard deviation of scores from the mean. There are three basic types of standardized tests. *Achievement tests* gauge whether students have learned what they have been taught, and if they gained specific knowledge or skills. Their test results are compared to other students' results, and are tracked over time to measure progressive learning. Results are also used to modify current teaching strategies in subject areas where students scored the lowest. *Scholastic aptitude tests* are used to predict a student's capability to learn over a short time period, such as the first year of college. Predictability is based upon students' responses to questions about what they have learned from their formal education and personal experiences. *Specific aptitude tests* are designed to predict how students will perform in a specific content area such as law or history.

Standardized tests have been criticized for creating an adverse impact on minorities, who score lower than their white peers due to cultural, ethnic, and language challenges. Many view these tests as being biased and developed unfairly in favor of white students, not an adequate means of measuring student preparedness, and outdated in terms of usefulness. Because minorities, and particularly blacks, have always scored lower on these tests, they are continually denied equal access to opportunities including admission to better colleges and thus equal job opportunities after completing college. This academic gap is estimated to impact at least half of all African Americans (Ford and Helms 2012).

As the data in Table 1.5 shows regarding the SAT, as well as what the scores from most other standardized tests demonstrate, the primary implication from using these tests is the negative impact on minority students, particularly African Americans and Hispanics. Because minorities are not provided the same level of preparation as students from wealthier families and educational backgrounds, they are the least prepared for these tests. They are therefore more prone to failing and being retained in their grade, placed in a lower education track, or being put in special or remedial programs. Students from white and middle and upper income families are more likely to be placed in gifted and talented or college preparatory programs. In comparison, minority students are not well-prepared for college entrance tests such as the SAT, ACT, GMAT, or GRE. Some therefore cannot get into top colleges, compete for scholarships, or attend college at all. Colleges and universities will lose diversity and become racially and economically segregated. High schools that consistently have larger percentages of students failing standardized tests face being taken over, being merged with other schools, or closed.

It must be stressed that the conclusion from these scores is not that black students are not as smart as other students. Once admitted to gifted programs and college preparatory programs, they are able to learn at the same pace as other students. However, standardized testing prohibits them from being given equal opportunities in education.

SCHOOL-TO-PRISON PIPELINE

The school-to-prison pipeline is a result of policies and practices school systems systemically take against students deemed as "high risk" in terms of behavior or academic performance to remove them from school through disciplinary actions that ultimately results in the student quitting school. This leads to students becoming active in criminal behavior, leading them to jail and prison. This practice disproportionately impacts minority students (particularly blacks and Hispanics) and those from the lowest economic backgrounds. Reasons for this "pipeline" include: the increase in zero-tolerance policies established in response to school violence from gangs and school shootings, overzealous policing in schools, and education policies that penalize school systems for students not passing standardized tests. An article from PBS (Public Broadcasting Service) about the

Table 1.5 SAT Mean Scores of College-Bound Seniors, by Race/Ethnicity, Selected Years, 1990–1991 through 2009–2010

Race/Ethnicity	1990–1991	1996–1997	1998–1999	1999–2000	2000–2001	2001–2002	2002–2003	2003–2004	2004–2005	2005–2006	2006–2007	2007–2008	2008–2009	2009–2010
SAT—Critical Reading														
All students	499	505	505	505	506	504	507	508	508	503	502	502	501	501
White	518	526	527	528	529	527	529	528	532	527	527	528	528	528
Black	427	434	434	434	433	430	431	430	433	434	433	430	429	429
Mexican American	454	451	453	453	451	446	448	451	453	454	455	454	453	454
Puerto Rican	436	454	455	456	457	455	456	457	460	459	459	456	452	454
Other	458	466	463	461	460	458	457	461	463	458	459	455	455	454
Asian/ Pacific Islander	485	496	498	499	501	501	508	507	511	510	514	513	516	519
American Indian/ Alaska Native	470	475	484	482	481	479	480	483	489	487	487	485	486	485
Other	486	512	511	508	503	502	501	494	495	494	497	496	494	494
SAT—Mathematics														
All students	500	511	511	514	514	516	519	518	520	518	515	515	515	516
White	513	526	528	530	531	533	534	531	536	536	534	537	536	536
Black	419	423	422	426	426	427	426	427	431	429	429	426	426	428
Mexican American	459	458	456	460	458	457	457	458	463	465	466	463	463	467
Puerto Rican	439	447	448	451	451	451	453	452	457	456	454	453	450	452
Other His-panic	462	468	464	467	465	464	464	465	469	463	463	461	461	462

Asian/ Pacific Islander	548	560	560	565	566	569	575	577	580	578	578	581	587	591
American Indian/ Alaska Native	468	475	481	481	479	483	482	488	493	494	494	491	493	492
Other	492	514	513	515	512	514	513	508	513	513	512	512	514	514

Note: Data are for seniors who took the SAT any time during their high school years through March of their senior year. If a student took a test more than once, the most recent score was used. The SAT was formerly known as the Scholastic Assessment Test and the Scholastic Aptitude Test. Possible scores on each part of the SAT range from 200 to 800. The critical reading section was formerly known as the verbal section.

Source: U.S. Department of Education, National Center for Education Statistics (2011). *Digest of Education Statistics, 2010* (NCES 2011–2015). Table 151.

school-to-prison pipeline (Amurao 2013) provides data to highlight the impact on both blacks and Latinos:

- 40% of students expelled from U.S. schools each year are black.
- 70% of students arrested in school or referred to law enforcement officers are black or Latino.
- Black students are three and a half times more likely to be suspended than whites.
- Black and Latino students are twice as likely to not graduate high school as whites.
- 68% of all males in state and federal prison do not have a high school diploma.

The National Education Association (NEA) has committed itself to combating the school-to-prison pipeline not only due to the severity of its impact on students in general, but also because of the targeted actions of certain student demographics. In a recent NEA report (Flannery 2015), it was noted that more than 3 million students were suspended from school in 2010, which was double the number in the 1970s. More than a quarter-million students were referred to the police, mostly for offenses that were once handled by verbal admonishment. The NEA contributes these numbers to zero-tolerance policies, the presence of police officers in schools, cuts to school funding, and the stress school administrators and teachers are under for their students to pass standardized tests. As a result, school practices result in suspensions, expulsions, and arrests of tens of millions of public school students, particularly those who are minorities, disabled, or identify as lesbian, gay, bisexual or transgender (LGBT).

The concerns raised by the NEA are supported by other data sources. Table 1.6 shows the percentage of students suspended from U.S. schools during the 2011–2012 school year. Notice the highest suspension rates were for black students in both elementary (7.6%) and secondary schools (23.2%). In comparison, the rate for all students was 2.6% and 10.1%, respectively; and for whites, 2.9% and 11.9%, respectively. The second highest rates by race were for American Indians, at 2.9% and 11.9%, respectively. Race aside, high rates of suspension were also seen for students with disabilities, 5.4% in elementary schools and 18.1% in secondary schools.

Analysis

Carla Amurao (2013) describes the school-to-prison pipeline as an "epidemic that is plaguing schools across the nation." Black students are subjected to disciplinary behavior for even minor offenses in schools. Many of them have a history of abuse, neglect, poverty, and learning disabilities. However, these factors are often ignored by school systems in rendering punishment rather than providing these students supportive rehabilitation. The goal of punishment is to remove

Table 1.6   Nationwide Suspension Rates (%) at U.S. Schools, 2011–2012

	School Level	
	Elementary	Secondary
All	2.6	10.1
American Indian	2.9	11.9
Pacific Islander	1.2	7.3
Asian	0.5	2.5
Black	7.6	23.2
Latino	2.1	10.8
White	1.6	6.7
English learner	1.5	11.0
With disability	5.4	18.1

Source: Redfield, Sarah E. and Jason P. Nance (2016). *School-to-Prison Pipeline: Preliminary Report.* The School-to-Prison Pipeline Task Force (Coalition on Racial and Ethnic Justice, Criminal Justice Section and Council for Racial & Ethnic Diversity in the Educational Pipeline). Retrieved from http://jjie.org/files/2016/02/School-to-Prison-Pipeline-Preliminary-Report-Complete-Final.pdf on May 20, 2016.

these students from the school environment or coerce them to quit. This often results in removing students from the one positive place in their lives, leading to the students' increased feelings of isolation, resentment, and confusion. Some end up dropping out of school completely after having repeated courses or grades. That then leads to committing crimes and eventually winding up in the penal system as a minor or adult.

Standardized testing requirements are considered a contributing factor to this issue. Because of the implications from laws such as "No Child Left Behind" and "Race to the Top," primary and secondary schools are under tremendous pressure for students to do well on standardized tests. These laws penalize schools whose students do not do well on standardized tests, either through withholding or taking away education funds. Therefore, schools have been accused of creating strategies to permanently remove students who are perceived to drag down overall test schools, including African American and developmentally disabled students.

According to the American Civil Liberties Union (Scott 2010), students face harsh penalties as a result of school pressures to have students succeed on standardized tests. Policies such as No Child Left Behind incentive schools to push out low-performing students so that a school's overall test score averages are higher. Further, "One study found that schools meted out longer suspensions to students who performed poorly on standardized tests than to high-performing students for similar offenses. This 'punishment gap' grew substantially during the period of time when standardized tests were administered, indicating that schools may use 'selective discipline' to keep low-performing students out of school during testing days."

The National Advancement of Colored People (NAACP) Legal Defense Fund (2013) is highly critical of school-to-prison pipelines because they target black youth and have no rehabilitative purposes. They report that "these practices harm academic achievement for all students while increasing the chances that those excluded will be held back, drop out, and become involved with the juvenile and criminal justice systems." Further, "African-American students overall are now nearly three times as likely to be suspended, and Latino students are nearly one-and-a-half times as likely to be suspended, as their white peers."

Studies show black students are targeted more than other students by school disciplinary policies. Predominantly, black schools are equipped with metal detectors, police officers, and methods to quickly remove problem students from classrooms. Statistics supporting the contention that black youth are the primary targets of the school-to-prison pipeline reveal the following (Sealey-Ruiz 2011, p. 117):

- In public schools nationwide, while black students account for 17% of the population, they represent 34% of school suspensions.
- Special education students represent 8.6% of public school students, but 32% of youth in juvenile detention worldwide.
- Black students with learning disabilities are three times more likely to be suspended than their white counterparts and four times more likely to end up in correctional facilities.

School-to-prison programs and policies have part of their roots in the Gun-Free School Zones Act of 1990, which set penalties for any person found possessing a gun on school grounds. The act states that "Whoever violates the Act shall be fined not more than $5,000, imprisoned for not more than 5 years, or both. Notwithstanding any other provision of law, the term of imprisonment imposed under this paragraph shall not run concurrently with any other term of imprisonment imposed under any other provision of law." The act was found unconstitutional by the Supreme Court in *United States v. Alfonso Lopez, Jr.*, 514 U.S. 549 (1995) and in violation of the Commerce Clause (which gives Congress the power "to regulate commerce with foreign nations, and among the several states, and with the Indian tribes"). The court held that while Congress had broad lawmaking authority under the Commerce Clause, the power was limited, and did not extend so far from "commerce" as to authorize the regulation of the carrying of handguns, especially when there was no evidence that carrying them affected the economy on a massive scale. Therefore, Attorney General Janet Reno's proposed changes to the act were adopted in the Omnibus Consolidated Appropriation Act of 1997 that required firearms under the act that affected interstate commerce. This change has yet to be challenged. Schools across the country have thus adopted the concept of zero tolerance from the act. Zero tolerance would apply to the possession of any type of fireman on school property.

Many schools extended or adopted new types of zero-tolerance policies after the Columbine High School massacre in 1999, and subsequent policies have been developed as a result of later tragedies involving mass shootings at schools around the country. These policies were not only developed to target individual students who could potentially be a threat, but applied to entire school populations as a pro-active safeguard. These policies mandate severe punishments for certain offenses, regardless of the circumstances of the event. These offenses include possession of illegal or illicit substances, possessing handguns, fighting on school grounds, or threatening teachers or other students. But the policies have also resulted in students being suspended for much lesser offenses, such as passing gas, possessing water guns, taking another student's food, raising one's voice in class, and turning off another student's computer during class (Aull 2012). Some schools also suspend students for bringing nail clippers or scissors to school. The punishments result in students being suspended, expelled, failed, and/or referred to law enforcement agencies for further punishments. Student failure in school can lead to a cycle of criminal behavior. González (2012, pp. 282–283) further explains the result of these "restorative justice" practices based upon no tolerance, particularly its impact on African American students. The author cites the Advancement Project's 2010 report, entitled *Test, Punish and Push Out: How Zero Tolerance and High-Stakes Testing Funnel Youth Into The School*, which blames these punitive disciplinary practices on the tripling of the national prison population from 1987 to 2007. Between the years of 1974 and 2000, the number of students suspended from school each year nearly doubled from 1.7 million to 3.1 million.

African American students end up in the criminal system not only due to school-to-prison pipeline effects, but also due to a systematic targeting of black youth by the criminal justice system. Black youth, as well as those from other minority groups, face racism in schools and elsewhere in their everyday lives. They are often the victims of racial profiling by law enforcement officers. Studies show that police are more likely to search vehicles driven by blacks and Latinos in comparison to whites (Holley and Van Vleet 2006). Racial profiling is especially tied to the War on Drugs instituted by federal and state laws, where black youths are targeted, in particular, for drug offenses. Perry and Bright discussed drug profiling and how blacks receive much harsher sentences from even small amounts of drug possession:

> Crack cocaine, the cheaper alternative to powder cocaine, which is more likely to be found in poor communities of color carried with it a 100 to 1 sentencing disparity relative to powder cocaine. This means that it takes 500 grams of powder cocaine to trigger the same 5-year mandatory minimum sentence that accompanies 5 grams of crack cocaine. These policies are also related to the increase in racial profiling in which African Americans are disproportionately stopped, searched, and arrested by the police and eventually sentenced despite being no more likely to possess or abuse drugs than whites. (2012, p. 188)

Once students have been expelled, placed in rehabilitative schools, or incarcerated, it is very difficult for them to return to normal schools. They face additional discrimination because of their past behavior and are labeled as troublemakers. Schools establish intentional roadblocks to their reentry in the school system or pressure them to quit if they do return. Schools fear these students may be disruptive, become bad influences on other students, or do poorly on standardized testing, thereby impacting overall school performance. Those who attempt to reenroll may be asked to produce "multiple documents to enroll in school, including documents that will establish the student's residency, age, or immunization status. If the juvenile justice system does not forward the documents and the student cannot otherwise provide them, the student may be denied enrollment. . . . A national study reports that more than 66% of youth in custody drop out of school after they are released" (Feierman, Levick, and Mody 2009, p. 1116). If allowed to enroll, they may be immediately placed in remedial courses, vocational classes, or enrolled in alternative education programs. Part or all of their credits from their prior schooling may also be rejected.

DISCIPLINARY ACTIONS

Data from the U.S. Department of Education Office for Civil Rights highlights the problem of black students being disproportionately disciplined. For example, the office reports that "black students represent only 16% of the student population, but 32%–42% of students suspended or expelled. In comparison, white students also represent a similar range of between 31%–40% of students suspended or expelled, but they are 51% of the student population." This means black students are suspended or expelled at three times the rate of white students. This has a tremendous negative impact on their education, given that, for example, 20% of black boys and 12% of black girls in grades K–12 are given out-of-school suspensions (2014).

Table 1.7 shows the types of punishment levied on students by race and ethnicity. Notice black or African American students receive 34% of all expulsions, 42% of multiple out-of-school suspensions, and 33% of single out-of-school suspensions. These rates are extremely high, considering that blacks comprise a little over 12% of the U.S. population. Comparatively, white students received 36% of all expulsions, 31% of multiple out-of-school suspensions, and 36% of single out-of-school suspensions. The majority of lesser punishments are given to white students, namely those whose punishments allow them to stay enrolled (51%) and receive in-school suspension (40%). The following are additional highlights provided by the Office of Civil Rights:

• Suspension of preschool children, by race/ethnicity and gender: Black children represent 18% of preschool enrollment, but 48% of preschool children receive more than one out-of-school suspension; in comparison, white students represent 43% of preschool enrollment, but 26% of preschool children receive more than one out-of-school suspension. Boys represent 79% of preschool children suspended once and 82% of preschool children suspended multiple times, although boys represent 54% of preschool enrollment.

Table 1.7   Students (%) Receiving Suspensions and Expulsions, by Race/Ethnicity

Type of Disciplinary Actions	White	Black/ African American	Native Hawaiian/ Other Pacific Islander	American Indian/ Alaska Native	Hispanic/ Latino	Two or More Races
Enrollment	51	16	0.5	0.5	24	2
In-school suspension	40	32	0.2	0.2	22	3
Out-of-school suspension (single)	36	33	0.4	2	23	3
Out-of-school suspension (multiple)	31	42	0.3	2	21	3
Expulsion	36	34	0.3	3	22	3

Note: Detail may not sum to 100% due to rounding. Totals: Enrollment is 49 million students, in-school suspension is 3.5 million students, single out-of-school suspension is 1.9 million students, multiple out-of-school suspension is 1.55 million students, and expulsion is 130,000 students. Data reported in this figure represents 99% of responding schools.
Source: U.S. Department of Education Office for Civil Rights (2014). *Civil Rights Data Collection (2011–12), Data Snapshot: School Discipline*. Washington, DC: U.S. Department of Education. Retrieved from http://ocrdata.ed.gov/Downloads/CRDC-School-Discipline-Snapshot.pdf on March 1, 2016.

- Disproportionately high suspension/expulsion rates for students of color: Black students are suspended and expelled at a rate three times greater than white students. On average, 5% of white students are suspended, compared to 16% of black students. American Indian and Alaska Native students are also disproportionately suspended and expelled, representing less than 1% of the student population but 2% of out-of-school suspensions and 3% of expulsions.

- Disproportionate suspensions of girls of color: While black boys receive more than two out of three suspensions, black girls are suspended at higher rates (12%) than girls of any other race or ethnicity and most boys; American Indian and Alaska Native girls (7%) are suspended at higher rates than white boys (6%) or girls (2%).

- Suspension rates, by race, sex, and disability status combined: With the exception of Latino and Asian American students, more than one out of four boys of color who have disabilities (served by Individuals with Disabilities Education Act [IDEA])—and nearly one out of five girls of color who have disabilities—receives an out-of-school suspension.

- Arrests and referrals to law enforcement, by race and disability status: While black students represent 16% of student enrollment, they represent 27% of students referred to law enforcement and 31% of students subjected to a school-related arrest. In comparison, white students represent 51% of enrollment, 41% of those referred to law enforcement, and 39% of those arrested. Students with disabilities (served by IDEA) represent a quarter of students who are arrested and referred to law enforcement, even though they are only 12% of the overall student population.

• Restraint and seclusion, by disability status and race: Students with disabilities (served by IDEA) represent 12% of the student population, but 58% of
those placed in seclusion or involuntary confinement, and 75% of those physically restrained at school to immobilize them or reduce their ability to move
freely. Black students represent 19% of students with disabilities served by
IDEA, but 36% of these students who were restrained at school through the
use of a mechanical device or equipment designed to restrict their freedom of
movement.

These findings were corroborated by data published in 2014 from the Kirwan
Institute for the Study of Race and Ethnicity, which showed that 70% of students who were involved in school-related arrests or referred to law enforcement
were black or Hispanic. Pointing to a 2009–2010 survey, the Kirwan Institute
also reported that black students only comprised 18% of the school enrollments
during that year, but accounted for 46% of students who were suspended more
than once, and 3% of all expulsions. Black students were disciplined to the point
that they were three and half times as likely as white students to be suspended
or expelled.

The Department of Education has found issues that go beyond disciplinary
actions that highlight racial disparities in American school systems. The Department's Office of Civil Rights (Press Office 2014a) released findings after a comprehensive evaluation of civil rights data from every public school in the country
from the 2011–2012 school year. The data was compiled from all of the nation's
97,000 public schools comprising 16,500 school districts, or 49 million students.
This study concluded that rates for suspension of students of color are significantly higher than those for white students. In addition, students of color, notably
black and Latino students, are significantly more likely to have inexperienced,
lower paid teachers. Finally, male students of color are disproportionally affected
by zero-tolerance policies, leading them to be more likely to repeat a grade, drop
out, or become involved in the juvenile justice system. Racial disparities also
impact Native Hawaiian/Pacific Islanders, who are held back a year at nearly
twice the rate of white students in kindergarten. Among the other key findings, the
Office of Civil Rights reported the following:

• Access to preschool: About 40% of public school districts do not offer preschool, and where it is available, it is mostly part-day only. Of the school districts that operate public preschool programs, barely half are available to all
students within the district.

• Access to advanced courses: Eighty-one percent of Asian American high school
students and 71% of white high school students attend high schools where a
full range of math and science courses are offered (algebra I, geometry, algebra
II, calculus, biology, chemistry, physics). However, less than half of American
Indian and Alaska Native high school students have access to a full range of
math and science courses in their high school. Black students (57%), Latino

students (67%), students with disabilities (63%), and English language learner students (65%) also have less access to a full range of courses.

- Access to college counselors: Nationwide, one in five high schools lacks a school counselor; in Florida and Minnesota, more than two in five students lack access to a school counselor.

Analysis

Studies have shown that schools that focus on student punishment instead of rehabilitation eventually place less emphasis on teaching and more on policing students. In some cases, schools even become less safe. Elbert Aull finds that, "This new culture of discipline has added an additional layer of instability to an already fragile learning environment at many schools. Far from being a silver bullet that has made schools safer and more conducive to learning, the overbearing police presence and overly punitive disciplinary policies appear to have transformed schools into places where administrators are far more concerned with controlling student behavior than encouraging scholarship and the free flow of ideas" (2012, pp. 185–186). As teachers and administrators focus their efforts on discipline, they are distracted from instructing students. The long-term consequence of this will be academic deficiencies passed from generation to generation because parents who dropped out or were kicked out of school tend to have a negative attitude toward education. They then often pass this negativity to their children, and place less emphasis on their children's academic achievement due to their own experiences.

It is recognized that some students genuinely pose disciplinary challenges. Some are involved in gangs, are abusing alcohol or drugs, or have violent behaviors that pose a risk to other students and teachers. In some cases, there are few alternatives except removing these children from the classroom. However, schools must work with local agencies to develop strategies whereby even these students are given educational opportunities. More schools should consider alternatives such as placing these students in special schools or after-school programs, utilizing juvenile camps, and mandating counseling services with local agencies to attempt to correct negative behaviors. These students should not be allowed to disrupt classroom instruction for other students who do not have behavior issues. At the same time, these "problem students" should not be denied an education. This will only increase the likelihood that they will become criminals, thus becoming a bigger issue for the local community. The costs to the nation would include increased costs of incarcerations, broken homes, and increased unemployment.

DROPOUT RATES

The National Center for Education Statistics defines the status dropout rate as "the percentage of 16- through 24-year-olds who are not enrolled in school and have not earned a high school credential (either a diploma or an equivalency credential such as a General Educational Development [GED] certificate). This rate is different from graduation rate measures that reflect the percentage of students earning a regular diploma within 4 years of entering high school. Status dropouts are no longer attending school (public or private) and do not have a high school level of educational attainment" (Kena et al. 2015, p. 178).

Table 1.8 outlines the percentage of high school dropouts (called the "status dropout rate") among persons 16 through 24 years old, by sex and race/ethnicity between the years 1970 and 2013. The rate for all races, ethnicities, and sexes has fallen drastically since 1960, when the rate for all Americans was 27.2%. In 1970, it was 15.0%, and by 2013, the rate had fallen to 6.8%. The dropout rate for blacks in 1970 was 27.9%, compared to 7.3% in 2013. Hispanics continue to have the highest dropout rate, although it fell from over 30% in the 1970s to 11.7% in 2013. Males continue to have higher dropout rates than females across all races and ethnicities. For example, black males in 2013 had dropout rates of 8.2% compared to 6.6% for black females.

The students with the highest status dropout rates tend to live in poverty, come from single-parent homes, and are raised by parents who also have lower levels of education. Data in Table 1.9 shows that the majority of American children (36.3%) between the ages of 6 and 18 in 2012 lived in homes where at least one parent had a bachelor's degree or higher. However, this rate of parental education varied by race and ethnicity. For example, 36.5% of Hispanic children between 6 and 18 years lived in a single-parent household where the parent had not obtained a high school diploma. The number of Hispanic children living in two-parent households in which neither parent held a high school diploma was 25.4%. For black youth, 15.4% lived in single-parent homes with a parent who had not completed high school, compared to 2.7% of black youths living with two parents who had not completed high school. The respective comparative rates for whites were 8.8% and 1.7%. For households where parents had a bachelor's degree or higher, 53.8% of whites from two-parent households and 23.7% of single-parent households fell in this category. In comparison, 40.2% of black parents from two-parent homes and 12.5% from single-parent householders, and 22.1% and 8.8% of Hispanic parents, respectively, also held bachelor's degrees or higher.

COLLEGE ENROLLMENT

There were over 20 million students in Title IV colleges and universities in 2013. These institutions have a written agreement with the Secretary of Education that allows them to participate in any of the Title IV federal student financial assistance programs, with the exception of the State Student Incentive Grant (SSIG) and the National Early Intervention Scholarship and Partnership (NEISP) programs. By sex, more women (11.8 million) were enrolled in higher education institutions than men (9 million). As shown in Table 1.10, the majority of

Table 1.8 Percentage of High School Dropouts among Persons 16 through 24-Years-Old (Status Dropout Rate), by Sex and Race/Ethnicity, Selected Years, 1970–2013

Year	Total Status Dropout Rate				Male Status Dropout Rate				Female Status Dropout Rate			
	All races[1]	White	Black	Hispanic	All races[1]	White	Black	Hispanic	All races[1]	White	Black	Hispanic
1970[2]	15.0	13.2	27.9	NA	14.2	12.2	29.4	NA	15.7	14.1	26.6	NA
1972	14.6	12.3	21.3	34.3	14.1	11.6	22.3	33.7	15.1	12.8	20.5	34.8
1974	14.3	11.9	21.2	33.0	14.2	12.0	20.1	33.8	14.3	11.8	22.1	32.2
1976	14.1	12.0	20.5	31.4	14.1	12.1	21.2	30.3	14.2	11.8	19.9	32.3
1978	14.2	11.9	20.2	33.3	14.6	12.2	22.5	33.6	13.9	11.6	18.3	33.1
1980	14.1	11.4	19.1	35.2	15.1	12.3	20.8	37.2	13.1	10.5	17.7	33.2
1982	13.9	11.4	18.4	31.7	14.5	12.0	21.2	30.5	13.3	10.8	15.9	32.8
1984	13.1	11.0	15.5	29.8	14.0	11.9	16.8	30.6	12.3	10.1	14.3	29.0
1986	12.2	9.7	14.2	30.1	13.1	10.3	15.0	32.8	11.4	9.1	13.5	27.2
1988	12.9	9.6	14.5	35.8	13.5	10.3	15.0	36.0	12.2	8.9	14.0	35.4
1990	12.1	9.0	13.2	32.4	12.3	9.3	11.9	34.3	11.8	8.7	14.4	30.3
1992[3]	11.0	7.7	13.7	29.4	11.3	8.0	12.5	32.1	10.7	7.4	14.8	26.6
1994[3]	11.4	7.7	12.6	30.0	12.3	8.0	14.1	31.6	10.6	7.5	11.3	28.1
1996[3]	11.1	7.3	13.0	29.4	11.4	7.3	13.5	30.3	10.9	7.3	12.5	28.3
1998[3]	11.8	7.7	13.8	29.5	13.3	8.6	15.5	33.5	10.3	6.9	12.2	25.0
2000[3]	10.9	6.9	13.1	27.8	12.0	7.0	15.3	31.8	9.9	6.9	11.1	23.5
2002[3]	10.5	6.5	11.3	25.7	11.8	6.7	12.8	29.6	9.2	6.3	9.9	21.2
2004[3,4]	10.3	6.8	11.8	23.8	11.6	7.1	13.5	28.5	9.0	6.4	10.2	18.5
2006[3,4]	9.3	5.8	10.7	22.1	10.3	6.4	9.7	25.7	8.3	5.3	11.7	18.1
2008[3,4]	8.0	4.8	9.9	18.3	8.5	5.4	8.7	19.9	7.5	4.2	11.1	16.7
2010[3,4,5]	7.4	5.1	8.0	15.1	8.5	5.9	9.5	17.3	6.3	4.2	6.7	12.8

(Continued)

Table 1.8 (Continued)

Year	Total Status Dropout Rate				Male Status Dropout Rate				Female Status Dropout Rate			
	All races[1]	White	Black	Hispanic	All races[1]	White	Black	Hispanic	All races[1]	White	Black	Hispanic
2011[3,4,5]	7.1	5.0	7.3	13.6	7.7	5.4	8.3	14.6	6.5	4.6	6.4	12.4
2012[3,4,5]	6.6	4.3	7.5	12.7	7.3	4.8	8.1	13.9	5.9	3.8	7.0	11.3
2013[3,4,5]	6.8	5.1	7.3	11.7	7.2	5.5	8.2	12.6	6.3	4.7	6.6	10.8

NA, not available.

Note: "Status" dropouts are 16- to 24-year-olds who are not enrolled in school and who have not completed a high school program, regardless of when they left school. People who have received GED credentials are counted as high school completers. All data except for 1960 are based on October counts. Data are based on sample surveys of the civilian noninstitutionalized population, which excludes persons in prisons, persons in the military, and other persons not living in households. Race categories exclude persons of Hispanic ethnicity except where otherwise noted.

[1] Includes other racial/ethnic categories not separately shown.

[2] For 1967 through 1971, white and black include persons of Hispanic ethnicity.

[3] Because of changes in data collection procedures, data may not be comparable with figures for years prior to 1992.

[4] White and black exclude persons identifying themselves as two or more races.

[5] Beginning in 2010, standard errors were computed using replicate weights, which produced more precise values than the generalized variance function methodology used in prior years.

Source: U.S. Department of Commerce, Census Bureau. *Current Population Survey (CPS), October 1967 through 2013.* (This table was prepared in July 2014.) Retrieved from https://nces.ed.gov/fastfacts/display.asp?id=16 on February 21, 2016.

Table 1.9 Percentage Distribution of 6- to 18-Year-Olds, by Parent's Highest Level of Educational Attainment, Household Type, and Child's Race/Ethnicity, 2012

Year, Household Type, and Race/Ethnicity	Less Than High School Completion	High School Completion[2]	Some College, No Degree	Associate's Degree	Bachelor's or Higher Degree[1]			
					Total	Bachelor's Degree	Master's Degree	Doctor's Degree
Total, both household types	**11.0**	**19.5**	**22.6**	**10.6**	**36.3**	**20.8**	**10.7**	**4.8**
White	3.5	16.6	21.8	11.9	46.1	26.1	13.8	6.2
Black	11.0	24.9	30.7	11.2	22.2	13.7	6.5	1.9
Hispanic	29.8	24.9	21.1	7.3	16.9	10.9	4.2	1.8
Asian	10.1	11.8	11.8	7.1	59.3	28.8	19.3	11.3
Pacific Islander	5.2	30.9	31.2	11.6	21.2	14.0	4.7	2.5
American Indian/Alaska Native	10.8	27.1	30.8	12.0	19.3	12.3	5.4	1.5
Two or more races	4.7	16.3	27.0	11.8	40.2	22.5	11.5	6.2
Two-parent household	7.2	15.2	19.9	11.1	46.5	25.6	14.2	6.7
White	1.7	12.7	19.6	12.1	53.8	29.5	16.6	7.7
Black	2.7	16.6	26.6	13.8	40.2	23.0	12.8	4.5
Hispanic	25.4	23.9	20.5	8.0	22.1	13.9	5.8	2.5
Asian	8.3	10.2	10.6	6.9	64.1	29.8	21.7	12.6
Pacific Islander	2.5	28.2	29.4	13.8	26.1	16.5	6.3	3.3
American Indian/Alaska Native	3.5	23.1	30.9	14.7	27.8	16.7	8.9	2.2
Two or more races	1.5	10.2	22.4	11.8	54.1	28.0	16.7	9.4
Single-parent household	18.1	27.6	27.8	9.6	16.9	11.6	4.0	1.3
White	8.8	27.7	28.4	11.4	23.7	16.0	5.8	2.0
Black	15.4	29.4	32.8	9.8	12.5	8.8	3.2	0.5
Hispanic	36.5	26.6	21.9	6.3	8.8	6.3	1.8	0.6
Asian	19.0	19.5	17.7	7.8	36.1	23.9	7.5	4.7
Pacific Islander	11.2	37.0	35.3	6.6	9.9	8.3	‡	‡
American Indian/Alaska Native	17.6	30.8	30.6	9.5	11.5	8.4	2.2	1.0
Two or more races	9.2	24.9	33.6	11.9	20.4	14.6	4.1	1.7

Note: Table includes only 6- to 18-year-olds who resided with at least one parent (including an adoptive or stepparent). Race categories exclude persons of Hispanic ethnicity. Detail may not sum to totals because of rounding.

[1]Includes adoptive and stepparents, but excludes parents not residing in the same household as their children.

[2]Includes parents who completed high school through equivalency programs, such as a GED program.

Source: U.S. Department of Commerce, Census Bureau. *American Community Survey, 2007 and 2012.* (This table was prepared in January 2014.) Retrieved from https://nces.ed.gov/programs/coe/indica tor_saa.asp and https://nces.ed.gov/programs/digest/d13/tables/dt13_104.70.asp on January 2, 2016.

Table 1.10 Number and Percentage of Students Enrolled at All Title IV Institutions, by Control of Institution, Student Level, Level of Institution, and Other Selected Characteristics, United States, Fall 2013

	Total		Public		Private			
					Nonprofit		For-profit	
	Number	Percent	Number	Percent	Number	Percent	Number	Percent
Student level								
Total students	20,847,787	100	14,855,412	100.0	3,993,462	100.0	1,998,913	100.0
4-year	13,407,463	64.3	8,120,461	54.7	3,942,175	98.8	1,344,827	67.3
2-year	7,097,068	34.0	6,677,519	45.0	41,499	1.0	378,050	18.9
Less than 2-year	343,256	1.6	57,432	0.4	9,788	0.2	276,036	13.8
Attendance status								
Full time	12,965,148	62.2	8,526,174	57.4	3,003,284	75.2	1,435,690	71.8
Part time	7,882,639	37.8	6,329,238	42.6	990,178	24.8	563,223	28.2
Gender								
Men	9,015,068	43.2	6,624,332	44.6	1,699,239	42.6	691,497	34.6
Women	11,832,719	56.8	8,231,080	55.4	2,294,223	57.4	1,307,416	65.4
Race/ethnicity								
American Indian or Alaska Native	159,660	0.8	123,195	0.8	20,363	0.5	16,102	0.8
Asian	1,148,404	5.5	872,481	5.9	220,635	5.5	55,288	2.8
Black or African American	2,790,255	13.4	1,831,062	12.3	447,858	11.2	511,335	25.6
Hispanic or Latino	3,023,461	14.5	2,400,044	16.2	330,028	8.3	293,389	14.7
Native Hawaiian or Other Pacific Islander	59,438	0.3	38,620	0.3	9,379	0.2	11,439	0.6
White	11,103,704	53.3	8,068,115	54.3	2,271,499	56.9	764,090	38.2
Two or more races	542,293	2.6	401,604	2.7	94,791	2.4	45,898	2.3
Race/ethnicity unknown	1,180,020	5.7	586,534	3.9	315,932	7.9	277,554	13.9
Nonresident alien	840,552	4.0	433,757	3.6	282,977	7.1	23,818	1.2

Source: Ginder, Scott A., Janice E. Kelly-Reid, and Farrah B. Mann (2014). Enrollment in Postsecondary Institutions, Fall 2013; Financial Statistics, Fiscal Year 2013; and Employees in Postsecondary Institutions, Fall 2013. National Center for Education Statistics, U.S. Department of Education. Retrieved from http://nces.ed.gov/pubs2015/2015012.pdf.

students enrolled in Title IV schools in 2013 (64.3%) attended four-year schools, and the majority (62.1%) were also full-time students. White students comprised 53.3% of all Title IV institutions, compared to 13.4% of African Americans and 14.5% of Hispanics or Latinos. For public Title IV institutions, the rates were approximately the same, at 54.3%, 12.3% and 16.2%, respectively. For private Title IV nonprofits, whites comprised a large share at 56.9%, compared to 11.2% for African Americans and 8.3% for Hispanics or Latinos. The rates are much narrower for private for-profit Title IV schools. Here, whites comprised 38.2% of students, compared to 25.6% of African Americans and 14.7% of Hispanics or Latinos.

Data shows that different types of Title IV institutions chosen for postsecondary education vary by race and ethnicity. In reference to Table 1.10 again, according to data from the Department of Education's National Center for Education Statistics, African Americans comprise a large share of students attending for-profit Title IV schools over other types. One explanation why for-profit colleges are attractive is because they aggressively recruit African American students. According to Constance Iloh and Ivory Toldson, while black enrollment in public two-year and four-year Title IV institutions increased by only 24% and 27%, respectively, from 2004 to 2009, it increased by 218% in four-year for-profit schools over the same time period. Fourteen percent of undergraduate students were enrolled in for-profit institutions during the 2011–2012 school year. Of these, 10% were black men and 23% were black women. The top two schools producing these black graduates were the University of Phoenix and Ashford University (2013, p. 207).

However, there is a reported concern with for-profit colleges, particularly for black students. According to a report from the Center for Responsible Lending, "Although all races and ethnicities are more likely to attend either a public or private, nonprofit school, African-American and Latino students make up a relatively large portion of students at for-profit colleges" (Smith and Parrish 2014). The report finds that for-profit schools have high net costs that cause students to rely on student loans. Specifically, 70% of four-year for-profit college attendees borrow money, while only 48% and 60% of four-year public and private, nonprofit attendees do so, respectively. The report outlines that, "Among those who borrow at four-year institutions, over one-third of for-profit students take out $8,900 or more in a single year, compared with just 10% and 14% of students attending public and private, nonprofit schools, respectively. This disparity is even more pronounced at two-year institutions, with very few public college attendees taking on any debt" (p. 11). As a result, loan delinquencies and defaults are also higher. For those who graduated from public schools, the delinquency or default rate is 19% compared to 18% for private nonprofits, and 35% at for-profits. For those who do not graduate, the delinquency or default rate is 45% for public institutions, 38% for private nonprofits, and 64% at for-profits.

A final concern is that the report references studies that find those who attend for-profit colleges are less satisfied with their major or concentration and, among those who do not complete their degree, are less satisfied with their education. They are also less likely to report that their student loan debt is a worthwhile investment or be satisfied with their job, and are more likely to be unemployed than those who attend nonprofit schools. It is apparent that in some cases, schools may be more concerned about profit than supporting student needs and achievement. For example, some will push for students to take online courses (which have lower direct and overhead costs) rather than onsite courses, even if students specifically demand onsite courses to meet their learning needs. Some go so far as to purposely not offer courses over one or even several terms to force students to be enrolled in particular programs for longer periods of time. Some do not attract the best faculty due to efforts to maintain low administrative and overhead costs, even at the expense of the quality of their education programs.

Table 1.11 shows the number and percent of 14- to 24-year-old students by their high school graduate status and college enrollment from 2007 through 2014. In 2014, for example, 86.8% of students between 18 and 24 years had graduated from high school and 46.1% were enrolled in college. Only 6.9% had dropped out of high school. Comparative data is given for those between the ages of 14 and 24 years, showing approximately 46% were enrolled in college, and 72% were either enrolled or had completed some college. Those attending college continue to increase. From this same data source, the percentage of those enrolled in college in 1970 was 33.5% and those either enrolled or who had completed some college was 50.5%. In 1980, those rates were 32.1% and 51.1%, and in 1990 they were 39.6% and 58.9%, respectively.

The data shows that the rates of high school graduation and college attendance vary by race. For example, 72.1% of whites between 14 and 24 years were enrolled in or had completed some college. Since 2007, that rate has remained over 70%. For blacks, 65.9% had enrolled in or completed some college, compared to 91.7% of Asians and 62.8% of Hispanics. Notice that over this time period, the greatest increase in college attendance was for Hispanics, followed by blacks. The Pew Research Center reports the same findings. In their analysis, Mark Lopez and Richard Fry (2013) argued, "For the first time, a greater share of Hispanic recent high school graduates are enrolled in college than whites. College enrollment rates among 18- to 24-year-old Hispanics who had completed high school continued their upward march in 2012. According to the Census Bureau, 49% of young Hispanic high school graduates were enrolled in college. By comparison, 47% of white non-Hispanic high school graduates were enrolled in college. These findings reflect those of a May Pew Research Center report that showed the share of Hispanic high school graduates enrolled in college immediately after high school surpassed whites in 2012."

Table 1.11 Population of 14- to 24-Year-Olds by High School Graduate Status, College Enrollment, Attainment, Race, and Hispanic Origin, October 2007–2014

	Population 18- to 24-year-olds								High School Graduates, 14 to 24 Years Old		
	High School Graduates		Percent			High School Dropouts			Percent	
	Total	Enrolled in College	High School Graduates	Enrolled in College	Of High School Graduates Enrolled in College	Number	Percent	All graduates	Enrolled in College	Enrolled or Completed Some College
Total											
All races											
2014	30,304	26,311	12,132	86.8	40.0	46.1	2,090	6.9	26,700	46.3	72.0
2013	30,556	26,317	12,202	86.1	39.9	46.4	2,215	7.3	26,734	46.8	71.8
2012	30,377	25,866	12,456	85.1	41.0	48.2	2,319	7.6	26,255	48.5	72.9
2011	29,943	25,435	12,570	84.9	42.0	49.4	2,481	8.3	25,765	49.6	73.1
2010	29,659	25,224	12,213	85.0	41.2	48.4	2,590	8.7	25,564	48.7	72.6
2009	29,223	24,647	12,073	84.3	41.3	49.0	2,733	9.4	25,015	49.1	72.0
2008	28,950	24,568	11,466	84.9	39.6	46.7	2,702	9.3	24,922	47.0	70.6
2007	28,778	24,146	11,161	83.9	38.8	46.2	2,937	10.2	24,491	46.3	69.7
White alone											
2014	22,507	19,541	9,077	86.8	40.3	46.4	1,599	7.1	19,786	46.6	72.1
2013	22,658	19,660	9,049	86.8	39.9	46.0	1,599	7.1	19,985	46.5	72.1
2012	22,712	19,555	9,302	86.1	41.0	47.6	1,641	7.2	19,831	47.9	73.5
2011	23,089	19,760	9,813	85.6	42.5	49.7	1,885	8.2	20,007	49.8	74.0
2010	22,851	19,517	9,325	85.4	40.8	47.8	1,941	8.5	19,741	48.0	73.0
2009	22,606	19,241	9,327	85.1	41.3	48.5	2,059	9.1	19,512	48.6	72.1
2008	22,530	19,334	9,141	85.8	40.6	47.3	1,991	8.8	19,586	47.5	71.6
2007	22,392	18,913	8,780	84.5	39.2	46.4	2,248	10.0	19,170	46.5	70.3

(*Continued*)

Table 1.11 (Continued)

| | | Population 18- to 24-year-olds | | | | | | | High School Graduates, 14 to 24 Years Old | | |
| | High School Graduates | | Percent | | | High School Dropouts | | | | Percent | |
	Total	Total	Enrolled in College	High School Graduates	Enrolled in College	Of High School Graduates Enrolled in College	Number	Percent	All graduates	Enrolled in College	Enrolled or Completed Some College
Black alone											
2014	4,704	3,993	1,528	84.9	32.5	38.3	345	7.3	4,061	39.0	65.9
2013	4,746	3,885	1,600	81.9	33.7	41.2	393	8.3	3,929	41.5	65.7
2012	4,714	3,754	1,689	79.6	35.8	45.0	467	9.9	3,816	45.0	66.6
2011	4,503	3,649	1,639	81.0	36.4	44.9	399	8.9	3,702	45.3	66.3
2010	4,457	3,669	1,692	82.3	38.0	46.1	258	12.1	3,731	46.2	66.2
2009	4,346	3,458	1,604	79.6	36.9	46.4	505	11.6	3,532	46.4	67.5
2008	4,265	3,387	1,349	79.4	31.6	40.0	548	12.1	3,445	40.2	60.7
2007	4,182	3,423	1,396	81.8	33.4	40.8	425	10.2	3,483	40.9	61.4
Asian alone											
2014	1,590	1,504	1,023	94.6	64.3	68.0	17	1.1	1,541	67.6	91.7
2013	1,639	1,495	1,001	91.2	61.1	66.9	61	3.7	1,530	67.4	86.8
2012	1,537	1,385	915	90.1	59.5	66.0	54	3.5	1,418	66.3	84.9
2011	1,252	1,123	748	89.8	59.7	66.5	65	5.2	1,149	66.9	88.1
2010	1,303	1,193	811	91.5	62.2	68.0	64	4.9	1,232	68.4	89.8
2009	1,181	1,080	768	91.4	65.0	71.1	26	2.2	1,096	71.0	91.8
2008	1,113	1,021	655	91.8	58.9	64.1	42	3.8	1,056	64.6	90.4
2007	1,165	1,010	658	86.7	56.4	65.1	86	7.4	1,026	65.1	91.6

Hispanic origin

Year											
2014	6,568	5,324	2,282	81.1	34.7	42.9	777	11.8	5,409	43.1	62.8
2013	6,489	5,118	2,193	78.9	33.8	42.8	889	13.7	5,190	43.1	62.3
2012	6,416	4,902	2,403	76.4	37.5	49.0	972	15.1	4,987	49.4	68.1
2011	5,974	4,569	2,079	76.5	34.8	45.5	975	16.3	4,630	45.7	65.4
2010	5,685	4,138	1,814	72.8	31.9	43.8	1,050	18.5	4,199	44.2	63.2
2009	5,332	3,747	1,465	70.3	27.5	39.1	1,112	20.8	3,813	39.6	57.8
2008	5,176	3,618	1,338	69.9	25.8	37.0	1,155	22.3	3,691	37.7	58.7
2007	5,175	3,487	1,375	67.4	26.6	39.4	1,310	25.3	3,553	39.9	58.0

Note: Numbers in thousands. Civilian noninstitutionalized population. Hispanics may be of any race. High school graduates are people who have completed four years of high school or more, for 1967–1991. Beginning in 1992, they were people whose highest degree was a high school diploma (including equivalency) or higher.

Source: U. S. Census Bureau (2015). *Current Population Survey, 1967 to 2014*. Washington, DC. Retrieved from https://www.census.gov/hhes/school/data/cps/historical/index.html on February 27, 2016.

FURTHER READINGS

Arbuthnot, Keena (2015). *Filling in the Blanks: Understanding Standardized Testing and the Black-White Achievement Gap*. Charlotte, NC: Information Age Publishing.

Herrnstein, Richard J. and Charles Murray (1996). *The Bell Curve: Intelligence and Class Structure in American Life*. New York: Free Press Paperbacks.

Hilton, Adriel A., J. Luke Wood, and Chance W. Lewis (eds.) (2012). *Black Males in Postsecondary Education: Examining Their Experiences in Diverse Institutional Contexts*. Charlotte, NC: Information Age Publishing.

Jairrels, Veda (2009). *Standardized Tests: The Real Reason for Low Test Scores*. Cambridge, MA: The Belknap Press of Harvard University Press.

Mallett, Christopher A. (2016). *The School-to-Prison Pipeline: A Comprehensive Assessment*. New York: Springer.

Nocella, Anthony J., II, Priya Parmar, and David Stovall (2014). *From Education to Incarceration: Dismantling the School-to-Prison Pipeline*. New York: Peter Lang Publishing.

Paige, Rod and Elaine Witty (2010). *The Black-White Achievement Gap: Why Closing It Is the Greatest Civil Rights Issue of our Time*. New York: Amacom Books.

Strayhorn, Terrell L. (ed.) (2013). *Living at the Intersections: Social Identities and Black Collegians (Research on African American Education)*. Charlotte, NC: Information Age Publishing.

2

Health

Health data can be complex to analyze because information is often presented using medical jargon that is hard for nonmedical readers to fully understand. For this reason, it is important to investigate data variables to fully understand what they mean. Even for data categories that are generally known, care should be taken in understanding what exactly is represented. For example, there are different types of diabetes. The researcher should understand what types of diabetes are being represented by data when making health inferences by such factors as race and age groups. This is particularly important if the researcher is using data to develop policy recommendations or determinations of health impact causation.

Just as with crime data, there can be biases in how health data is collected and reported. Data can be represented as simple counts, such as the number of patients who were given a vaccine or the number of births that took place during a period of time. Alternatively, health data can be produced from surveys. The primary data issues are with data obtained from surveys or other self-reporting methods. Localities, states, and organizations may underreport some issues for their personal benefit. For example, a city may not want to fully disclose the true rate of communicable diseases there because that information could prohibit attracting new residents and businesses. Some health data is also based on surveys. Citizens, practitioners, and health organizations may submit biased results based on record keeping and even memory (e.g., some may not remember specific information such as dates of visits or medications prescribed). Some survey respondents refuse to answer some questions because they consider them to be too personal. Academic institutions, researchers, and health organizations also conduct individual surveys. Their results may vary based on survey methods, the sampled population, and the time frame of surveys. In all cases, surveys also depend on the availability of the respondents who researchers want to reach, and barriers to understanding questions clearly based on language, education, and medical aptitude.

A primary issue in using health data is that numbers are underreported and often based on estimates. This is particularly true for health data about African Americans, as they, on average, do not seek medical attention for even the most serious conditions. Therefore, estimates for the entire population must be extrapolated based on sampling. It is challenging for researchers to obtain a large and diverse enough sample in order to ensure significance in developing healthy population estimates. Diverse samples must encompass a range of responses from different age groups, income levels, education levels, and people in different parts of the country. Along with this, most health data is reported for the general and noninstitutionalized population. Given the millions of prisoners in the United States, this greatly understates the true reporting of overall population health data.

Still, health data is plentiful, particularly from such organizations as the Centers for Disease Control and Prevention, National Institutes of Health within the U.S. Department of Health and Human Services, medical journals, and numerous online sources. Government sources are recommended as the primary source of information, rather than private or for-profit sources. However, refereed books and articles are great sources for data and information on specific health issues. Many researchers have conducted extensive surveys and dedicated years of study to develop reports.

PRIMARY HEALTH ISSUES

African Americans suffer from many health conditions due to both generational and economic factors. For centuries, they have had socioeconomic disadvantages, including not being able to obtain healthy food due to cost and a lack of local access, not having access to quality health care, and lacking the means to practice healthy lifestyles. Diets high in sugar and salt, pork, and fried foods have led to African Americans having higher rates of diabetes, heart disease, and other complications indicative of poor eating habits. These foods are also the staple of the poor because of their availability and affordability in low-income areas, thus continuing the cycle of generational health problems. Foods that are most healthy (e.g., fruits, vegetables, and those high in protein) also often cost the most. Some poor blacks living in inner-city areas do not even have access to these foods. In rural areas, rezoning and a drastic reduction in farming have had the same impact. Many governmental programs tout success in combating issues of access to healthy foods, but most programs that support those in poverty only provide enough funds for recipients to afford milk, bread, cereals, and foods that are high in sugar, salt, and fat.

In addition to unhealthy diets, the impact of stress from discrimination, living in poverty, growing up in broken homes, and living in areas with high crime rates also affects the health of blacks. As discussed in a recent article on this topic (Hovick et al. 2011, pp. 1789–1790), socioeconomic factors such as lower levels of income and education are directly correlated with many chronic health conditions, including cancer, diabetes, and heart disease. The article asserts that these health conditions can be the result of increased levels of stress, the tendency to eat foods high in starch and sugars, lack of adequate exercise, and a tendency to abuse alcohol and drugs.

The health disparities of African Americans and Latinos contribute to the United States lagging behind other developed nations' overall health outcomes. According to a report in Forbes (Pearl 2015), the life expectancy for men in the United States is last in comparison to all men in the 17 wealthiest nations. Women in the United States are ranked second. When analyzing the 34 most developed nations, U.S. health care outcomes ranked 20th to 27th from 1990 to 2010. This was due to racial, ethnic, and socioeconomic groups in the United States having poor access to health care, particularly African Americans and Latinos.

The report outlines statistics supporting such claims as African Americans and Latinos experience 30–40% poorer health outcomes than whites, costing the nation more than $60 billion a year in lost worker productivity; the death rate from breast cancer is 50% higher for African American women than white women; and 25% of African Americans have elevated blood pressure compared to 10% of white Americans.

Table 2.1 shows the leading causes of death in 2013 for the entire U.S. population, specifically for whites and for blacks. It shows the percentage of deaths and rate per 100,000 people for each cause of death. For the entire population, heart disease, cancer, and chronic lower respiratory disease were the three leading causes of death. Comparatively, these causes had a greater impact on whites (per 100,000 people). For other causes of death, the data shows racial disparities. For example, among the top 15 causes of death, whites have much higher rates of Alzheimer's disease, suicide, Parkinson's disease, and pneumonitis due to solids and liquids. The latter three causes are not even among the top leading causes of deaths for blacks. Blacks, on the other hand, have much higher rates of death due to homicides, HIV/AIDS, diabetes, and hypertension. Notice HIV and homicides are not among the leading causes of death for the general population or whites. These are both preventable and/or treatable conditions that are influenced by awareness, education, and access to quality health care.

HEALTH INSURANCE

A primary issue that affects health is health insurance. As outlined by Kirby and Kaneda (2010), those without coverage are the least likely to obtain preventive and routine care for even chronic conditions. They are more frequently hospitalized for conditions that are potential avoidable, as they are less likely to seek care for issues judged by physicians to be serious.

In the United States, the poor, African Americans, and Hispanics are the least likely populations to have health insurance. Per the Census Bureau (Smith and Medalia 2015, p. 16):

> In 2014, non-Hispanic Whites had a higher rate of health insurance coverage (92.4%) compared with Blacks, Asians, and Hispanics. The health insurance coverage rates for Blacks and Asians were lower than for non-Hispanic Whites, at 88.2% and 90.7%, respectively.

Table 2.1 Leading Causes of Death for Whites and Blacks, United States, 2013 (Including Rates per 100,000 Population in Specific Group)

	All Races, Both Sexes, All Ages		White, Both Sexes, All Ages		Black, Both Sexes, All Ages	
	Percent of Total Deaths	Rate	Percent of Total Deaths	Rate	Percent of Total Deaths	Rate
All Causes	100.0	821.5	100.0	889.2	100.0	693.4
Diseases of heart (heart disease)	23.5	193.3	23.6	209.6	23.8	164.8
Malignant neoplasms (cancer)	22.5	185.0	22.5	199.8	22.4	155.5
Chronic lower respiratory diseases	5.7	47.2	6.2	54.8	3.3	22.7
Accidents (unintentional injuries)	5.0	41.3	5.1	45.2	4.4	30.7
Cerebrovascular diseases (stroke)	5.0	40.8	4.9	43.3	5.4	37.2
Alzheimer's disease	3.3	26.8	3.5	31.0	1.9	13.1
Diabetes mellitus (diabetes)	2.9	23.9	2.7	23.6	4.4	30.6
Influenza and pneumonia	2.2	18.0	2.2	19.7	1.8	12.7
Nephritis, nephrotic syndrome, and nephrosis (kidney disease)	1.8	14.9	1.7	14.9	2.8	19.2
Assault (homicide)					2.7	18.4
Intentional self-harm (suicide)	1.6	13.0	1.7	14.9		
Septicemia	1.5	12.1	1.4	12.4	2.1	14.3
Chronic liver disease and cirrhosis	1.4	11.5	1.4	12.8	1.0	7.0
Essential hypertension and hypertensive renal disease	1.2	9.7	1.1	9.7	1.8	12.5
Certain conditions originating in the perinatal period					1.3	9.3
Human immunodeficiency virus infection					1.2	8.6
Parkinson's disease	1.0	8.0	1.1	9.4		
Pneumonitis due to solids and liquids	0.7	5.9	0.7	6.6		
All other causes (residual)	20.7	170.0	20.4	181.4	19.7	136.7

Note: Cause of death based on the International Classification of Diseases, tenth revision.

Source: CDC/NCHS (2014). *National Vital Statistics System, Mortality 2013*. Retrieved from http://www.cdc.gov/nchs/data/dvs/LCWK2_2013.pdf on January 17, 2016.

Hispanics had the lowest rate of health insurance coverage in 2014, at 80.1%. Non-Hispanic Whites and Asians were among the most likely to have had private health insurance in 2014, at 72.9% and 72.1%, respectively. Hispanics, who had the lowest rate of any health insurance coverage, had the lowest rate of coverage by private health insurance, at 48.7%, while 54.1% of Blacks had private health insurance coverage.

Table 2.2 shows the above data by race as well as by other demographic factor. For example, single individuals had higher rates of being uninsured (14.2%) than those that were part of families (9.5%). Uninsured rates were also higher for those that lived in principal cities (14.2%) than those outside metropolitan statistical areas (10.7%) and outside principal cities (9.3%). The highest uninsured rates by nativity were those that were not citizens (31.2%), followed by foreign born (21.4%), naturalized citizens (10.2%), and then native born citizens (8.7%). By type of insurance, private insurance was the primary type of coverage (66%) in comparison to government health insurance (36.5%). However, a greater percentage of blacks relied on government health insurance (44.2%) than any other race or ethnicity. As outlined in the table, government health insurance includes Medicaid, Medicare, TRICARE, CHAMPVA (Civilian Health and Medical Program of the Department of Veterans Affairs), and care provided by the Department of Veterans Affairs and the military.

Analysis

A lack of health insurance impacts the prevalence and treatment of basic health issues that are preventable or controllable, and affects overall life expectancy. As Ayanian (2015) points out, "Racial disparities in life expectancy are a key indicator of inequity in health outcomes. Although the United States has made progress in narrowing the gap in life expectancy between blacks and whites, from 7.6 years in 1970 to 3.8 years in 2010, a disparity remains—largely from blacks' higher death rates at younger ages from heart disease, diabetes, and cancer, as well as higher risks for HIV infection, homicide, and infant mortality." Additionally, the annual national economic losses from racial health disparities include $35 billion in excess health care expenditures, $10 billion in illness-related lost productivity, and nearly $200 billion in premature deaths.

The Patient Protection and Affordable Care Act of 2010, commonly referred to as the Affordable Care Act, has increased the number of Americans who had insurance coverage. According to the Department of Health and Human Services, the act resulted in an estimated 20 million people acquiring health insurance coverage between 2010 and early 2016 (Department of Health and Human Services Press Office 2016). This included 6.1 million uninsured youth between the ages of 19 and 25. Between 2013 and 2016, strong gains in insurance rates were found across all racial and ethnic groups.

Table 2.2 Percentage of People by Type of Health Insurance Coverage and Selected Demographic Characteristics, 2013 and 2014

	Total		Any Health Insurance		Private Health Insurance[1]		Government Health Insurance[2]		Uninsured[3]	
	2013	2014	2013	2014	2013	2014	2013	2014	2013	2014
	Number	Number	Percent	Percent	Percent	Percent	Percent	Percent	Percent	Percent
Total	313,401	316,168	86.7	89.6	64.1	66.0	34.6	36.5	13.3	10.4
Family status										
In families	255,079	256,308	87.7	90.5	65.4	67.3	34.1	35.9	12.3	9.5
Unrelated individuals	56,857	58,307	82.1	85.8	59.1	60.5	36.5	39.2	17.9	14.2
Residence										
Inside metropolitan statistical areas (MSAs)	266,117	266,071	88.6	89.6	64.7	66.6	33.5	35.4	13.4	10.4
Inside principal cities	102,026	99,298	84.4	87.9	58.3	60.9	35.9	38.1	15.6	12.1
Outside principal cities	164,091	166,773	87.9	90.7	68.6	70.0	31.9	33.7	12.1	9.3
Outside MSAs[4]	47,284	50,097	87.2	89.3	61.2	62.6	40.7	42.7	12.8	10.7
Race[5] and Hispanic origin										
White	243,446	244,468	87.3	89.9	66.6	68.0	33.5	35.7	12.7	10.1
White, not Hispanic	195,489	195,352	90.3	92.4	72.1	72.9	32.8	34.7	9.7	7.6
Black	40,647	41,226	84.1	88.2	50.2	54.1	43.1	44.2	15.9	11.8
Asian	17,008	17,796	86.2	90.7	68.6	72.1	26.0	28.2	13.8	9.3
Hispanic (any race)	54,268	55,614	75.6	80.1	44.7	48.7	37.3	39.5	24.4	19.9
Nativity										
Native born	272,658	273,984	88.8	91.3	66.0	67.4	35.6	37.5	11.2	8.7
Foreign born	40,743	42,184	72.3	78.6	51.9	56.7	27.6	30.4	27.7	21.4
Naturalized citizen	19,134	19,733	84.6	89.8	60.9	65.5	33.7	35.3	15.4	10.2
Not a citizen	21,609	22,451	61.3	68.8	44.0	48.9	22.2	26.2	38.7	31.2

Note: Numbers in thousands, margins of error in percentage points. Population as of March of the following year. For information on confidentiality protection, sampling error, nonsampling error, and definitions, see www2.census.gov/programs-surveys/cps/techdocs/cpsmar15.pdf. The estimates by type of coverage are not mutually exclusive; people can be covered by more than one type of health insurance during the year.

1. Private health insurance includes coverage provided through an employer or union, coverage purchased directly by an individual from an insurance company, or coverage through someone outside the household.

2. Government health insurance coverage includes Medicaid, Medicare, TRICARE, CHAMPVA (Civilian Health and Medical Program of the Department of Veterans Affairs), and care provided by the Department of Veterans Affairs and the military.

3. Individuals are considered to be uninsured if they do not have health insurance coverage for the entire calendar year.

4. The "Outside metropolitan statistical areas" category includes both micropolitan statistical areas and territory outside of metropolitan and micropolitan statistical areas. For more information, see "About Metropolitan and Micropolitan Statistical Areas" at www.census.gov/population/metro/about.

5. Federal surveys now give respondents the option of reporting more than one race. Therefore, two basic ways of defining a race group are possible. A group such as Asian may be defined as those who reported Asian and no other race (the race-alone or single-race concept) or as those who reported Asian regardless of whether they also reported another race (the race-alone-or-in-combination concept). This table shows data using the first approach (race alone). The use of the single-race population does not imply that it is the preferred method of presenting or analyzing data. The Census Bureau uses a variety of approaches. Information on people who reported more than one race, such as White and American Indian and Alaska Native or Asian and Black or African American, is available from Census 2010 through American FactFinder. About 2.9% of people reported more than one race in Census 2010. Data for American Indians and Alaska Natives, Native Hawaiians and Other Pacific Islanders, and those reporting two or more races are not shown separately.

Source: Smith, Jessica C. and Medalia (2015). *Health Insurance Coverage in the United States: 2014.* Washington, DC: U.S. Bureau of Census, September. Retrieved from https://www.census.gov/content/dam/Census/library/publications/2015/demo/p60-253.pdf on May 13, 2016.

- The uninsured rate among black non-Hispanics dropped by more than 50% (from 22.4% to 10%); about 3 million black adults gained coverage.
- The uninsured rate among Hispanics dropped by more than 25% (from 41.8% to 30.5%); about 4 million Hispanic adults gained coverage.
- The uninsured rate among white non-Hispanics declined by more than 50% (from 14.3% to 7.0%); about 8.9 million white adults gained coverage.

OBESITY

As of 2016, obesity has reached epidemic proportions in the United States, particularly for African Americans. This is primarily due to the ease of obtaining fast food and decreased mobility resulting from the increased use of technology. The terms "overweight" and "obesity" define the ranges of body weight that are generally greater than what is considered healthy for particular heights. For adults, these ranges are determined by using weight and height to calculate a number called the "body mass index," or BMI. This index correlates to the amount of body fat for most people. An adult with a BMI between 25 and 29.9 is considered overweight. An adult with a BMI of 30 or higher is considered obese. The following data exemplifies the consideration of weight for a person who is 5 feet and 9 inches tall:

Weight Range	BMI	Considered
124 lbs. or less	Below 18.5	Underweight
125 –168 lbs.	18.5–24.9	Healthy weight
169 –202 lbs.	25.0–29.9	Overweight
203 lbs. or more	30 or higher	Obese

For children and teens, BMI ranges and weight consideration are measured differently to take into account normal differences in body fat between boys and girls and differences in height at various ages. Children's indexes are plotted on a scale in comparison to other children of the same sex and age. A percentile is then derived corresponding to the following percentile ranges:

Weight Status Category	Percentile Range
Underweight	Less than the 5th percentile
Healthy weight	5th percentile to less than the 85th percentile
Overweight	85th to less than the 95th percentile
Obese	Equal to or greater than the 95th percentile

Data shows that in the United States, 34.9% of adults and 17% of youth (12.7 million) are obese (Ogden et al. 2014). Also, according to the Centers for Disease Control and Prevention (2016), "Non-Hispanic blacks have the highest age-adjusted rates of obesity (48.1%) followed by Hispanics (42.5%), non-Hispanic whites (34.5%), and non-Hispanic Asians (11.7%). Obesity is higher among middle age adults, 40–59 years old (40.2%) than among younger adults, age 20–39 (32.3%) or adults over 60 or above (3.7%)." It is a critical health issue because obesity leads to many other adverse health problems, including asthma, diabetes, heart disease, and stroke.

Obesity in children can have lifelong impacts and shorten life expectancies. According to the authors of a study on race and childhood obesity, it is more prevalent in nonwhite populations due to such factors as genetics, physiology, culture, socioeconomic status, environment, and the interaction of these and other variables. Childhood obesity is often associated with a host of other problems such as sleep apnea, asthma, fatty liver, orthopedic problems, ovarian hyperandrogenism, and chronic kidney disease. "From the child's standpoint, an important consequence of obesity may be psychosocial, including social isolation, poor school performance, and poor self-image" (Caprio et al. 2008, p. 2212).

As shown in Table 2.3, obesity is prevalent in every state. In fact, no state in the United States had an obesity rate lower than 20% in 2014. Notice the highest obesity rates were in Southern states, specifically Mississippi, West Virginia, Arkansas, Louisiana, and Alabama. This is not surprising given that in the South, food is often fried and high in salt, sugar, and fat. However, there is a disparity in obesity rates by race and ethnicity that is shown in Table 2.4. In almost every state, obesity rates for non-Hispanic black and Hispanic adults are much higher than those for non-Hispanic whites. Looking at the nation as a whole, the average obesity rates for non-Hispanic whites were 26.5%, compared to 35.7% for non-Hispanic blacks and 29.8% for Hispanic adults. These disparities are based on not only national region, but also economic status. The greatest disparities between blacks and whites were in Washington, D.C., Hawaii, South Carolina, North Carolina, and Oregon.

DIABETES

Diabetes mellitus, usually just referred to as diabetes, is the name of a group of metabolic diseases in which a person's blood glucose level is high, resulting from defects in the body's ability to produce and/or use insulin. Insulin is a hormone that the body needs to convert sugar, starches, and other foods into energy. It regulates carbohydrate and fat metabolism, and causes the liver, muscle, and fat tissues to take glucose from blood and store it. The human body breaks sugars and starches into glucose, which is needed to fuel cells. The regulation of blood glucose levels is part of metabolic stabilization or homeostasis. Diabetes is caused by a reduced production of or resistance to the insulin, resulting in a build-up of glucose in blood.

While there are many types of diabetes, almost 90% occur as two types: type 1 diabetes, formerly called insulin-dependent diabetes mellitus or juvenile diabetes, is usually diagnosed in children and young adults and accounts for 5–10% of diabetes cases. It is an autoimmune disease in which the body's immune system attacks and destroys its own insulin-producing cells in the pancreas. As a result,

Table 2.3 Obesity Rates per State Based on Percentage of Obese (BMI > 30) in U.S. Adults, 2014

State	Obesity (%)	State	Obesity (%)	State	Obesity (%)	State	Obesity (%)
Alabama	33.5	Illinois	29.3	Montana	26.4	Rhode Island	27.0
Alaska	29.7	Indiana	32.7	Nebraska	30.2	South Carolina	32.1
Arizona	28.9	Iowa	30.9	Nevada	27.7	South Dakota	29.8
Arkansas	35.9	Kansas	31.3	New Hampshire	27.4	Tennessee	31.2
California	24.7	Kentucky	31.6	New Jersey	26.9	Texas	31.9
Colorado	21.3	Louisiana	34.9	New Mexico	28.4	Utah	25.7
Connecticut	26.3	Maine	28.2	New York	27.0	Vermont	24.8
Delaware	30.7	Maryland	29.6	North Carolina	29.7	Virginia	28.5
District of Columbia	21.7	Massachusetts	23.3	North Dakota	32.2	Washington	27.3
Florida	26.2	Michigan	30.7	Ohio	32.6	West Virginia	35.7
Georgia	30.5	Minnesota	27.6	Oklahoma	33.0	Wisconsin	32.2
Hawaii	22.1	Mississippi	35.5	Oregon	27.9	Wyoming	29.5
Idaho	28.9	Missouri	30.2	Pennsylvania	30.2		

Source: Centers for Disease Control and Prevention (2014). *Obesity Prevalence Maps*. Division of Nutrition, Physical Activity, and Obesity. Retrieved from http://www.cdc.gov/obesity/data/prevalence-maps.html on March 6, 2016.

Table 2.4   Prevalence of Self-Reported Obesity among Adults by Race/Ethnicity, by State, BRFSS, 2011–2013

State	Non-Hispanic White Adults	Non-Hispanic Black Adults	Hispanic Adults	State	Non-Hispanic White Adults	Non-Hispanic Black Adults	Hispanic Adults
Alabama	29.8	41.8	27.3	Montana	23.4	N/A	29.6
Alaska	26.1	37.9	28.4	Nebraska	28.6	33.7	30.4
Arizona	22.0	32.5	33.8	Nevada	24.7	34.9	27.3
Arkansas	32.0	42.2	34.3	New Hampshire	27.1	27.7	24.7
California	22.4	34.8	30.7	New Jersey	24.4	34.5	27.5
Colorado	18.8	30.5	28.0	New Mexico	22.2	30.1	29.8
Connecticut	23.5	33.2	32.5	New York	23.6	32.7	27.3
Delaware	27.4	37.3	29.2	North Carolina	26.6	40.4	27.0
District of Columbia	10.0	35.6	18.5	North Dakota	29.1	24.7	36.2
Florida	24.5	34.8	26.4	Ohio	29.4	36.0	30.9
Georgia	26.2	37.2	28.1	Oklahoma	31.0	38.7	31.3
Hawaii	19.3	41.1	29.4	Oregon	26.2	39.5	31.2
Idaho	26.8	N/A	35.3	Pennsylvania	28.7	35.6	34.8
Illinois	27.0	38.7	29.9	Rhode Island	25.9	31.4	27.5
Indiana	30.1	42.5	33.2	South Carolina	27.5	42.6	29.7
Iowa	30.1	39.5	37.6	South Dakota	28.1	26.1	31.5
Kansas	29.2	39.2	33.5	Tennessee	30.2	40.4	25.6
Kentucky	31.0	42.0	24.5	Texas	26.5	38.2	35.4
Louisiana	30.4	41.9	32.6	Utah	24.1	26.0	26.1
Maine	28.5	22.6	24.2	Vermont	24.5	20.2	27.1
Maryland	25.3	37.5	25.9	Virginia	26.3	38.5	24.1
Massachusetts	22.4	33.6	31.0	Washington	27.5	37.6	29.7
Michigan	30.1	39.3	35.4	West Virginia	33.8	36.5	32.1
Minnesota	25.5	29.8	30.5	Wisconsin	28.6	38.5	32.4
Mississippi	30.7	42.9	28.2	Wyoming	25.5	N/A	29.2
Missouri	28.8	40.0	33.6				

Source: Centers for Disease Control and Prevention (2015). *Prevalence of Self-Reported Obesity among Non-Hispanic Black Adults by State and Territory, BRFSS, 2012–2014.* Retrieved from http://www.cdc.gov/obesity/data/table-non-hispanic-black.html on January 18, 2016.

insulin must be injected into the body by an injection or a pump. Otherwise, a person can lapse into a life-threatening coma. Symptoms of type 1 diabetes include unusual thirst and frequent urination, constant hunger, weight loss, irritability, blurred vision, and extreme fatigue.

Type 2 diabetes, formerly called adult-onset diabetes, accounts for 90–95% of all adult cases of diabetes and is more common among minorities (African Americans, Latinos, Asian Americans, Native Americans, and other Pacific Islanders) and the elderly. With this type, the body does not produce enough insulin or cells ignore insulin (insulin resistance). Although type 2 diabetes usually develops in adults over 40, it is becoming more prevalent in younger age groups. Symptoms include any of those associated with type 1, but also feeling tired or ill, experiencing weight loss, tingling and numbness in the hands and feet, frequent infections, slow-healing wounds, and recurring skin, gum, or bladder infections. Type 2 is treated with oral medication.

According to the National Institute of Diabetes and Digestive and Kidney Diseases (2016), people are more likely to have type 2 diabetes if they:

- Have a family history of diabetes
- Are a member of certain ethnic groups, including African Americans
- Are overweight or obese
- Are 45 years old or older
- Had diabetes while pregnant (gestational diabetes)
- Have prediabetes (glucose levels are elevated but not high enough to be diagnosed as diabetes)
- Have high blood pressure (HBP)
- Have abnormal cholesterol (lipid) levels
- Are not getting enough physical activity
- Have polycystic ovary syndrome
- Have blood vessel problems affecting the heart, brain, or legs
- Have dark, thick, and velvety patches of skin around the neck and armpits (called *acanthosis nigricans*)

There are various other forms of diabetes. Gestational diabetes occurs in 18% of pregnancies, and occurs when the placenta produces hormones that block the action of insulin in the mother. This causes the mother's body to resist naturally produced insulin and glucose builds up in high levels in the blood (called hyperglycemia). The mother may therefore need up to three times as much insulin to compensate. This type of diabetes disappears when the pregnancy is over, but women who have had gestational diabetes are at a greater risk for developing type 2. Other forms of diabetes are the result of genetic defects of insulin secretion (congenital diabetes), conditions causing damage to the pancreas, and hormones.

Additionally, the disease can result from surgery, drugs, infections, and other illnesses.

According to the Centers for Disease Control (2016), the number of Americans with diagnosed diabetes has increased fourfold (from 5.5 million to 22 million). From 1990 to 2009, the rates per 100 of diagnosed diabetes in the U.S. population increased by 217% (from 0.6 to 1.9) for those aged 0–44 years, and by 150% (from 5 to 12.5) for those aged 45–64. There are clear disparities by race. Native Americans have the highest rate of any race or ethnicity in the United States. In 2014, their rate was almost three times the national average. For others from 1980 to 2014, the age-adjusted rates of diagnosed diabetes per 100 U.S. civilian, noninstitutionalized population increased 152% (from 2.5 to 6.3) for white males. For white females, the age-adjusted rates per 100 increased 116% (from 2.5 to 5.4) from 1990 to 2009. Rates in this group changed little from 1980 to 1990 and from 2009 to 2014. Comparatively, the age-adjusted rates per 100 for black males increased 136% (from 3.9 to 9.2) from 1980 to 2014. For black females, the age-adjusted rates per 100 didn't change much from 1980 to 1997, but then increased 30% (from 7.6 to 9.9) from 1997 to 2014. From 1997 to 2014, the age-adjusted rates per 100 increased 93% (from 3.0 to 5.8) for Asian males but didn't change much for Asian females.

These statistics can be seen in Table 2.5, which outlines the age-adjusted rates of diagnosed diabetes per 100 civilian, noninstitutionalized populations by race

Table 2.5   Age-Adjusted Rates of Diagnosed Diabetes per 100 Civilian, Noninstitutionalized Population, by Race and Sex, United States, Selected Years from 1980 to 2014

Race[1]	White		Black		Asian[2]	
Year	Male	Female	Male	Female	Male	Female
1980	2.5	2.7	3.9	4.7	–	–
1985	2.6	2.7	4.7	5.1	–	–
1990	2.5	2.5	4.1	5.1	–	–
1995	3.1	3.3	5.0	6.7	–	–
2000	4.5	3.8	7.2	7.8	3.9	3.0
2005	5.5	4.9	8.1	8.3	4.6	4.9
2010	6.8	5.4	10.0	9.1	8.4	5.4
2011	6.2	5.5	9.7	8.9	7.4	5.6
2012	6.0	5.7	9.4	9.4	7.5	5.8
2013	6.5	5.7	9.1	9.1	6.7	5.4
2014	6.3	5.3	9.2	9.9	5.8	5.7

Note: See data methodology and limitations at http://www.cdc.gov/diabetes/statistics/prev/national/methods.htm.

[1] The race groups include people of both Hispanic and non-Hispanic origin.

[2] No data were available for Asians before 1997. Source: Centers for Disease Control and Prevention (2016). *Diabetes Public Health Resource*. Atlanta, GA. Retrieved from http://www.cdc.gov/diabetes/statistics/prev/national/figraceethsex.htm on March 6, 2016.

and sex for select years from 1980 through 2014. This table clearly shows blacks had the greatest rates of diabetes compared to whites and Asians. Many more were at risk due to such issues as bad eating habits, high cholesterol, and obesity. All three of these preexisting issues are most prevalent in African American populations due to a higher prevalence of poor diets, hereditary issues, sedimentary lifestyles, and stress than other races.

Diabetes is often referred to as "sugar" by African Americans. This ethnic variation in how the disease is referred to has influenced how blacks seek treatment for the illness. In a study conducted by Schorling and Saunders (2000), 31% of respondents did not know "sugar" and diabetes were the same illness. This misunderstanding led some respondents to believe their condition was curable and the result of bad dietary issues. This was most prevalent among older African Americans with lower levels of education. Yet, their diabetic conditions were much worse than respondents who understood the conditions "sugar" and "diabetes" were in fact the same.

HEART DISEASE

Heart disease is the leading cause of death for all Americans (refer to Table 2.1). It is a general term for a number of different conditions that adversely impact the heart. Other terms used are cardiac disease, cardiovascular disease (CVD), or cardiopathy. These conditions range from hereditary defects to problems caused by stress or poor diet. Some conditions are fatal and others are treatable if detected in early stages.

African Americans have a genetically higher risk of heart disease than any other race. They are also more prone to suffer from most of the heart disease risk factors that are generally controllable. For example, they have the highest incidences of diabetes, the highest rate of HBP, and are more obese on average than any other race. They also have biological differences that increase their risk for heart disease. For example, African Americans excrete less sodium than whites and are more salt sensitive. This increases the risk of HBP. This is compounded by the higher levels of stress African Americans have historically faced due to racism and poverty. Long-term stress can lead to reductions in sodium excretion because the sympathetic nervous system activation of the kidney reduces salt excretion.

According to data from the Centers for Disease Control (2015), approximately 600,000 people die of heart disease in the United States every year. This equates to 1 in every 4 deaths. The majority of deaths occur in Southern states. Coronary heart disease (CHD) is the most common type of heart disease, killing more than 370,000 people annually. Each year, approximately 735,000 Americans have a heart attack. Of these, 525,000 experience their first heart attack and 210,000 have had a previous heart attack. By race, 23.8% of non-Hispanic African American deaths in 2008 were due to heart disease, compared to 23.8% of non-Hispanic whites, 22.2% of Asian or Pacific Islanders, and 18.4% of American Indians and Alaskan Natives. HBP, high low-density lipoprotein (LDL) cholesterol, and smoking are key heart disease risk factors for heart disease. About half of Americans (49%) have at least one of these three risk factors.

The American Heart Association (Mozaffarian et al. 2013) published the following statistics about obesity in the United States during the year 2013:

- Among non-Hispanic blacks age 20 and older in the United States, 44.4% of men and 48.9% of women had CVD.
- In 2009, CVD caused the deaths of 46,334 black males and 48,070 black females.
- The 2009 overall death rate from CVD was 236.1. Death rates for blacks were 387 for males and 267.9 for females.
- Among non-Hispanic blacks age 20 and older, 6.8% of men and 7.1% of women have CHD.
- Among non-Hispanic blacks age 20 and older, 42.6% of men and 47% of women have HBP (defined as systolic pressure of 140 mm Hg or higher; diastolic pressure of 90 mm Hg or higher; taking antihypertensive medicine; or being told twice by a physician or other professional that you have hypertension).
- In 2009, HBP caused the deaths of 6,574 black males and 6,951 black females. The 2009 overall death rate from HBP was 18.5. Death rates for blacks were 51.6 for males and 38.3 for females.
- Among non-Hispanic blacks age 20 and older:
  - 38.6% of men and 40.7% of women had total blood cholesterol levels of 200 mg/dL or higher.
  - 10.8% of men and 11.7% of women had levels of 240 mg/dL or higher.
  - 33.1% of men and 31.2% of women had an LDL cholesterol of 130 mg/dL or higher.
  - 20.3% of men and 10.2% of women had high-density lipoprotein cholesterol less than 40 mg/dL.
- The prevalence of inactivity was highest among black (26.7%) and Hispanic (21.3%) girls, followed by white girls (13.7%), black boys (12.3%), Hispanic boys (10.7%), and white boys (8.5%).
- The prevalence of watching television equal to or greater than 3 hours per day was highest among black girls (54.9%) and boys (54.4%), followed by Hispanic boys (38.4%) and girls (37.2%) and white boys (27.3%) and girls (23.9%). Only 18% of non-Hispanic blacks age 18 and older met the 2008 Federal Physical Activity Guidelines.
- An estimated 31.8% of children age 2 –19 were overweight or obese. Among non-Hispanic black children, 36.9% of boys and 41.3% of girls were obese or overweight. Of these groups, 24.3% of black boys and 24.3% of black girls were obese (BMI-for-age $\geq$ 95th percentile).

• An estimated 68.2% of Americans age 20 and older were overweight or obese. Among non-Hispanic black adults, 68.7% of men and 79.9% of women were defined as overweight. Of these, 37.9% of black men, and 53.9% of black women were obese (BMI of 30.0 kg/m^2 and higher).

The American Heart Association and the American Stroke Association (Mozaffarian et al., 2015) outline the following racial and ethnic statistics for the factors that primary lead to or result from heart diseases:

• Direct and indirect costs of CVD and stroke total more than $320.1 billion. That includes health expenditures and lost productivity.
• Nearly half of all African American adults have some form of CVD, 48% of women and 46% of men.
• Heart disease is the number one cause of death in the United States, killing over 375,000 people a year. Over 39,000 African Americans died from heart disease in 2011.
• Stroke kills someone in the United States about once every 4 minutes. African Americans have nearly twice the risk for a first-ever stroke than white people, and a much higher death rate from stroke.
• Among adults, those most likely to smoke were American Indian or Alaska Native men (26%), white men (22%), African American men (21%), white women (19%), American Indian or Alaska Native women (17%), Hispanic men (17%), African American women (15%), Asian men (15%), Hispanic women (7%), and Asian women (5%).
• About 43% of Americans have total cholesterol 200 mg/dL or higher. The race and gender breakdown is: 46% of Hispanic men, 46% of white women, 43% of Hispanic women, 41% of black women, 40% of white men, and 37% of black men.
• Rates of HBP among African Americans are among the highest of any population in the world. Here is the U.S. breakdown by race and gender: 46% of African American women, 45% of African American men, 33% of white men, 30% of white women, 30% of Hispanic men, and 30% of Hispanic women.
• About 21 million Americans have diagnosed diabetes. That's almost 9% of the adult population, but diabetes rates are growing. In fact, about 35% of Americans have prediabetes. African Americans, Hispanics/Latinos, and other ethnic minorities bear a disproportionate burden of diabetes in the United States.

SUBSTANCE ABUSE

Substance abuse includes using illegal drugs as well as legal substances that can be manipulated or misused to provide the same or similar effects as illegal drugs. Substance abuse issues have become common to all races and socioeconomic groups. Tables 2.6 and 2.7 show that 9.4% of Americans 12 years of age

Table 2.6   Past Month Illicit Drug Use among Persons Aged 12 or Older, by Race/Ethnicity, 2002–2013

Year	Black or African American (%)	White (%)	Hispanic or Latino (%)	Asian (%)
2013	10.5	9.5	8.8	3.1
2012	11.3	9.2	8.3	3.7
2011	10.0	8.7	8.4	3.8
2010	10.7	9.1	8.1	3.5
2009	9.7	8.8	7.9	3.7
2008	10.0	8.3	6.2	3.6
2007	9.5	8.2	6.6	4.2
2006	9.8	8.5	6.9	3.6
2005	9.7	8.1	7.6	3.1
2004	8.7	8.1	7.2	3.1
2003	8.7	8.3	8.0	3.8
2002	9.7	8.5	7.2	3.5

Note: Sample sizes for American Indians or Alaska Natives, Native Hawaiians or Other Pacific Islanders, and persons of two or more races were too small for reliable trend presentation for these groups. *Source*: Substance Abuse and Mental Health Services Administration (2014). *Results from the 2013 National Survey on Drug Use and Health: Summary of National Findings, NSDUH Series H-48, HHS Publication No. (SMA) 14–4863*. Rockville, MD: Substance Abuse and Mental Health Services Administration.

and older used some type of illicit drug in 2013, compared to 8.3% in 2002. This percentage increase was predominantly due to increased alcohol and marijuana use among the same age group. The nonmedical use of psychotherapeutic drugs and tobacco decreased during this period. Males used drugs more than females, but both showed increased rates of usage, and both used alcohol and marijuana more than other substances. Females showed the greatest increase in alcohol use.

The primary age group of illicit drug users was between 18 and 25. By race, American Indians and Alaskan Natives were the heaviest users, followed by Native Hawaiians or Other Pacific Islanders. Blacks had higher percentages than whites and Asians, and also higher rates than Hispanics (who could be of any race). Alcohol, including binge drinking, was the primary abused substance. Whites and then blacks were the primary users; whites had the highest rates of binge drinking. In all categories, blacks only exceeded whites in marijuana use.

Education plays a role in the use of illicit and illegal drugs. According to the Substance Abuse and Mental Health Services Administration, "Illicit drug use in 2013 varied by the educational status of adults aged 18 or older. The rate of current illicit drug use was lower among college graduates (6.7%) than those with some college education but no degree (10.8%), high school graduates with no further education (9.9%), and those who had not graduated from high school (11.8%)." Additionally:

In 2013, among persons aged 12 or older, the rate of current illicit drug use was 3.1% among Asians, 8.8% among Hispanics, 9.5% among

Table 2.7 Use of Selected Substances in the Past Month among Persons Aged 12 and over, by Age, Sex, Race, and Hispanic Origin, United States, Selected Years 2002–2013

	Any Illicit Drug[1]		Marijuana		Nonmedical Use of Any Psychotherapeutic Drug[2]		Alcohol Use		Binge Alcohol Use[4]		Heavy Alcohol Use[5]		Any Tobacco[6]	
							Percentage of Population							
Age, Sex, Race, and Hispanic origin	2002	2013	2002	2013	2002	2013	2002	2013	2002	2013	2002	2013	2002	2013
12 years and over	8.3	9.4	6.2	7.5	2.7	2.5	51.0	52.2	22.9	22.9	6.7	6.3	30.4	25.5
Age														
12–13 years	4.2	2.6	1.4	1.0	1.7	1.3	4.3	2.1	1.8	0.8	0.3	0.1	3.8	1.3
14–15 years	11.2	7.8	7.6	5.8	4.0	2.2	16.6	9.5	9.2	4.5	1.9	0.7	13.4	6.4
16–17 years	19.8	15.8	15.7	14.2	6.3	3.1	32.6	22.7	21.4	13.1	5.6	2.7	29.0	15.5
18–25 years	20.2	21.5	17.3	19.1	5.5	4.8	60.5	59.6	40.9	37.9	14.9	11.3	45.3	37.0
26–34 years	10.5	15.3	7.7	12.6	3.7	4.4	61.4	66.1	33.1	37.4	9.0	10.9	38.2	38.3
35 years and over	4.6	5.6	3.1	4.0	1.6	1.6	52.1	53.6	18.6	19.0	5.2	5.0	27.9	22.8
Sex														
Male	10.3	11.5	8.1	9.7	2.8	2.6	57.4	57.1	31.2	30.2	10.8	9.5	37.0	31.1
Female	6.4	7.3	4.4	5.6	2.6	2.3	44.9	47.5	15.1	16.0	3.0	3.3	24.3	20.2
Age and sex														
12–17 years	11.6	8.8	8.2	7.1	4.0	2.2	17.6	11.6	10.7	6.2	2.5	1.2	15.2	7.8
Male	12.3	9.6	9.1	7.9	3.6	2.0	17.4	11.2	11.4	6.6	3.1	1.4	16.0	9.1
Female	10.9	8.0	7.2	6.2	4.4	2.4	17.9	11.9	9.9	5.8	1.9	1.0	14.4	6.5
Hispanic origin and race[3]														
Not Hispanic or Latino														
White only	8.5	9.5	6.5	7.7	2.8	2.5	55.0	57.7	23.4	24.0	7.5	7.3	32.0	27.7
Black or African American only	9.7	10.5	7.4	8.7	2.0	2.3	39.9	43.6	21.0	20.1	4.4	4.5	28.8	27.1

American Indian or Alaska Native only	10.1	12.3	6.7	10.8	3.2	2.1	44.7	37.3	27.9	23.5	8.7	5.8	44.3	40.1
Native Hawaiian or Other Pacific Islander only	7.9	14.0	4.4	13.4	3.8	1.1	*	38.4	25.2	24.7	8.3	8.9	28.8	25.8
Asian only	3.5	3.1	1.8	2.2	0.7	0.8	37.1	34.5	12.4	12.4	2.6	2.0	18.6	10.1
2 or more races	11.4	17.4	9.0	16.0	3.5	2.5	49.9	47.4	19.8	19.6	7.5	7.5	38.1	31.2
Hispanic or Latino	7.2	8.8	4.3	6.5	2.9	2.9	42.8	43.0	24.8	24.1	5.9	4.8	25.2	18.8

Note: Data are based on household interviews of a sample of the civilian noninstitutionalized population aged 12 and over.

*Estimates are considered unreliable. Data not shown if the relative standard error is greater than 17.5% of the log transformation of the proportion, the minimum effective sample size is less than 68, the minimum nominal sample size is less than 100, or the prevalence is close to 0% or 100%.

[1] Any illicit drug includes marijuana/hashish, cocaine (including crack), heroin, hallucinogens (including LSD and PCP), inhalants, or any prescription-type psychotherapeutic drug used nonmedically. See Appendix II, Illicit drug use.

[2] Nonmedical use of prescription-type psychotherapeutic drugs includes the use of pain relievers, tranquilizers, stimulants, or sedatives and does not include over-the-counter drugs. Special questions on methamphetamine were added in 2005 and 2006. Data for years prior to 2007 have been adjusted for comparability.

[3] Persons of Hispanic origin may be of any race. Data on race and Hispanic origin were collected using the 1997 Revisions to the Standards for the Classification of Federal Data on Race and Ethnicity. Single-race categories shown include persons who reported only one racial group. The category 2 or more races includes persons who reported more than one racial group. See Appendix II, Hispanic origin; Race.

[4] Binge alcohol use is defined as drinking five or more drinks on the same occasion on at least 1 day in the past 30 days. Occasion is defined as at the same time or within a couple of hours of each other. See Appendix II, Alcohol consumption; Binge drinking.

[5] Heavy alcohol use is defined as drinking five or more drinks on the same occasion on each of 5 or more days in the past 30 days. By definition, all heavy alcohol users are also binge alcohol users.

[6] Any tobacco product includes cigarettes, smokeless tobacco (i.e., chewing tobacco or snuff), cigars, or pipe tobacco. See Appendix II, Cigarette smoking.

Source: Centers for Disease Control and Prevention (2016). *Health, United States, 2014.* Atlanta, GA. Retrieved from http://www.cdc.gov/nchs/hus/contents2014.htm#055 on March 6, 2016.

whites, 10.5% among blacks, 12.3% among American Indians or Alaska Natives, 14.0% among Native Hawaiians or Other Pacific Islanders, and 17.4% among persons reporting two or more races. There were no statistically significant differences in the rates of current illicit drug use between 2012 and 2013 for any of the racial/ethnic groups. Between 2002 and 2013, the rate of current illicit drug use increased from 8.5 to 9.5% for whites. Among blacks, the rate increased from 8.7% in 2003 and 2004 to 10.5% in 2013. (2014, p. 26)

Analysis

Substance abuse has serious health consequences and negatively impacts an individual's desire and ability to work. It creates tremendous stress on families, especially when the abuser is a parent or caregiver. The social, physical, mental, and public health consequences include the following. This list includes many issues African Americans are already the most prone to suffer from:

- CVD
- Stroke
- Cancer
- Teenage pregnancy
- Contracting sexually transmitted diseases
- Hepatitis
- Lung disease
- Domestic violence
- Child abuse
- Motor vehicle crashes
- Physical fights
- Crime
- Homicide
- Suicide

There are many implications of substance abuse; and even more so for African Americans compared to people of other races. This is partially due to a lack of education of the consequences, and also being more socioeconomically depressed. Cooper, Friedman, Tempalski and Friedman (2007) reported that blacks living in segregated communities are vulnerable to injection drug use and sniffing or snorting injectable drugs such as heroin and cocaine. The researchers of this report believe that blacks are especially vulnerable to these behaviors due to their elevated risk of depression, anxiety, and general psychological distress. They point to associated factors in these communities including rates of unemployment, poverty, arrest, and neighborhood disorder. A study conducted at Purdue University (Neubert 2012) found that blacks who feel mistreated and discriminated against are more likely to abuse illegal drugs and alcohol. Its results show that medical professionals treating blacks for substance abuse should be aware of this when developing treatment methods. Ninety percent of the 3,570 African Americans surveyed reported everyday discrimination and 62% reported major discrimination in such areas as hiring and applying for loans.

FURTHER READINGS

Hampton, Robert L., Thomas P. Gullotta, and Raymond L. Crowel (eds.) (2010). *Handbook of African American Health*. New York: The Guilford Press.

Jack, Leonard, Jr. (ed.) (2010). *Diabetes in Black America: Public Health and Clinical Solutions to a National Crisis*. Munster: Hilton.

Lemelle, Anthony J., Wornie Reed, and Sandra Taylor (eds.) (2013). *Handbook of African American Health: Social and Behavioral Interventions*. New York: Springer.

Liburd, Leandris C. (2010). *Diabetes and Health Disparities: Community-Based Approaches for Racial and Ethnic Populations*. New York: Springer.

Matthew, Dayna Bowen (2015). *Just Medicine: A Cure for Racial Inequality in American Health Care*. New York: New York University Press.

Pollock, Anne (2012). *Medicating Race: Heart Disease and Durable Preoccupation with Difference*. Durham, NC: Duke University Press.

Sanders, Mark (ed.) (2013). *Substance Use Disorders in African American Communities: Prevention, Treatment and Recovery*. New York: Routledge.

Shepard, Donald S. (2010). *Lifestyle Modification to Control Heart Disease: Evidence and Policy*. Sudbury, MA: Jones and Bartlett.

Waters, Elizabeth, Boyd Swinburn, Jacob Seidell, and Ricardo Uauy (2010). *Preventing Childhood Obesity: Evidence Policy and Practice*. Hoboken, NJ: Blackwell.

3

Crime and Criminal Justice

The primary caution in using criminal justice data is that it is often self-reported. This means that counties, cities, and states often manipulate data reporting for their own benefit. For example, some cities may underreport arrests, murder rates, or other data in order to make their localities appear safer than they are. Another issue is that crime incidents are most often only reported by law enforcement based on known incidents. For this reason, crime data seldom truly represents the actual number of crimes committed. Data may also be excluded when all facts of a crime incident are not known. For example, crime statistics will often exclude information when data such as the offender's age, sex, and race are all reported as unknown. Experts, including criminologists and sociologists, refer to the amount of unreported or undiscovered crime data as the "dark (or hidden) figure of crime." This is especially the case for less severe crimes, as they are the most unreported, and many of these are never investigated to find the culprits.

It is important to also fully understand the definition of data variables, as they can contain several subelements. For example, "violent crimes" can include the offenses of murder and nonnegligent manslaughter, rape, robbery, and aggravated assault. "Property crimes" can include offenses of burglary, larceny-theft, motor vehicle theft, and arson.

Two of the most cited sources of data on violence and other crimes are the Federal Bureau of Investigation (FBI) and the National Crime Victimization Survey (NCVS), which greatly differ in their data on crime statistics. The FBI's Uniform Crime Reporting (UCR) program is a nationwide, cooperative statistical effort of nearly 18,000 city, university, college, county, state, tribal, and federal law enforcement agencies. These agencies *voluntarily* report data on crimes that are reported to them or are otherwise brought to their attention. The NCVS is an annual data collection method used by the Department of Justice to estimate true rates of crime in the United States. According to the Department of Justice, "Each year data are obtained from a nationally representative sample of 76,000 households comprising nearly 135,300 persons on the frequency, characteristics and consequences of criminal victimization in the United States. The survey enables BJS to estimate the likelihood of victimization by rape, sexual assault, robbery, assault, theft, household burglary, and motor vehicle theft for the population as a whole as well as for segments of the population such as women, the elderly, members of various racial groups, city dwellers, or other groups. The NCVS provides the largest national forum for victims to describe the impact of crime and characteristics of violent offenders" (Bureau of Justice Statistics 2015).

The NCVS includes incidents reported to police and those that were not reported, and is also based upon the victim's suspicion of an offender's motivation for committing acts, such as a hate crime. The National Incident-Based Reporting System (NIBRS) is part of the UCR program. It resulted from the FBI's effort to revise the UCR by expanding crime tracking and reporting. The difference between the NIBRS and UCR can be viewed at http://www.nij.gov/topics/crime/pages/ucr-nibrs.aspx. It shows, for example, the former tracks 46 types of crimes and contains actual information about arrests, while the UCR only tracks 8 types of crimes and just reports arrests in specific incidents.

U.S. PRISON POPULATION AND ARRESTS

Crime continues to be a serious problem in the United States in terms of approaches to corrections that have resulted in a very large incarcerated population. The White House (2015a) outlined some key statistics as of 2015 that highlight the issue as part of President Obama's address to the NAACP's 106th national convention. His address called for reforms to the American criminal justice system:

- 2.2 million: The number of prisoners in the United States, which has quadrupled from only 500,000 in 1980.
- 25%: The share of the world's prisoners that are in the United States, even though we're only home to 5% of the world's population.
- 60%: The share of U.S. prisoners who are either African American or Latino. About 1 in every 35 African American men and 1 in every 88 Latino men were serving time as of 2015. Among white men, that number was 1 in 214.
- $80 billion: The amount Americans spend each year to keep people incarcerated in the United States.

During the year previous to this address, 2014, there were an estimated 6,851,000 persons under the supervision of U.S. adult correctional systems. This included 1,945,400 who were actually incarcerated (i.e., in a federal or state prison, or in a local jail) and 4,564,900 who were under community supervision (i.e., supervised by probation or parole agencies). Seven state jurisdictions had correctional populations of 300,000 or more offenders, including Texas (699,300), California (589,600), Georgia (579,600), Florida (382,600), Pennsylvania (360,800), the federal system (338,000), and Ohio (326,300). These seven jurisdictions made up almost half (48%) of those actually incarcerated or under supervision (Kaeble et al. 2016).

Table 3.1 shows the breakout of the U.S. prison population by age, race, and sex in 2013. Black males made up the majority of the prison population (over 36%), although less than 10% of U.S. adult population. Their rate exceeded that of all other races, and Hispanics. In general, males and females between the ages of 25–39 had the highest imprisonment rates. In this same age range, black males were imprisoned at rates at least 2.5 times greater than Hispanic males and 6 times greater than white males. Of those who were 18–19 years old, black males were more than 9 times more likely to be imprisoned than white males (115 inmates per 100,000 white males). The difference between black and white female inmates of the same age was smaller. Data from 2014 shows the disparity in prisoners by race. Per a Bureau of Justice Statistics report about prisoners in 2014, "2.7% of black males and 1.1% of Hispanic males were sentenced to more than 1 year in state or federal prison at yearend 2014. An estimated 516,900 black males were in state or federal prison at yearend 2014, accounting for 37% of the male prison population. White males made up 32% of the male prison population (453,500 prison inmates), followed by Hispanics (308,700 inmates or 22%). White females (53,100 prisoners) in state or federal prison at yearend 2014 outnumbered both black (22,600) and Hispanic (17,800) females" (Carson 2015).

Upon a first glance, these statistics might indicate that African Americans, particularly young blacks, commit more crimes than whites. However, data shows that prison statistics are a result of inequality in sentencing. The American Civil Liberties Union (ACLU) reports that on average, black males are given sentences that are nearly 20% longer than those given to white males convicted of similar crimes (2014). This trend is true even when both parties have comparable criminal histories. Further, the disparities between sentences increase in relation to the severity of the crime committed. The ACLU found disparities in death penalties and life sentencing (casually referred to as "lifers") without the possibility of parole (LWOP). For LWOP, they report "Although blacks constitute only about 13% of the U.S. population, as of 2009, blacks constituted 28.3% of all lifers, 56.4% of those serving LWOP, and 56.1% of those who received LWOP for offenses committed as a juvenile. As of 2012, the ACLU's research shows that 65.4% of prisoners serving LWOP for nonviolent offenses are Black" (American Civil Liberties Union 2014).

The Sentencing Project provided similar findings to the United Nations in 2013. They reported black males are six times more likely to be incarcerated than white males and 2.5 times more likely than their Hispanic counterparts. This equates to one of every three black African American males born today expecting to go to prison in their lifetime. They found racial disparities based on studies in

Table 3.1 Sentenced Prisoners under the Jurisdiction of State or Federal Correctional Authorities, by Age, Sex, Race, and Hispanic Origin, December 31, 2013

Age	Total (%)	Male					Female				
		Total Male (%)	White (%)	Black (%)	Hispanic (%)	Other (%)	Total Female (%)	White (%)	Black (%)	Hispanic (%)	Other (%)
18–19	1.0	1.1	0.6	1.3	1.3	1.1	0.6	0.4	0.9	1.1	0.8
20–24	11.4	11.4	8.6	13.0	12.7	12.4	10.2	8.7	11.3	12.5	10.9
25–29	15.3	15.2	13.2	15.5	17.2	17.2	17.3	16.6	16.5	20.5	20.2
30–34	16.7	16.6	15.1	16.8	18.6	17.9	18.3	18.4	16.9	19.9	21.0
35–39	13.9	13.9	12.7	14.1	15.5	14.2	14.4	14.5	13.9	14.8	14.3
40–44	12.5	12.5	13.0	12.2	12.3	12.4	13.2	13.7	13.4	11.4	11.8
45–49	10.8	10.8	12.2	10.5	9.1	9.5	11.3	11.7	12.1	9.1	9.2
50–54	8.4	8.5	10.4	8.2	6.3	7.0	7.7	8.2	7.8	5.7	6.7
55–59	4.9	5.0	6.4	4.6	3.6	4.0	3.8	3.9	4.3	2.8	3.4
60–64	2.5	2.6	3.7	2.1	1.8	2.1	1.7	2.0	1.7	1.1	1.7
65 or older	2.1	2.2	3.8	1.2	1.4	1.8	1.2	1.4	0.9	1.1	0.8
Total number of sentenced prisoners	1,516,879	1,412,745	454,100	526,000	314,600	118,100	104,134	51,500	23,100	17,600	11,900

Note: Those in the "Other" category includes American Indians, Alaska Natives, Asians, Native Hawaiians, Pacific Islanders, persons of two or more races, or additional racial categories in reporting information systems. Those in the "White" and "Black" categories exclude persons of Hispanic or Latino origin.

Sources: Bureau of Justice Statistics, National Prisoner Statistics Program (2014). *Federal Justice Statistics Program, 2012–2013; National Corrections Reporting Program, 2012; and Survey of Inmates in State and Federal Correctional Facilities, 2004.* http://www.bjs.gov/content/pub/pdf/p13.pdf.

every facet of the criminal justice system, from initial police stops to the assignment of legal defense to final sentencing. Using the results of the War on Drugs as but one example, the Sentencing Project (2013) reported: from 1999 to 2005, African American[s] constituted roughly 13% of drug users on average but 36% of those arrested for drug offenses and 46% of those convicted for drug offenses. While the War on Drugs creates racial disparity at every phase of the criminal justice process, disparities in sentencing laws for various types of drugs and harsh mandatory minimum sentences disproportionately contribute to disparity.

Statistics from The Sentencing Project and the ACLU were substantiated by the Department of Justice. On April 28, 2014, the U.S. Attorney General, Eric Holder, released a statement outlining the Department of Justice's plans to collect data on police stops and arrests as part of an effort to curb racial bias in the criminal justice system. In this release he stated "Racial disparities contribute to tension in our nation generally and within communities of color specifically, and tend to breed resentment toward law enforcement that is counterproductive to the goal of reducing crime. Of course, to be successful in reducing both the experience and the perception of bias, we must have verifiable data about the problem. As a key part of this initiative, we will work with grant recipients and local law enforcement to collect data about stops and searches, arrests, and case outcomes in order to help assess the impact of possible bias." He further pointed to a study that revealed that half of African American men have been arrested at least once by the time they reach age 23. Overall, in 2012, black men were 6 times, and Latino men were 2.5 times, more likely to be imprisoned than white men (Department of Justice 2014).

Table 3.2 shows the categories of crimes that led to charges in 2014, organized by race and ethnicity. Notice that whites committed the majority of crimes (69.4%), which is expected given the fact that they comprised the largest percentage of the population in 2014 (77.4% for all whites, and 62.1% for non-Hispanic whites). However, there is a disparity when analyzing the types of crimes committed by race. For example, the data shows that blacks or African Americans were charged for over half of all murders and nonnegligent manslaughters, robberies, and illegal gambling offenses. In addition, they were charged with at least one third of all aggravated assaults, violent arson crimes, charges of forgery and counterfeiting, embezzlements, carrying or possessing weapons, crimes of prostitution and commercialized vice, disorderly conduct, crimes of suspicion, and curfew and loitering law violations. Driving under the influence (DUI) is the only category in which the number of African Americans charged with the crime accurately correlated to the percentage of African Americans in the general U.S. population (blacks accounted for 13% of all offenders charged with DUIs).

RACIAL PROFILING

The justice system in the United States is not "color blind." This fact is evidenced by the overincarceration of African Americans in the American prison system, particularly when compared to the percentage of the population comprised of

Table 3.2 Arrests by Race, 2014

Offense Charged	Total Arrests by Race — Number by Race						Total Arrests by Race — Percent Distribution[1]					Total Arrests by Ethnicity — Number by Ethnicity		Total Arrests by Ethnicity — Percent Distribution[1]	
	Total	White	Black or African American	American Indian or Alaska Native	Asian	Native Hawaiian or Other Pacific Islander	White	Black or African American	American Indian or Alaska Native	Asian	Native Hawaiian or Other Pacific Islander	Total[2]	Hispanic or Latino	Hispanic or Latino	Not Hispanic or Latino
Total	8,730,665	6,056,687	2,427,683	135,599	100,067	10,629	69.4	27.8	1.6	1.1	0.1	6,541,125	1,234,324	18.9	81.1
Murder and nonnegligent manslaughter	8,230	3,807	4,224	83	107	9	46.3	51.3	1.0	1.3	0.1	6,045	1,308	21.6	78.4
Rape[3]	16,326	10,977	4,888	212	222	27	67.2	29.9	1.3	1.4	0.2	11,508	3,126	27.2	72.8
Robbery	74,077	31,354	41,379	616	617	111	42.3	55.9	0.8	0.8	0.1	55,913	11,437	20.5	79.5
Aggravated assault	291,600	185,612	96,511	4,372	4,507	598	63.7	33.1	1.5	1.5	0.2	232,910	57,750	24.8	75.2
Burglary	186,794	126,242	56,504	1,703	1,999	346	67.6	30.2	0.9	1.1	0.2	152,261	30,669	20.1	79.9
Larceny-theft	971,199	671,260	271,788	15,869	11,355	927	69.1	28.0	1.6	1.2	0.1	725,373	112,745	15.5	84.5
Motor vehicle theft	53,456	35,551	16,391	668	677	169	66.5	30.7	1.2	1.3	0.3	40,946	10,471	25.6	74.4
Arson	7,298	5,338	1,709	142	98	11	73.1	23.4	1.9	1.3	0.2	5,520	1,022	18.5	81.5
Violent crime[4]	390,233	231,750	147,002	5,283	5,453	745	59.4	37.7	1.4	1.4	0.2	306,376	73,621	24.0	76.0
Property crime[4]	1,218,747	838,391	346,392	18,382	14,129	1,453	68.8	28.4	1.5	1.2	0.1	924,100	154,907	16.8	83.2
Other assaults	853,887	558,181	272,068	13,618	9,173	847	65.4	31.9	1.6	1.1	0.1	639,100	114,589	17.9	82.1
Forgery and counterfeiting	44,336	28,272	15,095	279	646	44	63.8	34.0	0.6	1.5	0.1	34,657	5,601	16.2	83.8
Fraud	109,576	72,424	34,853	1,116	1,124	59	66.1	31.8	1.0	1.0	0.1	88,004	8,784	10.0	90.0
Embezzlement	12,678	7,851	4,518	87	210	12	61.9	35.6	0.7	1.7	0.1	10,325	1,065	10.3	89.7
Stolen property; buying, receiving, possessing	69,912	45,816	22,538	662	812	84	65.5	32.2	0.9	1.2	0.1	54,153	10,604	19.6	80.4
Vandalism	154,755	108,531	41,723	2,761	1,556	184	70.1	27.0	1.8	1.0	0.1	122,943	23,350	19.0	81.0
Weapons; carrying, possessing, etc.	109,891	62,920	44,705	803	1,307	156	57.3	40.7	0.7	1.2	0.1	81,630	19,194	23.5	76.5

Prostitution and commercialized vice	37,030	19,867	15,483	199	1,434	47	53.7	41.8	0.5	3.9	0.1	28,546	5,507	19.3	80.7
Sex offenses (except rape and prostitution)	43,125	31,279	10,462	640	688	56	72.5	24.3	1.5	1.6	0.1	31,963	8,173	25.6	74.4
Drug abuse violations	1,216,225	837,851	353,862	10,071	12,893	1,548	68.9	29.1	0.8	1.1	0.1	910,629	190,771	20.9	79.1
Gambling	4,363	1,560	2,568	16	192	27	35.8	58.9	0.4	4.4	0.6	2,059	403	19.6	80.4
Offenses against the family and children	79,075	50,912	26,048	1,521	574	20	64.4	32.9	1.9	0.7	*	51,746	6,051	11.7	88.3
Driving under the influence	863,598	722,451	112,107	12,048	15,938	1,054	83.7	13.0	1.4	1.8	0.1	646,288	151,675	23.5	76.5
Liquor laws	246,304	197,559	35,727	9,539	3,302	177	80.2	14.5	3.9	1.3	0.1	173,195	27,008	15.6	84.4
Drunkenness	327,325	264,906	51,485	6,952	3,552	430	80.9	15.7	2.1	1.1	0.1	305,049	72,574	23.8	76.2
Disorderly conduct	338,636	213,342	114,802	7,734	2,493	265	63.0	33.9	2.3	0.7	0.1	207,465	27,127	13.1	86.9
Vagrancy	21,577	14,819	6,116	443	182	17	68.7	28.3	2.1	0.8	0.1	16,903	2,656	15.7	84.3
All other offenses (except traffic)	2,546,822	1,726,091	750,488	42,980	23,946	3,317	67.8	29.5	1.7	0.9	0.1	1,876,766	323,498	17.2	82.8
Suspicion	1,057	557	472	15	13	0	52.7	44.7	1.4	1.2	0.0	157	7	4.5	95.5
Curfew and loitering law violations	41,513	21,357	19,169	450	450	87	51.4	46.2	1.1	1.1	0.2	29,071	7,159	24.6	75.4

Note: 12,320 agencies; 2014 estimated population 250,194,950.

[1] Because of rounding, the percentages may not add to 100.0.

[2] The ethnicity totals are representative of those agencies that provided ethnicity breakdowns. Not all agencies provide ethnicity data; therefore, the race and ethnicity totals will not equal.

[3] The rape figures in this table are aggregate totals of the data submitted based on both the legacy and revised Uniform Crime Reporting definitions.

[4] Violent crimes are offenses of murder and nonnegligent manslaughter, rape, robbery, and aggravated assault. Property crimes are offenses of burglary, larceny-theft, motor vehicle theft, and arson.

* Less than one-tenth of 1%.

Source: Federal Bureau of Investigation (2015). *Crime in the United States, 2014.* Washington, DC: Department of Justice. Retrieved from https://www.fbi.gov/about-us/cjis/ucr/crime-in-the-u.s/2014/crime-in-the-u.s.-2014/tables/table-43 on December 3, 2015.

African Americans. This also bears out because blacks do not commit anywhere near the highest number of crimes.

The likelihood of black males going to prison in their lifetime is higher than for males of other races and ethnicities; 16% of black males in the United States will go to prison, compared to 2% of white males and 9% of Hispanic males. Again, this is not because blacks commit more crimes, but because blacks are often the targets of racial profiling by police officers, and blacks are given longer prison sentences than whites are for the same crimes. Racial profiling results from law enforcement and private security practices that disproportionately target people of color for investigation and punishment. Many drivers and pedestrians who are minorities are stopped, held, and searched because of their race. Some are even unnecessarily arrested and held in jails and detention centers for a minimum number of hours. Additionally, black communities often lack the safety offered by a police presence. In economically and socially depressed areas where crime rates are the highest, residents are not afforded recurring or reliable police support. As discussed by the American Sociological Association (2007, p. 13):

> For racial and ethnic minorities, the two core issues are "under-policing and abusive policing." Empirical evidence indicates that minorities are still more likely than white Americans to be arrested far beyond their numbers in the population, to be victimized by excessive police force, to be stopped, questioned, and frisked on the street, pulled over for humiliating searches while driving (e.g., "racial profiling" or "DWB, driving while black"), or subjected to verbal abuse and harassment by police. Although these situations are not necessarily the result of explicit racial discrimination, research shows that blacks widely believe that police racism against blacks is widespread, that the criminal justice system treats blacks more harshly than whites, and that police provide too little protection for their neighborhoods.

Data on racial profiling is well documented. For example, the Sentencing Project extensively tracks and reports data on discrimination and racial profiling. The report they submitted to the United Nations in 2013 outlines the following statistics (The Sentencing Project 2013, p. 4):

> The effects of racial bias are particularly well demonstrated in the areas of traffic stops and drug law enforcement. Between 1980 and 2000, the U.S. black drug arrest rate rose from 6.5 to 29.1 per 1,000 persons; during the same period, the white drug arrest rate increased from 3.5 to 4.6 per 1,000 persons. Yet the disparity between the increase in black and white drug arrests does not correspond to any significant disparity in black drug activity. In 2012, for instance, the National Institute on Drug Abuse published a study surveying drug usage among secondary school students in the United States from 1975–2011. The study found that white

students were slightly more likely to have abused an illegal substance within the past month than black students. Yet from 1980–2010, black youth were arrested for drug crimes at rates more than double those of white youth. Disparity between black drug activity and black arrest rates is also present in adult populations: in Seattle in 2002, for instance, African Americans constituted 16% of observed drug dealers for the five most dangerous drugs but 64% of drug dealing arrests for those drugs. While these arrests were for trafficking rather than possession, the modest evidence available suggests that most drug users purchase drugs from a dealer of their own race.

An example of racial profiling is the use of "stop and frisk" tactics. Here, police officers detain any persons they feel may fit the profile of a suspected criminal even if they have no probable cause. On the surface, this would seem to be a violation of the Fourth Amendment, which protects "The right of the people to be secure in their persons, houses, papers, and effects, against unreasonable searches and seizures, shall not be violated, and no Warrants shall issue, but upon probable cause, supported by Oath or affirmation, and particularly describing the place to be searched, and the persons or things to be seized." In the case of *Terry v. Ohio*, 392 U.S. 1 (1968), however, the Supreme Court ruled that unreasonable searches and seizures are not committed when police officers have a reasonable suspicion that a person has, is, or is about to commit a crime, even without probable cause.

Several cases since 1968 have given strength to the court's prior ruling. For example, in *Arizona v. Johnson*, 555 U.S. 323 (2009), the Supreme Court ruled unanimously that police officers could conduct "pat downs"—physically search the passenger of a motor vehicle stopped for a routine traffic violation—if the police had a reasonable suspicion the passenger was armed and dangerous. The results of these rulings and "stop-and-frisk" laws in general have affected African Americans more than anyone else. A *Michigan Journal of Race and Law* article data that supports this claim says:

> The practice is particularly troubling in the nation's most populous city. In 2011 alone, New York police officers made over 680,000 stops. 87% of those stopped were Black and Hispanic, despite constituting only slightly more than half of the city's population. The practice is not even particularly effective. For instance, in eight-square blocks of a low-income Brooklyn neighborhood, from January 2006 to March 2010, NYPD officers made nearly 52,000 stops. Yet, less than 1% of those stops resulted in an arrest, and the police recovered a paltry twenty-five guns. Such aggressive policing tactics targeted largely at Black men have correlated with their extraordinarily high incarceration rates, leading many to conclude that the criminal justice system is the new Jim Crow. (2012, pp. 135–136)

Data shows that many states still lack laws that effectively deal with racial profiling. For example, the NAACP conducted an analysis of state racial profiling laws in "analyzing these policies to ascertain whether they include the necessary components to make these policies effective and enforceable." Their analysis found the following:

- 20 state laws do not explicitly prohibit racial profiling.
- 30 states have some form of racial profiling laws on the books.
- 17 state laws ban the use of pretextual traffic stops.
- 16 states criminalize violations of their anti-profiling laws.
- 3 states allow individuals to seek injunctive relief to stop officers or police departments from racial profiling.
- 18 states require mandatory data collection for all stops and searches; 15 require analysis and publication of racial profiling data.
- 18 states require the creation of commissions to review and respond to complaints of racial profiling.
- 17 states require the creation of commissions to review and respond to complaints of racial profiling.
- No states meet all of the NAACP criteria of an effective racial profiling law.
                                         (Brooks, Brock, and Bolling-Williams 2014)

In summarizing their findings, the report concluded that even though 30 states have one or more antiracial profiling laws on the books,

> not one adequately meets all the provisions required for an effective law, making them inadequate tools to significantly curb the practice of racial profiling. Most state laws do not include a definition of profiling that is inclusive of all significantly impacted groups. They also tend to lack a ban on pretextual stops of pedestrians and motorists, in which officers use minor violations (such as not using a seat belt or jay walking) as a pretext to search for illegal contraband. In addition, most state laws do not include a provision allowing individuals to seek court orders to stop police departments from engaging in racial profiling or obtain remedies for violations. (p. 19)

The New York Civil Liberties Union and the NAACP continue to file legal oppositions to the practices in New York. The racial profiling rates in that state are purported to be among the highest in the nation. In August 2013, Federal Judge Shira A. Scheindlin ruled that the city's tactics violated the constitutional rights of minorities and were an indirect form of racial profiling in which many blacks would not have been stopped if they were white. She ordered several remedies, including a pilot program in which body cameras would be worn by police officers in at least five precincts in addition to community meetings being held to reform police department tactics as part of "a joint remedial process."

"The judge named Peter L. Zimroth, a partner in Arnold & Porter L.L.P., and a former corporation counsel and prosecutor in the Manhattan district attorney's office, to monitor the Police Department's compliance with the United States Constitution. The installation of a monitor will leave the department under a degree of judicial control that is certain to shape the policing strategies under the next mayor" (Goldstein 2013). Mayor Michael R. Bloomberg immediately filed an appeal, vowing to continue the stop and frisk policies until the appeal was heard.

The use of stop-and-frisk is so dramatic in New York that many blacks fail to even report being stopped. An article in the *Huffington Post* (2013) reports on a survey of 500 men and women between the ages of 18 and 25 conducted by the Vera Institute of Justice in five "highly patrolled" New York City neighborhoods: Jamaica in Queens, East Harlem, Bedford-Stuyvesant and East New York in Brooklyn, and the South Bronx. Those surveyed were stopped at least once by police. Forty-five percent reported they encountered an officer who threatened them, and 46% experienced physical force at the hands of an officer. Twenty-five percent said they'd been involved in a stop in which a police officer had drawn a weapon. Forty-four percent had been stopped at least nine different times by police officers. Some reported being stopped more than 20 times. Only 29% said they'd been informed why they had been stopped.

The fact that blacks receive longer jail and prisoner sentences than their white counterparts is recognized by all levels of government, but actions to reverse this trend are not being put in place. Attorney General Eric Holder spoke of his concern over the issue in 2013. During a speech to Al Sharpton's 15th Annual National Action Network Convention in New York on April 4, 2013, Holder cited a government report on the disparity in stating:

> I am concerned by a troubling report released by the United States Sentencing Commission in February, which indicates that—in recent years—black male offenders have received sentences that are nearly 20% longer than those imposed on white males convicted of similar crimes. The Department of Justice is determined to continue working alongside Congressional leaders, judges, law enforcement officials, and independent groups—like the American Bar Association—to study the unintended collateral consequences of certain convictions; to address unwarranted sentencing disparities; and—where appropriate—to explore ways to give judges more flexibility in determining certain sentences. Too many people go to too many prisons for far too long for no good law enforcement reason. It is time to ask ourselves some fundamental questions about our criminal justice system. Statutes passed by legislatures that mandate sentences, irrespective of the unique facts of an individual case, too often bear no relation to the conduct at issue, breed disrespect for the system, and are ultimately counterproductive. It is time to

examine our systems and determine what truly works. We need to ensure that incarceration is used to punish, to rehabilitate, and to deter—and not simply to warehouse and forget. . . . Too many people go to too many prisons for far too long for no good law enforcement reason. It is time to ask ourselves some fundamental questions about our criminal justice system. Statutes passed by legislatures that mandate sentences, irrespective of the unique facts of an individual case, too often bear no relation to the conduct at issue, breed disrespect for the system, and are ultimately counterproductive. It is time to examine our systems and determine what truly works. We need to ensure that incarceration is used to punish, to rehabilitate, and to deter—and not simply to warehouse and forget. (Department of Justice 2013)

The practice of disparate treatment of black youth, which pushes them toward prison instead of rehabilitation, begins while they are young with the school-to-prison pipeline. Nicholson-Crotty, Birchmeier, and Valentine (2009, p. 1003) find minority youth comprise over 60% of children detained by juvenile justice systems, and they are more than eight times as likely as their white peers to be housed in juvenile detention facilities. While in school they are subject to exclusionary discipline, such as out-of-school suspension and expulsion, at much higher rates than are white students.

Being black, poor, and living in urban areas increases the potential of being pushed into the school-to-prison pipeline. It is systemic of the inequality in the overall U.S. justice system, which has been found to be biased toward minorities and the poor. The following 14 points were raised as examples of racism in the U.S. criminal justice system as outlined by Quigley (2010):

- The United States has seen an increase in arrests and jail populations over the last 40 years, mostly as a result of the war on drugs. However, whites and blacks are cited for drug offenses, possession, and sales at rates that are roughly comparable.

- The police stop and question blacks and Latinos at much higher rates than whites. In New York City, where minorities account for close to half of the population, 80% of those stopped by NYPD were blacks and Latinos. Of the whites who were stopped, only 8% were frisked. In stark contrast, 85% of blacks and Latinos who were stopped were frisked, according to information provided by the NYPD. In a California study, the ACLU reported that blacks were three times more likely to be stopped than whites.

- Since 1970, drug arrests have risen dramatically: from 320,000 to almost 1.6 million, according to the Bureau of Justice Statistics of the U.S. Department of Justice. African Americans are reportedly arrested 2–11 times more often than whites are for drug-related offenses.

- African Americans are frequently excluded (illegally) from serving on criminal juries, according to a June 2010 study by the Equal Justice Initiative. To cite one example, 8 out of 10 African Americans in Houston County, Alabama, who were qualified for jury services were prevented by prosecutors from serving on death penalty cases.

- Only 3–5% of criminal cases reportedly go to trial; the additional 95–97% are plea bargained. As a result of this, a majority of African American defendants never have a trial. Most plea bargains entail the promise of a longer sentence if a person exercises their constitutional right to a trial. The American Bar Association reports that, as a result, many innocent people plead guilty.
- In March 2010, the U.S. Sentencing Commission reported that black offenders who are in the federal system tend to receive sentences that are 10% longer than those of white offenders who were convicted of the same crimes.
- Marc Mauer of the Sentencing Project reported that African Americans are 21% more likely to receive mandatory minimum sentences than white defendants, and 20% more likely to be sentenced to prison than white drug defendants.
- A July 2009 report by the Sentencing Project found that two-thirds of the people in the United States who have been given life sentences are minorities. In New York, 83% of those serving life sentences are minorities.
- African Americans make up 13% of the U.S. population and 14% of drug users, but account for 37% drug-related arrests and 56% of state prisoners accused of drug offenses.
- According to the U.S. Bureau of Justice Statistics, a black male born in the year 2001 has a 32% (1 in 3) chance of going to jail in his lifetime. Similarly, white males have a 6% chance and Latino males have a 17% chance. Black boys are five times more likely (and Latino boys nearly three times as likely) to go to jail compared to white boys.
- African American juvenile youth make up only 16% of the population, but account for 28% of juvenile arrests, 37% of the juvenile jail population, and 58% of the number of juveniles who are sent to adult prisons.
- A study by Professor Devah Pager of the University of Wisconsin found that 17% of white job applicants who had criminal records received employer callbacks, compared to only 5% of black job applicants who had criminal records.

VIOLENT CRIMES

Violent crimes are those that involve the perpetrator using physical force or the threat of physical force. This includes the crimes of murder and nonnegligent manslaughter, forcible rape, robbery, and aggravated assault. Table 3.3 shows the number of U.S. citizens 12 years and older in 2005, 2013, and 2014, and the percentage of those citizens who were victims of a violent crime at least once during each respective year. Generally, the number of violent crimes across all races and sexes has decreased since 2005. Males accounted for the highest percentage of violent crime victims. Note that the percentages across all categories in this table seem small (e.g., 1.2%), but consider how many people this represents (e.g.,

Table 3.3   Prevalence of Violent Crime, by Victim Demographic Characteristics, 2005, 2013, and 2014

Victim Demographic Characteristic	2005	2013	2014	2005	2013	2014
Total	3,350,630	3,041,170	2,948,540	1.4%	1.2%	1.1%
Male	1,972,270	1,567,070	1,497,430	1.7	1.2	1.2
Female	1,378,360	1,474,090	1,451,110	1.1	1.1	1.1
Race/Hispanic origin:						
White	2,192,670	1,860,870	1,848,860	1.3	1.1	1.1
Black/African American	474,420	430,380	453,650	1.7	1.3	1.4
Hispanic/Latino	489,410	540,130	457,320	1.5	1.3	1.1
Other	194,130	209,800	188,710	1.4	1.1	1.0

Notes: Data columns represent the number of persons age 12 and older who experienced at least one victimization during the year for violent crime, and percentage of persons age 12 or older who experienced at least one victimization during the year for violent crime.

White and Black/African American categories exclude persons of Hispanic or Latino origin.

The "Other" category includes American Indians and Alaska Natives; Asians, Native Hawaiians, and other Pacific Islanders; and persons of two or more races; however, it excludes persons of Hispanic or Latino origin.

Source: Bureau of Justice Statistics (2015). *Criminal Victimization, 2014*. Office of Justice Programs, U.S. Department of Justice, September 29. Retrieved from http://www.bjs.gov/content/pub/pdf/cv14.pdf on December 19, 2015.

17,969 people) who were victims of violent crimes that involve force (or threat of force), including murder, nonnegligent manslaughter, rape, robbery, and aggravated assault.

Blacks have the highest victimization rates compared to all others. The rate of violent crimes against blacks decreased from 1.7% in 2005 to 1.4% in 2014. This is significant because the black population did not decrease as much as the white population did during that time. The white population decreased by 16% between 2005 and 2014, so a decrease in victimization rates has greater significance. The black population only decreased by 4% during the same years, but the victimization rate decreased at a slower rate than whites.

Black-on-black crime continues to be an issue, leading to instances of victimization. While blacks do not commit the most crimes overall, they commit the most crimes against those of the same race. This is particularly the case in crimes involving drugs and inner city gang violence. This is evidenced in Table 3.3, which shows that black males have the highest rates of crime victimization. It can also more clearly be seen in the data shown in Table 3.4. While 83% of reported homicides committed against white victims were by white offenders in 2011, 91% of black homicides were committed by black offenders. Eighty-eight percent of black homicide victims were murdered by black males.

Table 3.4   Race and Sex of Homicide Victims by Race and Sex of Offender, 2011 (Single Victim/Single Offender)

Race of Victim	Total	Race of Offender				Sex of Offender		
		White	Black	Other	Unknown	Male	Female	Unknown
White	3,172	2,630	448	33	61	2,810	301	61
Black	2,695	193	2,447	9	46	2,385	264	46
Other race	180	45	36	99	0	155	25	0
Unknown race	84	36	27	3	18	63	3	18

Sex of Victim	Total	Race of Offender				Sex of Offender		
		White	Black	Other	Unknown	Male	Female	Unknown
Male	4,304	1,834	2,289	87	94	3,760	450	94
Female	1,743	1,034	642	54	13	1,590	140	13
Unknown sex	84	36	27	3	18	63	3	18

Note: This table is based on incidents where some information about the offender is known by law enforcement; therefore, when the offender's age, sex, and race are all reported as unknown, these data are excluded from the table.

Source: Federal Bureau of Investigation (2016). *Crime Statistics in the United States, 2011*. Retrieved from https://www.fbi.gov/about-us/cjis/ucr/crime-in-the-u.s/2011/crime-in-the-u.s.-2011/tables/expanded-homicide-data-table-6 on February 5, 2016.

According to FBI data, the cities with the highest homicide rates in 2011 were Flint, Michigan; Detroit, Michigan; St. Louis, Missouri; Oakland, California; Memphis, Tennessee; Little Rock, Arkansas; Birmingham, Alabama; Atlanta, Georgia; Baltimore, Maryland; and Stockton, California. These cities share several factors in common. First, they all had high unemployment rates in 2011. These ranged from a low of 7.2% in Little Rock, Arkansas, to a high of 20.2% in Stockton, California. The average unemployment rate was 8.95% nationally. The average median U.S. income was $50,054. The median income for each of these cities was below that, ranging from $49,190 in Oakland to $22,672 in Flint (Sauter et al. 2012). Poverty is a primary cause of violent crimes, including murder. Inequality and deprivation lead to crime, particularly when deprived groups are concentrated together in areas such as inner cities. These areas often lack investments from local, state, and federal governments to foster economic improvements or tackle issues of violence.

Murder rates increase when socioeconomic depression is coupled with the ease of obtaining guns by those who seek to harm others and by those who feel the need to protect themselves. The majority of murders committed in the United States are by offenders with guns, and blacks lead the nation in the number of murders due to firearm use. Of the 16,799 homicides in the United States in 2009, 11,493 (or 68%) were due to firearm use (Kochanek et al. 2011, p. 39). Lax national and state gun laws have led to a growth in the number of weapons in the hands of Americans and, most troubling, a growth in more complex and deadly weapons. In 1994, there were 192 million firearms in the possession of civilians. By 2009, the number had grown to approximately 310 million: 114 million handguns, 110 million rifles, and 86 million shotguns (Krouse 2012, p. 12). This is compared to 900,000 guns in the hands of law enforcement and 3 million firearms used by the military services in 2009.

HATE CRIMES

Hate crimes, also called *bias crimes*, are criminal offenses committed against a person, property, or society that are motivated, in whole or in part, by the offender's bias against a race, religion, disability, sexual orientation, or ethnicity/national origin. The criminal behavior inflicted on victims includes physical or verbal assault, injury to person or property, harassment through any form of verbal or written communication, and murder. Victims of hate crimes can include individuals, businesses, institutions, or society in general. The term "hate crime" entered federal laws and became a part of the nation's vocabulary during the 1980s due to an increase in crimes by individual citizens and hate groups (such as Skinheads) that were motivated by biases such as race and sexual orientation.

Table 3.5 shows the incidents, offenses, and victims of hate crimes in 2014, per data from the FBI. Note the data is based on "known offenders," which means information was only based on reported incidents. This also means there were many more offenses that were not reported, including offenses with known and

Table 3.5 Incidents, Offenses, Victims, and Known Offenders by Bias Motivation, 2014

Bias Motivation	Incidents	Offenses	Victims[1]	Known Offenders[2]
Total	**5,479**	**6,418**	**6,727**	**5,192**
Single-bias incidents	**5,462**	**6,385**	**6,681**	**5,176**
Race	**2,568**	**3,081**	**3,227**	**2,431**
Antiwhite	593	701	734	635
Antiblack or African American	1,621	1,955	2,022	1,442
Anti–American Indian or Alaska Native	130	142	148	108
Anti-Asian	140	168	201	187
Anti–Native Hawaiian or Other Pacific Islander	3	4	4	3
Anti–multiple races, group	81	111	118	56
Religion	**1,014**	**1,092**	**1,140**	**687**
Anti-Jewish	609	635	648	380
Anti-Catholic	64	67	70	35
Anti-Protestant	25	28	28	12
Anti-Islamic (Muslim)	154	178	184	148
Anti–other religion	107	120	125	70
Anti–multiple religions, group	44	51	71	29
Anti–atheism/agnosticism/etc.	11	13	14	13
Sexual orientation	**1,017**	**1,178**	**1,248**	**1,154**
Antigay (Male)	599	683	703	732
Anti-lesbian	129	168	174	126
Anti–lesbian, gay, bisexual, or transgender (mixed group)	241	278	305	249
Antiheterosexual	18	18	19	10
Antibisexual	30	31	47	37
Ethnicity	**648**	**790**	**821**	**668**
Anti–Hispanic or Latino	299	376	389	325
Anti–not Hispanic or Latino[3]	349	414	432	343
Disability	**84**	**95**	**96**	**74**
Antiphysical	23	26	26	25
Antimental	61	69	70	49
Gender	**33**	**40**	**40**	**25**
Antimale	10	12	12	10
Antifemale	23	28	28	15
Gender identity	**98**	**109**	**109**	**137**
Antitransgender	58	69	69	104
Anti–gender nonconforming	40	40	40	33
Multiple-bias incidents[4]	**17**	**33**	**46**	**16**

[1] The term *victim* may refer to a person, business, institution, or society as a whole.

[2] The term *known offender* does not imply that the identity of the suspect is known, but only that an attribute of the suspect has been identified, which distinguishes him/her from an unknown offender.

[3] The term *anti–not Hispanic or Latino* does not imply the victim was targeted because he/she was not of Hispanic origin, but it refers to other or unspecified ethnic biases that are not Hispanic or Latino.

[4] A *multiple-bias incident* is an incident in which one or more offense types are motivated by two or more biases.

Source: Federal Bureau of Investigation (2015). *2014 Hate Crime Statistics*. Washington, DC: Department of Justice. Retrieved from https://www.fbi.gov/about-us/cjis/ucr/hate-crime/2014/tables/table-1 on January 23, 2016.

unknown offenders. The FBI only provides data on reported incidents. However, jurisdictions have been found to underreport these crimes in order to protect the image of their communities. Additionally, the majority of victims do not report incidents. According to the U.S. Department of Justice (Langton and Planty 2010), fewer than half (45%) of all hate crimes were reported to the police between 2003 and 2009. Reasons for this include victims feeling fearful to report incidents, not recognizing that the crimes are hate crimes, or simply wanting to forget the incidents ever happened. In a 2015 *Washington Post* article, Christopher Ingraham (2015) writes, "FBI hate crime data show that more than 50 out of every 1 million black citizens was the victim of a racially motivated hate crime in 2012, the highest among any racial group. But this is almost certainly an undercount. The FBI is reliant on state and local law enforcement agencies to categorize and report hate crimes correctly. Some agencies do a much better job of this than others, and there is general agreement that the FBI numbers are significantly lower than they should be."

As shown, the majority of reported hate crimes are due to racial bias. According to the FBI (2015), 5,479 incidents involving 6,418 offenses were committed against 6,727 victims in 2014. Of these incidents, 46.8% were motivated by race, 18.5% by religion, 18.5% by sexual orientation, 11.8% by an ethnicity/national origin bias, and 1.5% by physical or mental disability. As shown in Table 3.5, the majority of all hate crime incidents (29.5%) and specifically race-based crimes (63.1%) in 2014 were against blacks. In comparison, only 10.8% of hate crimes were against whites.

Table 3.6 shows hate crimes by the types of offenses committed. A reported 3,303 incidents were crimes against persons, with intimidation accounting for 41.7% of these incidents, simple assault for 39.5%, and aggravated assault for 18.1%. Of the 2,317 reported incidents of crimes against property, the majority (73.1%) were acts of destruction/damage/vandalism.

POLICE SHOOTINGS

In recent years, the issue of police shootings has come to the forefront of media and political attention due to several reports of unarmed blacks being victims of armed police officers. National outrage ensued from media coverage showing victims who were unarmed or already in custody when actions by police officers directly led to their deaths. For this reason, data is becoming more available on police shootings. For example, the *Washington Post* has a dedicated website showing data on police shootings, based on news reports, public records, internet databases, and original reporting (found at https://www.washingtonpost.com/graphics/national/police-shootings/). During the year 2015, this source reported 1,037 police shootings, 654 of which were fatal. The total shootings so far that year involved 993 males and 44 females. By race and ethnicity, the total shootings involved 512 white suspects, 263 blacks, 170 Hispanics, 38 categorized as "Other," and 54 categorized as "Unknown." By age of the victims, 19 were under

Table 3.6 Hate Crime Incidents, Offenses, Victims, and Known Offenders by Offense Type, 2014

Offense Type	Incidents[1]	Offenses	Victims[2]	Known Offenders[3]
Total	**5,479**	**6,418**	**6,727**	**5,192**
Crimes against persons	**3,303**	**4,048**	**4,048**	**3,925**
Murder and nonnegligent manslaughter	4	4	4	5
Rape (revised definition)[4]	9	9	9	10
Rape (legacy definition)[5]	0	0	0	0
Aggravated assault	599	770	770	899
Simple assault	1,307	1,514	1,514	1,664
Intimidation	1,378	1,745	1,745	1,336
Other[6]	6	6	6	11
Crimes against property	**2,317**	**2,317**	**2,624**	**1,455**
Robbery	122	122	138	255
Burglary	162	162	208	185
Larceny-theft	239	239	256	152
Motor vehicle theft	22	22	22	15
Arson	26	26	39	20
Destruction/damage/vandalism	1,694	1,694	1,907	792
Other[6]	52	52	54	36
Crimes against society[6]	**53**	**53**	**55**	**61**

[1] The actual number of incidents is 5,479. However, the column figures will not add to the total because incidents may include more than one offense type, and these are counted in each appropriate offense type category.

[2] The term *victim* may refer to a person, business, institution, or society as a whole.

[3] The term *known offender* does not imply that the identity of the suspect is known, but only that an attribute of the suspect has been identified, which distinguishes him/her from an unknown offender. The actual number of known offenders is 5,192. However, the column figures will not add to the total because some offenders are responsible for more than one offense type, and are, therefore, counted more than once in this table.

[4] The figures shown in the rape (revised definition) row include only those reported by law enforcement agencies that used the revised Uniform Crime Reporting (UCR) definition of rape.

[5] The figures shown in the rape (legacy definition) row include only those reported by law enforcement agencies that used the legacy UCR definition of rape. See the data declaration for further explanation.

[6] Includes additional offenses collected in the National Incident-Based Reporting System.

Source: Federal Bureau of Investigation (2015). *2014 Hate Crime Statistics.* Washington, DC: Department of Justice. Retrieved from https://www.fbi.gov/about-us/cjis/ucr/hate-crime/2014/tables/table-2 on January 23, 2016.

18 years of age, 342 were 18–29, 371 were 30–44, 286 were 45 and over, and 19 were "Unknown."

Private sources also report data on police shootings. For example, the website Mapping Police Violence (http://mappingpoliceviolence.org) provides extensive data by city, and also a list of individual shootings, with details on each specific incident. *The Guardian* also provides extensive data, as well as details on individual cases at http://www.theguardian.com/us-news/ng-interactive/2015/jun/01/the-counted-police-killings-us-database.

Data from the federal government is much less conclusive. In fact, public organizations are being criticized for a lack of action to capture and report data on police shootings. For example, author Cody Ross (2015), from the University of California, points out that "The failure of the nation's police to critically evaluate their own use of force, has led the United Nations Committee Against Torture to sharply criticize the ever growing militarization of police departments in the United States, especially as evidence of significant race-based and sexuality-based brutality and excessive use of force has been uncovered, including bona fide acts of torture (e.g., those committed by Chicago Police Commander Jon Burge and others under his command, between 1972 and 1991). The UN Committee Against Torture specifically noted that it: 'regrets the lack of statistical data available on allegations of police brutality and the lack of information on the result of the investigations undertaken in respect of those allegations.'"

The U.S. Congress has taken action to attempt to rectify reporting. In 2014, it passed the Death in Custody Reporting Act, a reauthorization of an act by the same name that was passed in 2000 and expired in 2006. It requires each state to "report to the Attorney General, on a quarterly basis and pursuant to guidelines established by the Attorney General, information regarding the death of any person who is detained, under arrest, or is in the process of being arrested, is en route to be incarcerated, or is incarcerated at a municipal or county jail, State prison, State-run boot camp prison, boot camp prison that is contracted out by the State, any State or local contract facility, or other local or State correctional facility (including any juvenile facility)." Information required in the report shall include, at a minimum, the name, gender, race, ethnicity, and age of the deceased; the date, time, and location of death; the law enforcement agency that detained, arrested, or was in the process of arresting the deceased; and a brief description of the circumstances surrounding the death [from http://www.gpo.gov/fdsys/pkg/CREC-2008-01-23/pdf/CREC-2008-01-23-house.pdf].

There are still issues, such as self-reporting by police departments, and the penalty for not complying with the act is relatively small; states are in danger of losing only 10% of federal law enforcement grants. Further, police departments are very decentralized, so even the states will have a difficult time capturing full and even complete information from their different police jurisdictions.

Some information is currently available by the government. For example, the Bureau of Justice Statistics reports data on arrest-related deaths (http://www.bjs.gov/index.cfm?ty=dcdetail&iid=428). Per its most recent report (Bureau of

Justice Statistics 2015), "After the passage of the Death in Custody Reporting Act (DICRA) of 2000 (P.L. 106–297), the Bureau of Justice Statistics (BJS) began collecting data on deaths that occurred in the process of arrest. Provisions in the 2000 DICRA called for collecting all deaths occurring within the process of arrest in any state, county, or local law enforcement agency nationwide." The report estimated that 7,427 law enforcement homicides took place between 2003 and 2009 and in 2001. However, approximately 50% of homicides were not reported to the bureau's Arrest-Related Deaths (ARD) program or the FBI's Supplementary Homicide Reports (SHR). Based on an upper-bound estimate of 9,937 homicides, the estimate of reported homicides reduces even further to under 40% (see Table 3.7).

According to a Gallup poll (Jones 2015), confidence in police reached a 22-year low in 2015. While the poll shows the majority of Americans (52%) expressed "a great deal" or "quite a lot" of confidence, reductions were seen in every demographic group surveyed. Comparing results from 2012–2013 to 2014–2015, adult confidence declined from 57% to 53%. By race and ethnicity, whites who felt confident fell from 60% to 57%, for blacks from 36% to 30%, and for Hispanics from 60% to 52%. Reductions were seen for both men and women, every age group, level of education, income level, and geographic region of the country. Interestingly, the only increase in confidence was seen for those who viewed themselves as politically conservative (60–63%), while reductions were seen for those who considered themselves moderate (57–49%) and liberal (51–44%).

A poll by the Pew Research Center (Drake 2015) revealed similar results. The percentage polled who had a great deal of confidence that local police treated whites and blacks equally fell from 2007 to 2009, and then fell again in 2014. A decline was also seen for those who reported only having some confidence. By race, reductions in confidence were reported by whites (from 43%, to 38% to 35%, respectively). The number of blacks who reported having a great deal of confidence actually increased from 2009 (12%) to 2014 (17%). However, the percentage who only reported a fair amount of confidence decreased from 24% to 19%, and the percentage who reported very low confidence increased from 24% to 46%.

Table 3.7   Number and Percentage of Law Enforcement Homicides Captured, by Source and Estimation Approach, 2003–2009 and 2011

Law Enforcement Homicides	Lower-Bound Estimate		Upper-Bound Estimate	
	Number	Percentage of Universe	Number	Percentage of Universe
Estimated universe	7,427	100	9,937	100
Observed deaths	5,324	72	5,324	54
ARD	3,620	49	3,620	36
SHR	3,385	46	3,385	34
Unobserved deaths	2,103	28	4,613	46

Source: Bureau of Justice Statistics, Arrest-Related Deaths (ARD) Program, 2003–2009 and 2011; and FBI, Supplementary Homicide Reports (SHR), 2003–2009 and 2011.

A very interesting data point reveals that this issue is unique to the United States. According to a report by Graham (2015), encounters are more likely to end in a killing in the United States than in other countries. "According to the Bureau of Justice Statistics, police shot and killed 828 people in 2011, a figure that includes all killings, justifiable or not. By comparison, during the same year, there were two fatal police shootings in England and Wales; six in Australia; and six in Germany." A report in *The Economist* (2014) noted that in 2013, there were 458 deaths from police shootings in the United States, compared to 0 in Japan and Great Britain.

The militarization of local police departments is partly due to military weapons that were provided by the federal government. Under the 1033 Program, billions of dollars of military equipment were transferred from the Department of Defense to thousands of law enforcement agencies. This program was authorized under the National Defense Authorization Act for Fiscal Year 1997. President Obama (The White House 2015b) announced efforts to reverse the results of this program in 2015 and stated the following:

> Today, we're also releasing new policies on the military-style equipment that the federal government has in the past provided to state and local law enforcement agencies. We've seen how militarized gear can sometimes give people a feeling like there's an occupying force, as opposed to a force that's part of the community that's protecting them and serving them. It can alienate and intimidate local residents, and send the wrong message. So we're going to prohibit some equipment made for the battlefield that is not appropriate for local police departments. There is other equipment that may be needed in certain cases, but only with proper training. So we're going to ensure that departments have what they need, but also that they have the training to use it.

FURTHER READINGS

Alexander, Michelle (2012). *The New Jim Crow: Mass Incarceration in the Age of Colorblindness*. New York: The New Press.

Altschiller, Donald (2015). *Hate Crimes: A Reference Handbook, 3rd edition*. Santa Barbara, CA: ABC-CLIO.

Barak, Gregg, Paul Leighton, and Allison Cotton (2015). *Class, Race, Gender, and Crime: The Social Realities of Justice in America, 4th edition*. Lanham, MD: Rowman & Littlefield.

Epp, Charles R., Steven Maynard-Moody, and Donald Haider-Markel (2014). *Pulled Over: How Police Stops Define Race and Citizenship*. Chicago: The University of Chicago Press.

Gabbidon, Shaun L. and Helen Taylor Greene (2016). *Race and Crime, 4th edition*. Thousand Oaks, CA: Sage.

Newton, Michael (2014). *Hate Crime in America, 1968–2013: A Chronology of Offenses, Legislation and Related Events*. Jefferson, NC: McFarland.

Spence, Gerry (2015). *Police State: How America's Cops Get Away with Murder*. New York: St. Martin's Press.

Walker, Samuel, Cassia Spohn, and Miriam Delone (2012). *The Color of Justice: Race, Ethnicity, and Crime in America*. Belmont, CA: Wadsworth.

4

Employment

The primary source of data on employment is the U.S. Department of Labor. It derives data from a monthly survey called the Current Population Survey (CPS) that has been in use since 1940, and was assumed by the U.S. Census Bureau in 1942. The Bureau of Labor Statistics is the Labor Department's principal fact-finding agency for the federal government in the fields of labor, economics, and statistics. It provides data on employment, wages, inflation, productivity, and many other topics. One important point is that the survey is not limited to those who have U.S. citizenship, so respondents include documented and undocumented people. Full details on how the government currently measures unemployment can be found at http://www.bls.gov/cps/cps_htgm.htm.

Employment data is reported by employed and unemployed people. "Employed" includes working full-time and part-time, which also accounts for temporary or seasonal workers (i.e., hired during major holidays and times of the year such as spring or summer). People who have jobs are considered to be employed even if they are on vacation, sick leave, maternity leave, or in a labor dispute when they take the survey.

Those who are defined as "unemployed" are defined as those who are jobless but actively looking for a job (generally within four weeks prior to taking the survey) and are available for work. "Actively looking for work" means a person is submitting resumes or completing job applications, placing or answering job advertisements, using unions or professional registers for their employment search, or using other means to actively seek a job. It does not include those passively looking for work through such activities as just attending a job training program or reading about a job opening. The Bureau of Labor Statistics also defines unemployment as by saying "Persons who were not working and were waiting to be recalled to a job from which they had been temporarily laid off are also included as unemployed. Receiving benefits from the Unemployment Insurance (UI) program has no bearing on whether a person is classified as unemployed." (2013)

These two categories comprise those who are actually in the labor force. Thus those not considered to be in the labor force are those who aren't working and are also not looking for a job or available for work. These definitions are very important, as the unemployment rate only includes those "in the labor force" and excludes those "not in the labor force." Not considering this gives an inaccurate and underestimated view of the actual workforce.

Another important factor is that, unless otherwise noted, the labor force includes members of the population who are 16 years and older, and who are part of the noninstitutional population. That means that the Department of Labor excludes data from anyone living in a correctional institution, residing in a nursing or mental care facility, and those on active duty in the Armed Forces.

EMPLOYMENT AND UNEMPLOYMENT

According to the U.S. Bureau of Labor Statistics (2015), African Americans and American Indians/Alaska Natives had the highest unemployment rates in 2014. Their rates were each 11.3%, compared to 5% for Asians, 5.3% for whites, 6.1% for Native Hawaiians and Other Pacific Islanders, and 10.2% for those who identified as being "Two or More Races." For Hispanics, the rate was 7.4%, compared to 5.9% for non-Hispanics. Being unemployed not only includes being completely out of the workforce, but also includes those who were previously employed full-time, but are now working part-time and at lower wages. This is referred to as underemployed.

Table 4.1 shows selected employment statistics by race and ethnicity. By race and ethnicity, Asians and whites had higher rates of labor force participation than blacks in 2014, with the latter at 61.2%. Disparities can be seen across educational levels, as well. For example, the majority of employed whites and Asians had a bachelor's degree or higher. Comparatively, the majority of blacks and Hispanics only had a high school diploma. This means most blacks and Hispanics also earned much lower average incomes. In fact, the Bureau of Labor Statistics (2015) reports whites (39%) and Asians (51%) are predominantly employed in management, professional, and related occupations. A larger percentage of blacks (25%) and Hispanics (26%) work in the service industry, and 16% of blacks and Hispanics work in jobs related to production, transportation, and material moving.

The U.S. Bureau of Labor Statistics offers the following important points on long-term unemployment on minorities (see Table 4.2):

- In 2014, 33.5% of all unemployed people were jobless for 27 weeks or longer.
- Men were slightly more likely than women to be unemployed 27 weeks or longer (34.0% versus 32.8%).

Table 4.1 Selected Employment Statistics by Race, 2014

	Unemployment Rate	Labor Force Participation Rate	Educational Attainment of the Labor Force Age 25 and Older				
			Less Than High School Diploma	High School Graduate, No College	Some College, No Degree	Associate's Degree	Bachelor's Degree and Higher
White	5.3	63.1	8	27	16	11	38
Black or African American	11.3	61.2	8	31	22	11	27
Asian	5.0	63.6	6	17	10	7	60
Hispanic or Latino	7.4	66.1	28	30	15	8	19

Source: U.S. Bureau of Labor Statistics (2015). *Labor Force Characteristics by Race and Ethnicity, 2014 (Report 1057).* Washington, DC, November. Retrieved from http://www.bls.gov/opub/reports/cps/labor-force-characteristics-by-race-and-ethnicity-2014.pdf on January 23, 2016.

Table 4.2   Percentage of the Unemployed Who Were Jobless for 27 Weeks or Longer and 99 Weeks or Longer, by Gender, Race, and Hispanic and Latino Ethnicity, 2014 Annual Averages

	Percentage of the Unemployed Who Were Jobless for 27 Weeks or Longer	Percentage of the Unemployed Who Were Jobless for 99 Weeks or Longer
Men	34.0	11.8
Women	32.8	10.9
White	31.5	10.7
Black or African American	39.6	13.0
Asian	37.7	14.7
Hispanic or Latino ethnicity	29.9	10.1

Source: Kosanovich, Karen and Eleni Theodossiou Sherman (2015). *Trends in Long-term Unemployment*. Washington, DC: U.S. Bureau of Labor Statistics. Retrieved from http://www.bls.gov/spotlight/2015/long-term-unemployment/pdf/long-term-unemployment.pdf on January 2, 2016.

Among the major race and Hispanic ethnicity groups, 39.6% of blacks and 37.7% of Asians who were unemployed had been looking for work for 27 weeks or longer. Data showed that whites and Hispanics were less likely to be unemployed long term, reported at 31.5% and 29.9%, respectively. (Bureau of Labor Statistics 2015)

The incidence of extreme long-term unemployment has fallen in recent years but remains high by historical standards. In 2014, 11.4% of all unemployed people had been looking for work for 99 weeks or longer. Men were more likely than women to be unemployed for 99 weeks or longer (11.8% versus 10.9%). Unemployed Asians and blacks (14.7% and 13.0%, respectively) were more likely to be jobless for 99 weeks or longer than unemployed whites (10.7%) and Hispanics (10.1%). (Kosanovich and Sherman 2015)

African Americans even face job discrimination because of their greater propensity to have "ethnic sounding" names (i.e., names that are used exclusively for people of a particular race or ethnicity). A 2014 *Huffington Post* article about modern issues with racism revealed that applicants with "white-sounding" names receive, on average, one callback from employment reviews per every 10 resumes sent. In comparison, those with "African-American-sounding names" get one callback per 15 resumes. The report further found that resumes with "white-sounding name" yielded as many callbacks as African American applicants who had eight more years of experience in their work history. Aura and Hess (2010) discuss the findings of a study that analyzed whether those with ethnic names were more likely to obtain interviews after sending in resumes. They reference a study by Bertrand and Mullainathan (2004) that was undertaken to determine the extent to which an African American's first name affects his or her job prospects. Resumes with African American ("ethnic") names and others with "traditional white names" were sent to job openings listed in the newspapers of major cities. They reported the following from their findings:

> To receive one job interview, a resume with a black name needs to be sent to 15 openings. In contrast, to receive one job interview, a resume with a white name needs to be sent to only ten job openings. Furthermore, by using auxiliary information from birth certificates from Massachusetts that also list a mother's education, Bertrand and Mullainathan construct measures of expected maternal education level for each name in their sample. Their results imply that it is the racial information conveyed in the name and not the parental background factor signaled by the name (i.e. parental education) that potential employers are using as the basis to select between resumes. They conclude that this shows that racial discrimination is a factor in the job market. (p. 215)

Heslin, Bell, and Fletcher (2012) reported similar findings:

> Access discrimination has been extensively documented in field studies. In one study, job applicants with names such as LaKisha, Tyrone, and Jamal (common to blacks) had to send out 50 per cent more resumes than applicants named Emily, Brad, and Greg (common to whites) to be offered a job interview (Bertrand & Mullainathan 2004). Having a White-sounding name enhanced the chance of being given a job interview as much as adding an additional eight years of experience to the resume of a Black person. These results were consistent across occupation, industry type, and employer size. (p. 845)

In 2006, the news program 20/20 (Stossel and Kendall 2006) conducted an experiment on the same topic. On the show, the results of their on-air experiment showed that African Americans with "ethnic-sounding names" were less likely to be called back for interviews, even when their resumes met the job requirements and their qualifications were equal to other applicants'. In the experiment, African Americans posted resumes on popular job search web sites. One resume listed the applicant's real name, while the other listed a fictitious name that sounded more "traditionally white." The resumes with the "traditional" names were downloaded almost 20% more often by job recruiters.

HOMEOWNERSHIP

Homeownership is one of the fundamental determinants of well-being in the United States. From an economic viewpoint, a home is one of the best financial investments. A home and accompanying land are long-term assets that can grow in equitable value over time, serve as sources for substantial tax deductions, and can be passed from generation to generation as a wealth inheritance asset. Even in the short term, there is the benefit of stable home prices. Unlike rent that increases each year, home principal, interest, and tax rates remain relatively stable from year to year. The predominant economic and social benefit is having a safe and secure place to live. There is also the satisfaction of owning one's residence, and being able to provide a stable environment for oneself and one's family. In essence, buying a house has long been seen as a core part of the "American Dream."

Table 4.3 shows homeownership rates by race and ethnicity from 2011 through 2015. The rate of homeownership nationwide decreased a little; from around 66% in 2011 to approximately 63% in 2015. Non-Hispanic whites had the highest rate, with 72.2% by the fourth quarter of 2015. The rate for blacks alone was 41.9%. The rates for blacks were also lower than all other races combined and Hispanics of any race.

The disparity among race and ethnicity in homeownership can be attributed to a number of factors, including historical and current discriminatory practices by sellers and lenders. As pointed out by DeSilva and Elmelech (2012, pp. 2–3), "In neoclassical economic theory, racial and ethnic inequality in homeownership is viewed as a reflection of between-group differences in income, wealth, life-cycle characteristics and household preferences. Studies focusing on the black-white divide have supported this view, concluding that racial differences in household income, household and parental wealth, preference for urban location and demographic characteristics contribute to racial differences in homeownership. There is also a consensus in the literature that these variables only partially explain the black-white differential. Some studies have attributed the unexplained black-white disparity to the presence of racial preferences and institutional discrimination in the credit and housing markets."

Speaking on historical discrimination and strategies to overcome the recession impacts of the early 21st century, Correa (2014, p. 25) outlined:

As the housing "recovery" continues and its long-term ramifications become clear, two areas merit attention: emphasizing fair housing enforcement and viewing homeownership as an indicator rather than an end. In terms of strengthening enforcement of fair housing laws, the Housing Discrimination Survey's fourth decennial wave of audits in the field (U.S. Department of Housing and Urban Development 2012) revealed ongoing discrimination against buyers and renters. The Survey recommends a multi-pronged strategy, including vigorous enforcement of anti-discrimination protections. That should be coupled with education about the availability and desirability of diverse neighborhoods, with the goal being "to open up exclusive communities and preserve affordable options in gentrifying neighborhoods," as well as providing "neighborhood reinvestment—to equalize the quality of services, resources, and amenities in minority neighborhoods."

Perhaps the greatest impediment to African Americans and other minorities in obtaining equal housing opportunities is discriminatory practices that either exclude them or apply extra criteria for loan approval. For example, some neighborhood realtors purposefully do not advertise houses for sale so that minorities

Table 4.3 Homeownership Rates by Race/Ethnicity of Householder, 2011–2015

		Homeownership Rates[1] (%)			
Year/Quarter	United States	Non-Hispanic White Alone	Black Alone[2]	All Other Races[3]	Hispanic (of Any Race)
2015					
Fourth quarter	63.8	72.2	41.9	53.3	46.7
Third quarter	63.7	71.9	42.4	53.7	46.1
Second quarter	63.4	71.6	43.0	52.6	45.4
First quarter	63.7	72.0	41.9	55.4	44.1
2014					
Fourth quarter	64.0	72.3	42.1	55.3	44.5
Third quarter	64.4	72.6	42.9	54.2	45.6
Second quarter	64.7	72.9	43.5	54.7	45.8
First quarter	64.8	72.9	43.3	55.8	45.8
2013					
Fourth quarter	65.2	73.4	43.2	56.0	45.5
Third quarter	65.3	73.3	43.1	55.2	47.6
Second quarter	65.0	73.3	42.9	54.5	45.9
First quarter	65.0	73.4	43.1	54.6	45.3
2012					
Fourth quarter	65.4	73.6	44.5	55.2	45.0
Third quarter	65.5	73.6	44.1	54.6	46.7
Second quarter	65.5	73.5	43.8	55.0	46.5
First quarter	65.4	73.5	43.1	55.1	46.3
2011					
Fourth quarter	66.0	73.7	45.1	56.5	46.6
Third quarter	66.3	73.8	45.6	56.4	47.6
Second quarter	65.9	73.7	44.2	56.0	46.6
First quarter	66.4	74.1	44.8	56.7	46.8

Note: Beginning in 2003, the question on race on the CPS was modified to comply with the revised standards for federal statistical agencies. Respondents may now report more than one race, but small sample sizes preclude showing all race categories. The question on Hispanic origin is asked separately, and is asked before the question on race. For further information on each major race group and the Two or More Races populations, see reports from the Census 2000 Brief series (C2KBR/01), available on the Census 2000 website at: http://www.census.gov/population/www/cen2000/briefs.html.

[1] Standard errors for quarterly homeownership rates by race and ethnicity of householder generally are 0.3% for non-Hispanic white (single race) householders, 0.6% for black (single race) householders, 0.7% for All Other Races householders, and 0.6% for Hispanic householders.

[2] The homeownership rate for fourth quarter 2015 for householders who reported black whether or not they reported any other race was 41.6%.

[3] Includes people who reported Asian, Native Hawaiian or Other Pacific Islander, or American Indian or Alaska Native regardless of whether they reported any other race, as well as all other combinations of two or more races.

Source: Callis, Robert R. and Kresin, Melissa (2016). *Residential Vacancies and Homeownership in the Fourth Quarter 2015.* Washington, DC: Social, Economic and Housing Statistics Division, U.S. Census Bureau, U.S. Department of Commerce. Retrieved from http://www.census.gov/housing/hvs/files/currenthvspress.pdf on February 24, 2016.

do not know they are vacant. Many lending institutions have been found to violate laws in lending to minorities. A 2013 article in the *Huffington Post* illustrated the experiences of minorities who tried renting or buying homes, only to be shown fewer real estate properties than their white peers, who were equally qualified. The article points out that the study, done by the Department of Housing and Urban Development (HUD), ran 8,000 such tests in 28 different metropolitan areas. The minorities were compared to white home hunters of the same age, sex, and qualifications to own or rent properties. Although minorities were typically able to get some appointments (viewing a minimum of one housing unit), the authors of the study cited subtle discrimination in the results, which suggested that whites were shown more units, thus expanding their location and financial options in comparison to the limited options of minorities (Gamboa 2013).

Federal, state, and local prosecution is the primary means to end housing discrimination. The Department of Justice's Civil Rights Division (2017) reports:

> The Housing and Civil Enforcement Section of the Civil Rights Division is responsible for the Departments' enforcement of the Fair Housing Act (FHA), along with the Equal Credit Opportunity Act, the Servicemembers Civil Relief Act (SCRA), the land use provisions of the Religious Land Use and Institutionalized Persons Act (RLUIPA) and Title II of the Civil Rights Act of 1964, which prohibits discrimination in public accommodations.
>
> Under the FHA, the Department of Justice may bring lawsuits where there is reason to believe that a person or entity is engaged in a "pattern or practice" of discrimination or where a denial of rights to a group of persons raises an issue of general public importance. The Department of Justice also brings cases where a housing discrimination complaint has been investigated by the Department of Housing and Urban Development, HUD has issued a charge of discrimination, and one of the parties to the case has "elected" to go to federal court. In FHA cases, the Department can obtain injunctive relief, including affirmative requirements for training and policy changes, monetary damages and, in pattern or practice cases, civil penalties.

FURTHER READINGS

Conrad, Cecilia A., John Whitehead, Patrick Mason, and James Stewart (eds.) (2005). *African Americans in the U.S. Economy*. Lanham, MD: Rowman & Littlefield.

Morris, Monique W. (2015). *Black Stats: African Americans by the Numbers in the Twenty-First Century*. New York: The New Press.

Oliver, Melvin L. and Thomas M. Shapiro (2006). *Black Wealth/White Wealth: A New Perspective on Racial Inequality, 2nd edition*. New York: Routledge.

Shapiro, Thomas M. (2004). *The Hidden Cost of Being African American: How Wealth Perpetuates Inequality*. New York: Oxford University Press.

Smiley, Tavis (2016). *The Covenant with Black America-Ten Years Later*. Carlsbad, CA: Hay House.

Williams, Walter E. (2011). *Race & Economics: How Much Can Be Blamed on Discrimination?* Stanford, CA: Hoover Institution Press.

5

Voting

The primary issue with voting data is obtaining it from reputable sources. There are many news organizations, polling organizations, and private organizations that report voting information in addition to government sources. As with other types of data, care must be taken to ensure the data is not biased, and that it is also complete (based upon completed versus forecasted election results). Since 1964, the U.S. Census Bureau has fielded the Voting and Registration Supplement to the Current Population Survey (CPS) every two years. The Census Bureau surveys the civilian noninstitutionalized population in the United States. The results provide data about presidential and congressional elections. However, the official count of votes cast can be found on the web page of the Clerk of the U.S. House of Representatives at http://history.house.gov/Institution/Election-Statistics/Election-Statistics/ or on the web page of the Federal Election Commission at www.fec.gov/pubrec/electionresults.shtml. State and local agencies must be used to obtain official data on election results at lower levels of government.

The next issue is that voter information by sex, race, and ethnicity must be obtained from surveys and polls. Information is not collected on voter registration forms or during elections. Care must be taken in understanding the methodology used to obtain the data, such as the sample size used and the geographic region the sample was taken from. Data may be collected by telephone calls, online surveys, face-to-face interviews, or from people arriving at or leaving voting locations. Here, results will vary based on such factors as the time, length, and method of surveying. Be mindful that voter perceptions on issues are based on surveys of respondents who may not actually be registered to vote or have a true intention of voting. Thus, care should be taken to avoid assuming that the results are directly representative of the actual voting population.

There are also issues in the final data from the surveys because responses are voluntarily given by respondents. Respondents are not always truthful, given the fact that politics is such a sensitive and sometimes personal issue. Some don't know how to answer such questions as "what is your political ideology," while some will refuse to respond. Responses can also vary based on how interview questions are worded. These types of issues should be revealed in study results.

VOTING RATES

Historically, voting rates for African Americans have lagged behind whites during every major election. Although decades were spent fighting for equality in voting, the majority of blacks still do not exercise their voting rights. The reasons for this range from feeling disenfranchised from the political process to discriminatory practices used by localities and states that attempt to discourage minorities and the poor from voting. This began with Jim Crow laws in the South after the Civil War, and is seen in current laws imposing more voter identification requirements. Blacks have the most to lose from not being involved in the political process because they are at greater risk for issues, such as unemployment and adverse treatment by the court system, and are in the greatest need of government assistance programs. Their absence from the political process leads to politicians and appointed leaders ignoring the needs of those who do not vote in favor of active voters. Elected officials give the greatest support to those who will keep them in office and provide financial support to their campaigns.

Data shows, however, that the voting rates of African Americans are increasing in comparison to whites. Blacks are most likely to vote during years when elections appear to have racial implications, such as supporting social programs that blacks depend on for economic and social well-being more than whites. The continuation of this trend is contingent upon the income and education levels of blacks because both factors have a direct correlation to the propensity to vote. Increases in black voter turnouts also depend on whether politicians pass laws and institute policies that are most salient to blacks, and lastly on the growing political clout of the increasing Hispanic population.

Table 5.1 shows voting by race during the 2000, 2004, 2008, and 2012 presidential elections, as well as the voting rate by race/ethnicity. Notice the voting rates for blacks had the widest gap from whites in the two earlier elections. More blacks voted than Asians and Hispanics did during all elections. For the latter two elections, the black voting rate reached and then surpassed that of whites. Blacks voted at a higher rate (66.2%) than non-Hispanic whites (64.1%) for the first time since the Census Bureau started publishing voting rates by the eligible citizenship population in 1996.

Table 5.1 Voter Turnout, by Race and Hispanic Origin, 2000, 2004, 2008, and 2012

Year and Race and Hispanic Origin	Total Votes Cast	Net Change from Previous Presidential Election	Voting Rates
2012			
Total	132,948	1,804	
White, non-Hispanics	98,041	–2,001	64.1
Blacks	17,813	1,680	66.2
Asians	3,904	547	47.3
Hispanics	11,188	1,443	48.0
2008			
Total	131,144	5,408	
White, non-Hispanics	100,042	475	66.1
Blacks	16,133	2,117	64.7
Asians	3,357	589	47.6
Hispanics	9,745	2,158	49.9
2004			
Total	125,736	14,910	
White, non-Hispanics	99,567	10,098	67.2
Blacks	14,016	1,099	60.0
Asians	2,768	723	44.2
Hispanics	7,587	1,653	47.2
2000			
Total	110,826	5,809	
White, non-Hispanics	89,469	2,865	61.8
Blacks	12,917	1,531	56.8
Asians	2,045	304	43.4
Hispanics	5,934	1,006	45.1

Notes: Numbers in thousands. Federal surveys now give respondents the option of reporting more than one race. Therefore, two basic ways of defining a race group are possible. A group such as Asian may be defined as those who reported Asian and no other race (the race-alone or single-race concept) or as those who reported Asian regardless of whether they also reported another race (the race-alone-or-in-combination concept). The body of this report (text, figures, and tables) shows data for people who reported they were the single race White and not Hispanic, people who reported the single race Black, and people who reported the single race Asian. Use of the single-race populations does not imply that it is the preferred method of presenting or analyzing data.

Data for the American Indian and Alaska Native and the Native Hawaiian and Other Pacific Islander populations are not shown in this report because of their small sample size in the November 2012 Current Population Survey.

Source: File, Thom (2013). *The Diversifying Electorate—Voting Rates by Race and Hispanic Origin in 2012 (and Other Recent Elections)*. Washington, DC: United States Census Bureau, U.S. Department of Commerce, May. Retrieved from https://www.census.gov/prod/2013pubs/p20-568.pdf on February 5, 2016.

Higher voting rates were also prevalent by certain regions. For example, in the 2012 election, blacks had the highest voter rates in parts of the eastern United States. This included the states of Mississippi, Alabama, Tennessee, Kentucky, Pennsylvania, and New York. Per the Census Bureau:

> In the eastern part of the country, Blacks tended to vote at higher rates than non-Hispanic Whites. The New England division was an exception, as voting rates for Blacks and non-Hispanic Whites were not statistically different in that part of the country. Voting disparities were high in the East South Central division, where Blacks voted at higher rates than non-Hispanic Whites by 7.6 percentage points. In the middle part of the country voting rates for Blacks and non-Hispanic Whites were generally not statistically different from one another, but in the two most western census divisions, the rates for non-Hispanic Whites were higher than those of Blacks by margins of 12.8 percentage points in the Mountain division and 5.9 percentage points in the Pacific division. (File 2013)

The trends shown in Table 5.1 are a result of blacks generally voting at higher rates during years when they are most interested in the presidential candidates. Because the vast majority of blacks vote Democrat, the years with the highest rates were those in which there were extraordinary heated presidential elections. The following are the years when the voting rates for blacks exceeded 60% and the presidential candidates running in those years:

- 1984 Ronald Reagan (Republican) vs. Walter Mondale (Democrat)
- 1992 Bill Clinton (Democrat) vs. George Bush (Republican)
- 2004 George W. Bush (Republican) vs. John Kerry (Democrat)
- 2008 Barack Obama (Democrat) vs. John McCain (Republican)
- 2012 Barack Obama (Democrat) vs. Mitt Romney (Republican)

Besides interest in candidates, there are many factors that influence general voting behavior. These include trust in the government, belief that government will look out for black interests, general interest in politics, and a belief in the efficacy of voting. Other factors that affect voting are socioeconomic. Voter participation increases for those with higher levels of education. For example, during the 2008 election, only 39.4% of those who didn't graduate high school voted. The rate for those who graduated high school or possessed a General Education Development (GED) was 54.9%; 68% for those with some college or an associate's degree; 77% for those with a bachelor's degree; and 82.7% for those with an advanced degree (File and Crissey 2012, p. 4). Income level is another determining factor of voting. The following are the voting rates by income during the 2008 election (File and Crissey 2012, p. 4):

- Less than $20,000: 51.9%
- $20,000–29,999: 56.3%

- $30,000–39,999: 62.2%
- $40,000–49,999: 64.7%
- $50,000–$74,999: 70.9%
- $75,000–$99,999: 76.4%
- $100,000 and over: 91.8%

One area that may increase overall minority voting rates are the growing number of minorities in Congress. While still predominantly white, there were more blacks in the 114th Congress than ever before. According to the Congressional Research Service (Manning 2015, pp. 6–7), the following data outlines minority representation in the House and Senate in 2015–2016:

- There are a record 48 African American Members (8.9% of the total membership) in the 114th Congress, 3 more than at the beginning of the 113th Congress.20 Forty-six serve in the House, including two Delegates, and two serve in the Senate. This number includes one Member of the House who is of African American and Asian ancestry and is counted in both ethnic categories in this report. Forty-four of the African American House Members, including two Delegates, are Democrats, and two are Republicans. There is a Senator of each party. Twenty African American women, including two Delegates, serve in the House.

- There are 38 Hispanic or Latino Members in the 114th Congress, 7.0% of the total membership and a record number.21 Thirty-four serve in the House and four in the Senate. Of the Members of the House, 25 are Democrats (including 1 Delegate and the Resident Commissioner from Puerto Rico), 9 are Republicans, and 9 are women. There are four male Hispanic Senators (three Republicans, one Democrat). One set of Hispanic Members, Representatives Linda Sánchez and Loretta Sanchez, are sisters.

- A record 14 Members of the 114th Congress (2.6% of the total membership and 1 more than at the beginning of the 113th Congress) are of Asian, South Asian, or Pacific Islander ancestry. Thirteen of them (12 Democrats, 1 Republican) serve in the House, and 1 (a Democrat) serves in the Senate. These numbers include one House Member who is also of African American ancestry and another of Hispanic ancestry; these Members are counted in both ethnic categories. Of those serving in the House, two are Delegates. Seven of the Asian Pacific American Members are female: six in the House and one in the Senate.

- There are two American Indian (Native American) Members of the 114th Congress, both of whom are Republican Members of the House.

Table 5.2 shows more detailed voting information from 1964 through 2014. By total and race/ethnicity, it shows the total number and percentage of people registered to vote versus those that actually voted. For example, the total percentage of registered voters has decreased since the 1960s, when 70% of the population was

Table 5.2 Reported Voting and Registration by Race, Hispanic Origin, Sex, and Age Groups, November 1964-2014

Year	Total Voting-Age Population	Total Percent Total Population	Total Percent Citizen Population	White Total Population	White Citizen Population	White Non-Hispanic Total Population	White Non-Hispanic Citizen Population	Black Total Population	Black Citizen Population	Asian[1] Total Population	Asian[1] Citizen Population	Hispanic (of Any Race) Total Population	Hispanic (of Any Race) Citizen Population	Total Population Male	Total Population Female
Voted															
2014	239,874	38.5	41.9	40.3	43.4	45.0	45.8	37.3	39.7	19.1	27.1	18.4	27.0	37.2	39.6
2012	235,248	56.5	61.8	57.6	62.2	63.0	64.1	62.0	66.2	31.3	47.3	31.8	48.0	54.4	58.5
2010	229,690	41.8	45.5	43.4	46.7	47.8	48.6	40.7	43.5	21.3	30.8	20.5	31.2	40.9	42.7
2008	225,499	58.2	63.6	59.6	64.4	64.8	66.1	60.8	64.7	32.1	47.6	31.6	49.9	55.7	60.4
2006	220,603	43.6	47.8	45.8	49.7	50.5	51.6	38.6	41.0	21.8	32.4	19.3	32.3	42.4	44.7
2004	215,694	58.3	63.8	60.3	65.4	65.8	67.2	56.3	60.0	29.8	44.1	28.0	47.2	56.3	60.1
2002	210,421	42.3	46.1	44.1	47.5	48.0	49.1	39.7	42.3	19.4	31.2	18.9	30.4	41.4	43.0
2000	202,609	54.7	59.5	56.4	60.5	60.4	61.8	53.5	56.8	25.4	43.4	27.5	45.1	53.1	56.2
1998	198,228	41.9	45.3	43.3	46.3	46.5	47.4	39.6	41.8	19.3	32.4	20.0	32.8	41.4	42.4
1996	193,651	54.2	58.4	56.0	59.6	59.6	60.7	50.6	53.0	25.7	45.0	26.8	44.0	52.8	55.5
1994	190,267	45.0	48.4	47.3	50.0	50.1	51.0	37.1	38.9	21.8	39.4	20.2	34.0	44.7	45.3
1992	185,684	61.3	67.7	63.6	69.2	66.9	70.2	54.1	59.2	27.3	53.9	28.9	51.6	60.2	62.3
1990	182,118	45.0	49.3	46.7	50.5	49.0	51.4	39.2	42.4	20.3	40.0	21.0	36.0	44.6	45.4
1988	178,098	57.4	62.2	59.1	63.4	61.8	64.2	51.5	55.0	NA	NA	28.8	48.0	56.4	58.3
1986	173,890	46.0	49.4	47.0	50.1	48.9	50.7	43.2	45.5	NA	NA	24.2	38.0	45.8	46.1
1984	169,963	59.9	64.9	61.4	65.7	63.3	66.4	55.8	60.6	NA	NA	32.7	50.0	59.0	60.8
1982	165,483	48.5	51.9	49.9	52.8	51.5	53.4	43.0	45.5	NA	NA	25.3	38.5	48.7	48.4
1980	157,085	59.3	64.0	60.9	65.4	62.8	66.2	50.5	53.9	NA	NA	29.9	46.1	59.1	59.4
1978	151,646	45.9	48.9	47.3	50.1	48.6	50.6	37.2	39.5	NA	NA	23.5	35.7	46.6	45.3
1976	146,548	59.2	NA	60.9	NA	NA	NA	48.7	NA	NA	NA	31.8	NA	59.6	58.8
1974	141,299	44.7	NA	46.3	NA	NA	NA	33.8	NA	NA	NA	22.9	NA	46.2	43.4
1972	136,203	63.0	NA	64.5	NA	NA	NA	52.1	NA	NA	NA	37.5	NA	64.1	62.0
1970	120,701	54.6	NA	56.0	NA	NA	NA	43.5	NA	NA	NA	NA	NA	56.8	52.7
1968	116,535	67.8	NA	69.1	NA	NA	NA	57.6	NA	NA	NA	NA	NA	69.8	66.0
1966	112,800	55.4	NA	57.0	NA	NA	NA	41.7	NA	NA	NA	NA	NA	58.2	53.0
1964	110,604	69.3	NA	70.7	NA	NA	NA	58.5	NA	NA	NA	NA	NA	71.9	67.0
Registered															
2014	239,874	59.3	64.6	61.3	65.9	66.9	68.1	59.7	63.4	34.4	48.8	34.9	51.3	57.2	61.2
2012	235,248	65.1	71.2	66.7	71.9	72.4	73.7	68.5	73.1	37.2	56.3	38.9	58.7	63.1	67.0
2010	229,690	59.8	65.1	61.6	66.4	67.0	68.2	58.8	62.8	34.1	49.3	33.8	51.6	57.9	61.5
2008	225,499	64.9	71.0	66.6	72.0	72.0	73.5	65.5	69.7	37.3	55.3	37.6	59.4	62.6	67.0

96

Year	Population													
2006	220,603	61.6	67.6	64.0	69.5	69.7	71.2	57.4	60.9	32.9	49.1	32.1	53.7	59.5	63.5
2004	215,694	65.9	72.1	67.9	73.6	73.5	75.1	64.4	68.7	34.9	51.8	34.3	57.9	64.0	67.6
2002	210,421	60.9	66.5	63.1	67.9	67.9	69.4	58.5	62.4	30.7	49.2	32.6	52.5	58.9	62.8
2000	202,609	63.9	69.5	65.7	70.4	70.0	71.6	63.6	67.5	30.7	52.4	34.9	57.4	62.2	65.6
1998	198,228	62.1	67.1	63.9	68.2	67.9	69.3	60.2	63.6	29.1	48.9	33.7	55.2	60.6	63.5
1996	193,651	65.9	71.0	67.7	72.0	71.6	73.0	63.5	66.4	32.6	57.2	35.7	58.6	64.4	67.3
1994	190,267	62.5	67.1	64.6	68.4	68.1	69.4	58.5	61.3	28.7	51.9	31.3	52.9	61.2	63.7
1992	185,684	68.2	75.2	70.1	76.3	73.5	77.1	63.9	70.0	31.2	61.6	35.0	62.5	66.9	69.3
1990	182,118	62.2	68.2	63.8	69.1	66.7	69.9	58.8	63.5	28.4	56.0	32.3	55.2	61.2	63.1
1988	178,098	66.6	72.1	67.9	72.8	70.8	73.6	64.5	68.8	NA	NA	35.5	59.1	65.2	67.8
1986	173,890	64.3	69.0	65.3	69.5	67.7	70.2	64.0	67.3	NA	NA	35.9	56.4	63.4	65.0
1984	169,963	68.3	73.9	69.6	74.5	71.6	75.1	66.3	72.0	NA	NA	40.1	61.4	67.3	69.3
1982	165,483	64.1	68.5	65.6	69.4	67.5	70.1	59.1	62.6	NA	NA	35.3	53.7	63.7	64.4
1980	157,085	66.9	72.3	68.4	73.4	70.3	74.1	60.0	64.1	NA	NA	36.4	56.0	66.6	67.1
1978	151,646	62.6	66.7	63.8	67.5	65.4	68.2	57.1	60.6	NA	NA	32.9	50.1	62.6	62.5
1976	146,548	66.7	NA	68.3	NA	NA	NA	58.5	NA	NA	NA	37.8	NA	67.1	66.4
1974	141,299	62.2	NA	64.6	NA	NA	NA	54.2	NA	NA	NA	34.9	NA	62.8	61.7
1972	136,203	72.3	NA	73.4	NA	NA	NA	65.5	NA	NA	NA	44.4	NA	73.1	71.6
1970	120,701	68.1	NA	70.8	NA	NA	NA	64.5	NA	NA	NA	NA	NA	69.6	66.8
1968	116,535	74.3	NA	75.4	NA	NA	NA	66.2	NA	NA	NA	NA	NA	76.0	72.8
1966	112,800	70.3	NA	71.7	NA	NA	NA	60.2	NA	NA	NA	NA	NA	72.2	68.6
1964	110,604	NA	NA	NA	NA	NA	NA	NA	NA	NA	NA	NA	NA	NA	NA

Note: Numbers in thousands.

Prior to 1972, data are for people 21–24 years of age with the exception of those aged 18–24 years in Georgia and Kentucky, 19–24 years in Alaska, and 20–24 years in Hawaii.

Prior to 1996, the CPS did not collect information on citizenship in a uniform way. Estimates for the citizenship population presented in this table prior to 1996 should be interpreted with caution, as they are not directly comparable to estimates from 1996 and after.

Because of changes in the Current Population Survey race categories beginning in 2003, 2004–2012 data on race are not directly comparable with data from earlier years.

Federal surveys now give respondents the option of reporting more than one race. Therefore, two basic ways of defining a race group are possible. A group such as Asian may be defined as those who reported Asian and no other race (the race-alone or single-race concept) or as those who reported Asian regardless of whether they also reported another race (the race-alone-or-in-combination concept). This table shows data for people who reported they were the single race White and not Hispanic, people who reported the single race Black, and people who reported the single race Asian. Use of the single-race populations does not imply that it is the preferred method of presenting or analyzing data.

[1] Prior to 2004, this category was "Asian and Pacific Islanders," therefore rates are not directly comparable with prior years.

Source: U.S. Census Bureau (2016). *Historical Reported Voting Rates, Current Population Survey, November 2014 and Earlier Years.* Retrieved from https://www.census.gov/data/tables/time-series/demo/voting-and-registration/voting-historical-time-series.html on May 15, 2016.

registered and over 60% of the public voted, on average. Voting rates remained high in presidential election years compared to years in which only congressional elections were held. From the chart, it can be seen that Hispanics had the lowest registration and voting rates. For blacks, the voter registration rate and voting rate exceeded non-Hispanic whites in 2012 for the first time.

POLITICAL PARTY IDENTIFICATION

Prior to the 1960s, blacks typically supported the Republican Party, particularly since the party was formed by abolitionists, and Republican president Abraham Lincoln ended slavery. After the Civil War and through most of the 20th century, the Democratic Party was very hostile toward blacks and opposed equal rights. Southern Democratic political leaders supported Jim Crow laws and opposed civil rights legislation, and members of the Klu Klux Klan were part of the Democratic Party. A significant number of blacks changed their party affiliation during the 1960 election when President John F. Kennedy defeated Republic contender Richard Nixon. Ironically, Kennedy was not a civil rights advocate, and Nixon was a friend of Dr. Martin Luther King Jr. However, when Dr. King was arrested in 1960, Nixon was unable to get the civil rights leader released. Kennedy was convinced by his brother-in-law, Sargent Shriver, to call Dr. King's wife, Corretta Scott King, to share his concern.

Robert Kennedy, John's brother, was managing the campaign, and was outraged when he first heard about the call for fear that Southern Democratic governors and others would oppose Kennedy's bid for president as a result, particularly with the election only 13 days away. However, Robert ended up using the opportunity to his political advantage. He called the Georgia judge who had denied King a bond for release. The next day, as a result of the political pressure placed on the judge, Dr. King was released from prison. As a result, blacks overwhelmingly supporting Kennedy and contributed to his winning the presidential election by a very slim margin. This was the foundation of blacks supporting Democrats versus Republicans. The passage of the Civil Rights Act of 1964 and Voting Rights Act of 1965 under President Lyndon Johnson, which were both opposed by Republican leaders, solidified black support for the Democratic Party.

Today, blacks and white are politically divided when it comes to political parties. While whites tend to lean more right and give greater support to the Republican Party, blacks are often more liberal and the majority of African Americans support the Democratic Party. According to survey results from Gallup (Newport 2013), "Non-Hispanic whites accounted for 89% of Republican self-identifiers nationwide in 2012, while accounting for 70% of independents and 60% of Democrats. Over one-fifth of Democrats (22%) were black, while 16% of independents were Hispanic." Within racial and ethnic groups, Gallup's results showed that 35% of respondents definitively identify themselves as Republican, while 26% as Democrat. The remainder identified as Independent or didn't know. Conversely, 64% of blacks identified as Democrat, only 5% as Republican, and half as Independent or "didn't know." The majority of Hispanics and Asians also identified as Democrats.

The Pew Research Center also conducted a survey of political affiliation to provide an array of demographics showing party support. Their data showed just some of the factors that indicated which Americans were statistically more likely to support Republicans and Democrats by sex, race, ethnicity, and other social, economic, and demographic factors. First, men were more likely to lean Republican (43%) than women (36%), while women leaned more Democrat (52%) than men (44%). By race and ethnicity, the majority of non-Hispanic blacks (80%) leaned Democrat, with only 11% leaning Republican. The Pew Research Center's data also showed additional demographic and economic factors that frequently influenced political ideology. Generally, all education levels tended to lean Democrat, but the strongest affiliations were tied to those with the highest levels of income. By income level, Republican support increased in tandem with increases in income levels. Republicans accounted for 48% of voters who made more than $75,000 a year, compared to 31% of Republican voters who reported making under $30,000 a year. Another interesting point is that those in urban areas leaned Democrat while those in rural areas leaned Republican.

In terms of religious affiliations, 70% of non-Hispanic white Evangelical Protestants leaned Republican, compared to 82% of black Protestants, 61% of Jews, 61% of those who are religiously unaffiliated, 72% of atheists, and 69% of agnostics. The survey also collected data specific to non-Hispanic blacks. While the majority of blacks in every economic and demographic area leaned Democrat, those blacks with a tendency to lean Republican are likely to have a high school diploma or less, be employed, and/or live in rural areas. In all three cases, the percentages were under a fourth of those surveyed.

VOTER DISENFRANCHISEMENT

Most states have laws that address voting by those convicted of felonies. These laws vary drastically across the United States. Felons in Maine and Vermont never lose their right to vote, not even while incarcerated. In Florida, Iowa, and Virginia, felons and ex-felons permanently lose their right to vote. Florida and Virginia do allow for supplementary programs where voting rights can be restored by gubernatorial pardons. As for the rest of the country, the National Conference of State Legislatures (2016a) details that in 38 states and the District of Columbia, most ex-felons automatically gain the right to vote upon the completion of their sentence. In some states, ex-felons must wait for a certain period of time after the completion of their sentence before rights can be restored, or they must apply to have their voting rights restored. Table 5.3 shows the felony disenfranchisement restrictions by state.

Due to these issues, the following actions have been taken since 2008:

- In 2009, Washington restored the right to vote to felons who completed their sentences, while requiring them to reregister to vote.
- In 2011, the Florida Board of Executive Clemency (composed of the governor and three cabinet members) reversed a 2007 policy change that automatically restored voting rights to nonviolent offenders upon the completion of

Table 5.3   Summary of Felony Disenfranchisement Restrictions in 2014

Restriction (Number of States) per States				
Nonrestriction (2)	Prison (14)	Prison and Parole (4)	Prison, Parole, and Probation (19)	Prison, Parole, Probation, and Postsentence—Some or All (12)
Maine	District of Columbia	California	Alaska	Alabama[1]
Vermont	Hawaii	Colorado	Arkansas	Arizona[2]
	Illinois	Connecticut	Georgia	Delaware[3]
	Indiana	New York	Idaho	Florida[4]
	Massachusetts		Kansas	Iowa[5]
	Michigan		Louisiana	Kentucky
	Montana		Maryland	Mississippi[1]
	New Hampshire		Minnesota	Nebraska[6]
	North Dakota		Missouri	Nevada[7]
	Ohio		New Jersey	Tennessee[8]
	Oregon		New Mexico	Virginia[9]
	Pennsylvania		North Carolina	Wyoming[4]
	Rhode Island		Oklahoma	
	Utah		South Carolina	
			South Dakota	
			Texas	
			Washington	
			West Virginia	
			Wisconsin	

[1] State disenfranchises postsentence for certain offenses.
[2] Arizona disenfranchises postsentence for a second felony conviction.
[3] Delaware requires a five-year waiting period for certain offenses.
[4] State requires a five-year waiting period.
[5] Governor Tom Vilsack restored voting rights to individuals with former felony convictions via executive order in 2005. Governor Terry Branstad reversed this executive order in 2011.
[6] Nebraska reduced its indefinite ban on voting to a two-year waiting period in 2005.
[7] Nevada disenfranchises post-sentence except for first-time nonviolent offenses.
[8] Tennessee disenfranchises those convicted of felonies since 1981, in addition to those convicted of select offenses prior to 1973.
[9] Virginia requires a five-year waiting period for violent offenses and some drug offenses. As of July 15, 2013, the state will no longer require a two-year waiting period for nonviolent offenses.
Source: Chung, Jean (2015). Felony Disenfranchisement: A Primer. Washington, DC: The Sentencing Project. Retrieved from http://www.sentencingproject.org/doc/publications/fd_Felony%20Disenfranchisement%20Primer.pdf on March 2, 2016.

their sentence. The new policy requires that all ex-felons wait between five and seven years before applying to regain voting rights. In Iowa, the governor in 2011 reversed an executive order issued in 2005 under the previous governor. The 2005 order automatically restored the voting rights of all ex-felons, but under the 2011 order they will now have to apply to regain rights. In Tennessee,

HB 1117 was enacted, adding to the list of felons who will not be eligible to vote again.

- In 2012, South Carolina mandated that felons on probation would not have voting rights restored. Previously, only felons on parole or incarcerated had their voting rights suspended.
- In 2013, Delaware eliminated the five-year waiting period before voting rights are restored. In Virginia, then governor McDonnell signed an executive order creating new rights restoration processes for persons with prior felony convictions.
- In 2015, Wyoming enacted HB 15 requiring the Department of Corrections to issue a certification of restoration of voting rights to certain nonviolent felons who are being released from the state's prisons.
- In 2015, outgoing Kentucky governor Steve Beshear signed an executive order to automatically restore the right to vote (and to hold public office) to certain offenders, excluding those who were convicted of violent crimes, sex crimes, bribery, or treason. However, the order was reversed by incoming Governor Matt Bevin as one of his first acts in office. Bevin's order does not retroactively affect felons who, between November 24 and December 22, 2015, received a certificate from the state Department of Corrections confirming their restoration of rights.

The impact of felon laws prohibiting voting is substantial for African Americans. According to The Sentencing Project (Uggen, Shannon, and Manza 2012), the total number of disenfranchised felons increased from 1,762,582 in 1960 to 5,852,180 in 2010. Over two million of these were African Americans who were in prison, jail, on felony probation, or ex-felons. This data is shown in Table 5.4, with details on the disenfranchised by each state. Notice the largest percentage of disenfranchised were in Florida (10.42%), Mississippi (8.27%), Kentucky (7.35%), Virginia (7.34%), and Alabama (7.19%). The number of African Americans of the total disenfranchised populations in these states ranged from 23.3% in Kentucky to 58.9% in Mississippi. This exemplifies the negative impact to African Americans, as they represent such a large percentage of current or ex-felons.

The impact of felony laws on voting has long been debated. Ochs (2006, p. 89) does a great job in outlining the negatives of these policies in stating, "Felon disenfranchisement policies threaten compelling government interests in several respects. Free and fair elections are necessary but insufficient for democracy and the right to vote in the United States is central to democratic principles of liberty, freedom, and self-expression. The fact that the franchise is not equally protected has threatened vital U.S. economic interests and international relations. Universal suffrage is the greatest compelling governmental interest in terms of the electoral process, particularly when there is no evidence that a felon has or will commit voter fraud. Furthermore, the Supreme Court in *Carrington v. Rash*, 380 U.S. 89 (1965) ruled that no class of voters may be prohibited from voting based on

Table 5.4 Estimates of Disenfranchised Felons, 2010

State	Prisoners	Parolees	Felony Probation	Jail	Ex-Felons	Total	Total African Americans	Voting Age Population	Percentage Disenfranchised
Alabama	31,764	9,006	22,017	1,536	198,031	262,354	137,478	3,647,277	7.19%
Alaska	5,597	2,089	6,959	7	0	14,652	1,471	522,853	2.80%
Arizona	40,130	7,993	54,135	1,583	95,893	199,734	23,083	4,763,003	4.19%
Arkansas	16,204	21,106	27,250	633	0	65,193	25,357	2,204,443	2.96%
California	165,062	105,133	0	8,282	0	278,477	78,164	27,958,916	1.00%
Colorado	22,815	11,014	0	1,370	0	35,199	6,648	3,803,587	0.93%
Connecticut	19,321	2,894	0	0	0	22,215	9,300	2,757,082	0.81%
Delaware	6,598	560	4,448	0	14,032	25,638	11,831	692,169	3.70%
Florida	104,306	4,093	103,318	6,525	1,323,360	1,541,602	520,521	14,799,219	10.42%
Georgia	49,164	25,091	197,013	4,597	0	275,866	159,942	7,196,101	3.83%
Hawaii	5,912	0	0	0	0	5,912	250	1,056,483	0.56%
Idaho	7,431	3,957	13,721	386	0	25,495	645	1,138,510	2.24%
Illinois	48,418	0	0	2,085	0	50,503	27,933	9,701,453	0.52%
Indiana	28,028	0	0	1,255	0	29,283	10,309	4,875,504	0.60%
Iowa	9,455	3,197	8,862	374	0	21,888	4,473	2,318,362	0.94%
Kansas	9,051	5,063	3,704	691	0	18,509	5,853	2,126,179	0.87%
Kentucky	20,544	14,628	25,688	1,998	180,984	243,842	56,920	3,315,996	7.35%
Louisiana	39,445	26,202	42,599	3,648	0	111,894	70,301	3,415,357	3.28%
Maine	0	0	0	0	0	0	3,300	1,053,828	0.00%
Maryland	22,645	13,195	26,164	1,584		63,588	41,562	4,420,588	1.44%
Massachusetts	11,312	0	0	1,448	0	12,760	3,300	5,128,706	0.25%
Michigan	44,113	0	0	1,820	0	45,933	24,573	7,539,572	0.61%
Minnesota	9,796	5,807	42,661	962	0	59,226	14,221	4,019,862	1.47%
Mississippi	21,067	6,434	26,793	1,173	127,346	182,814	107,758	2,211,742	8.27%
Missouri	30,623	19,421	54,916	1,064	0	106,024	35,172	4,563,491	2.32%
Montana	3,716	0	0	230	0	3,946	171	765,852	0.52%
Nebraska	4,587	941	4,080	312	7,819	17,739	3,368	1,367,120	1.30%
Nevada	12,653	4,964	8,067	717	59,919	86,321	21,823	2,035,543	4.24%
New Hampshire	2,761	0	0	184	0	2,945	200	1,029,236	0.29%

New Jersey	25,007	15,563	57,517	2,289	0	100,376	50,898	6,726,680	1.49%
New Mexico	6,659	3,146	17,781	781	0	28,367	1,811	1,540,507	1.84%
New York	56,656	48,542	0	2,935	0	108,133	51,318	15,053,173	0.72%
North Carolina	40,116	3,621	36,869	1,826	0	82,432	43,621	7,253,848	1.14%
North Dakota	1,487	0	0	97	0	1,584	132	522,720	0.30%
Ohio	51,712	0	0	2,130	0	53,842	25,280	8,805,753	0.61%
Oklahoma	26,252	2,627	21,642	970	0	51,491	13,526	2,821,685	1.82%
Oregon	14,014	0	0	683	0	14,697	1,616	2,964,621	0.50%
Pennsylvania	51,264	0	0	3,608	0	54,872	26,550	9,910,224	0.55%
Rhode Island	3,357	0	0	0	0	3,357	964	828,611	0.41%
South Carolina	23,578	6,412	11,739	1,427	0	43,156	32,425	3,544,890	1.22%
South Dakota	3,434	2,843	0	145	0	6,422	369	611,383	1.05%
Tennessee	27,451	12,157	52,178	2,221	247,808	341,815	145,943	4,850,104	7.05%
Texas	173,649	104,763	247,136	6,939	0	532,487	156,316	18,279,737	2.91%
Utah	6,807	0	0	672	0	7,479	691	1,892,858	0.40%
Vermont	0	0	0	0	0	0	0	496,508	0.00%
Virginia	37,410	2,624	56,654	2,840	351,943	451,471	242,958	6,147,347	7.34%
Washington	18,235	6,956	26,785	1,114	0	53,090	8,779	5,143,186	1.03%
West Virginia	6,681	1,796	6,876	288	0	15,640	1,822	1,465,576	1.07%
Wisconsin	22,724	19,572	22,602	1,361	0	66,259	22,574	4,347,494	1.52%
Wyoming	2,112	682	3,236	157	19,470	25,657	805	428,224	5.99%
Totals	1,391,123	524,092	1,233,410	76,947	2,626,605	5,852,179	2,234,325	234,063,163	2.50%

Source: Uggen, Christopher, Sarah Shannon, and Jeff Manza (2012). *State-Level Estimates of Felon Disenfranchisement in the United States, 2010.* Washington, DC: The Sentencing Project.

how they may or may not vote." The primary argument against felons voting is trust and a belief they lack sound judgment. Another is that criminals, if allowed to vote, would thus support politicians who would be more lenient on crime. It is clear to see this latter argument is based on political motives of conservatives favoring harsher prison sentences.

Some voting laws continue to negatively impact the democratic voting process. For example, new laws in many states require new voter identification requirements. This practice will negatively impact minorities by requiring various type of proof of identity including photo identifications, birth certificates, copies of utility bills, or bank statements. Many minorities, the elderly, students, people with disabilities, and particularly those with low-income will find it costly to produce some of these documents. This assertion is supported by data.

These laws were meant to reduce the incidents of voter fraud, but instead cause many valid voters to not cast ballots because of the extra proof of identification burdens. Some are unable to pay for new forms of identification, and others (such as the elderly and the poor) lack proper identification, such as birth certificates.

Historically, Southern states enacted laws that intentionally restricted blacks' ability to vote, such as requiring literacy tests or poll taxes. The Department of Justice has the ability to stop these activities under the Voting Rights Act. However, that was challenged in *Shelby County, Alabama v. Holder*, 570 U.S. (2013) involving plaintiffs asking the court to rule on:

> whether Congress acted within its authority to enforce the constitutional prohibition against discrimination in voting when it reauthorized Section 5 of the Voting Rights Act of 1965, 42 U.S.C. 1973c (Section 5), in 2006, on the basis of an extensive record demonstrating that, despite considerable progress under Section 5's remedial framework, discrimination against minority voters continues to be a serious problem in covered jurisdictions and that Section 5 remains a valuable tool in preventing, remedying, and deterring such discrimination.

Section 5 of the Voting Rights Act of 1965 required certain states to gain preclearance from the Department of Justice before making any changes to their voting laws or practices. The case also challenged Section 4, which contains a coverage formula to determine which jurisdictions are subject to preclearance based upon historical voting discrimination.

Oral arguments were heard by the court on February 27, 2013. The case ensued after the Department of Justice overturned voter identification laws in Southern states (including Texas, South Carolina, and Florida) based on its view that these laws were based on racial discrimination. The plaintiffs argued racial discrimination no longer existed in voting and that the federal government had a need to intervene in state and local elections. The defense countered this argument, mainly due to continued complaints by black voters of discrimination and concerns that voter tampering was occurring.

With a 5–4 ruling, the court ruled in favor of the plaintiffs. It found that Section 4 was based upon formulas developed in the 1960s and was no longer valid. It also ruled the section exceeded the federal government's authority to enforce the Fourteenth and Fifteenth Amendments under the concept of federalism because it violated the equal sovereignty of the states. Invalidating Section 4 in essence also invalidated Section 5, while the court would not specifically rule on Section 5. The court pointed out the nation had changed since the original passage and subsequent amendments to the Act. While it was still illegal to practice voting discrimination, the ruling gained widespread criticism due to the continued use of discriminatory voting practices, particularly in the South.

In response to the court's decision, President Obama remarked:

> I am deeply disappointed with the Supreme Court's decision today. For nearly fifty years, the Voting Rights Act—enacted and repeatedly renewed by wide bipartisan majorities in Congress—has helped secure the right to vote for millions of Americans. Today's decision invalidating one of its core provisions upsets decades of well-established practices that help make sure voting is fair, especially in places where voting discrimination has been historically prevalent. As a nation, we've made a great deal of progress towards guaranteeing every American the right to vote. But, as the Supreme Court recognized, voting discrimination still exists. And while today's decision is a setback, it doesn't represent the end of our efforts to end voting discrimination. I am calling on Congress to pass legislation to ensure every American has equal access to the polls. My Administration will continue to do everything in its power to ensure a fair and equal voting process. (The White House 2013)

After the court's finding in the case, Attorney General Eric Holder announced intentions by the Department of Justice to continue fighting racial discrimination under Section 3 of the Voting Rights Act. This section was not affected by the Supreme Court decision in *Shelby*. Part of the section states:

> If in a proceeding instituted by the Attorney General under any statute to enforce the guarantees of the fifteenth amendment in any State or political subdivision the court finds that a test or device has been used for the purpose or with the effect of denying or abridging the right of any citizen of the United States to vote on account of race or color, it shall suspend the use of tests and devices in such State or political subdivisions as the court shall determine is appropriate and for such period as it deems necessary.

The Fifteenth Amendment prohibits the federal and state governments from denying a citizen the right to vote based on that citizen's "race, color, or previous condition of servitude." The Department filed suit against the state of Texas for passing voting laws that were deemed in violation of the Fifteenth Amendment in

2013. In an address, Holder stated, "Thanks to the hard work of our Civil Rights Division, we are continuing to refine and re-focus current enforcement efforts across the country. And while the suits we've filed in Texas mark the first voting rights enforcement actions the Justice Department has taken since the Supreme Court ruling, they will not be the last" (Department of Justice 2013). In response to the Supreme Court's rulings, it's likely that continual battles will emerge between the federal government and individual states over these issues. States including Texas, Arkansas, Mississippi, Alabama, Florida, South Carolina, North Carolina, and Virginia passed new or amended voting laws after the ruling. For example, Governor Pat McCrory signed a new law in North Carolina that required government issued photo identifications at the polls, shortened the early voting period by one week, and ended same-day voter registration. Lawsuits were immediately filed by the NAACP and the American Civil Liberties Union (McCallister 2013).

Individual states continue to pass these laws. They vary by state in terms of being "strict" or "nonstrict," and whether they require a voter's photograph. Each of these is defined by the National Conference of State Legislatures (2016b):

- Non-strict: At least some voters without acceptable identification have an option to cast a ballot that will be counted without further action on the part of the voter. For instance, a voter may sign an affidavit of identity, or poll workers may be permitted to vouch for the voter. In some of the "nonstrict" states (Colorado, Florida, Montana, Oklahoma, Rhode Island, Utah, and Vermont), voters who do not show required identification may vote on a provisional ballot. After the close of Election Day, election officials will determine (via a signature check or other verification) whether the voter was eligible and registered, and therefore whether the provisional ballot should be counted. No action on the part of the voter is required. In New Hampshire, election officials will send a letter to anyone who signed a challenged voter affidavit because they did not show an ID, and these voters must return the mailing, confirming that they are indeed in residence as indicated on the affidavit.

- Strict: Voters without acceptable identification must vote on a provisional ballot and also take additional steps after Election Day for it to be counted. For instance, the voter may be required to return to an election office within a few days after the election and present an acceptable ID to have the provisional ballot counted. If the voter does not come back to show ID, the provisional ballot is not counted. Using the nonstrict/strict categorization, 21 states have nonstrict voter ID requirements, and 11 have strict requirements.

- Photo vs. nonphoto identification: Some states request or require voters to show an identification document that has a photo on it, such as a driver's license, state-issued identification card, military ID, tribal ID, and many other forms of ID. Other states accept nonphoto identification such as a bank statement with name and address or other document that does not necessarily have a photo. Using this categorization for laws that are in effect in 2016, 17 states ask for a photo ID and 16 states also accept nonphoto IDs.

FURTHER READINGS

Frymer, Paul (2013). *Uneasy Alliances: Race and Party Competition in America.* Princeton, NJ: Princeton University Press.

Kreider, Kyle L. and Thomas J. Baldino (eds.) (2015). *Minority Voting in the United States.* Santa Barbara, CA: ABC-CLIO.

Kreider, Rose M. and Renee Ellis (2011). *Number, Timing, and Divorce of Marriages and Divorces: 2009 (Household Economic Studies).* Washington, DC: U.S. Census Bureau.

Scher, Richard K. (2015). *The Politics of Disenfranchisement: Why Is It So Hard to Vote in America?* New York: Routledge.

Stout, Christopher T. (2015). *Bringing Race Back In: Black Politicians, Deracialization, and Voting Behavior in the Age of Obama.* Charlottesville: University of Virginia Press.

Walters, Ronald W. (2007). *Freedom Is Not Enough: Black Voters, Black Candidates, and American Presidential Politics.* Lanham, MD: Rowman & Littlefield.

6

Family

Data on such topics as marriage, divorce, teen pregnancy, and teen violence are best obtained from government sources. These areas of research are based on official government records, such as state-issued marriage licenses, legal proceedings, and court records. National information may be based on estimates from community surveys, state and local records, and other sources. Just as with other data, the researcher should be sure to research the methodology used to understand how and when data was collected, if any factors were not included, and how to fully understand what the variables presented represent. Some sources will publish a user's guide outlining methodology, variable definitions, and related information to reports produced.

Also be mindful that the definitions of some variables may have changed over time. For example, the definition of "family" has changed to adapt to societal trends. According to the Census Bureau, family groups prior to 2007 were restricted to married couple and single-parent families, and their own children. In 2007, unmarried two-parent families were added to the official definition. Unmarried two-parent family groups are opposite-sex partners who share joint custody of a child under 18 years of age.

The Census Bureau provides an array of data on families and living arrangements. The Bureau uses the following sources, as outlined at http://www.census.gov/hhes/families/data/:

- The American Community Survey (ACS): an annual national survey collected monthly that provides communities with reliable and timely demographic, housing, social, and economic data every year. Data about families and living arrangements are available for the U.S. states, counties, selected metropolitan and micropolitan statistical areas, and selected zip codes. There are over a thousand detailed tables in American FactFinder (AFF). There are over 700 recurring tables with data on families and living arrangements. Data are available from 2000 to the present.

- Current Population Survey (CPS): a monthly survey of about 50,000 households conducted by the U.S. Census Bureau for the Bureau of Labor Statistics. The survey has been conducted for more than 50 years. Data about families and living arrangements are collected annually as part of the Annual Social and Economic Supplement (ASEC). For CPS definitions and explanations, or for additional information about the Current Population Survey, visit the CPS website (http://www.census.gov/programs-surveys/cps.html). An annual table package is produced with national level living arrangements and characteristics for adults, children, married couples, unmarried couples, households, and families. These tables are among the most detailed published by the Bureau. CPS collects data about the presence and type (bio, step, adoptive) of two parents in the household for everyone, as well as the presence of a spouse or cohabiting partner. This allows for detail about children's living arrangements and subfamilies which is not possible in ACS and Decennial Census data. Data about families and living arrangements are available from about 1960 to present.

- The Survey of Income and Program Participation (SIPP): a longitudinal panel survey of demographic information, income, labor force characteristics, and program participation in the United States with supplemental topical modules including questions on topics such as child wellbeing, child care and details about household relationships. Data are available for the U.S. since the beginning of the SIPP program in 1985.

- The Decennial Census: occurs every 10 years, in years ending in zero, to count the population and housing units for the entire United States. Its primary purpose is to provide the population counts that determine how seats in the U.S. House of Representatives are apportioned. Data about families and living arrangements are available for all 50 U.S. states and the District of Columbia, as well as all counties, and subcounty statistical areas (such as zip codes and block groups) from 1790 to the present.

Although terms like "families" and "households" are familiar, they are used in particular ways in Census Bureau products. The following are the Census Bureau's definitions of some commonly used terms:

- Household: an occupied housing unit.
- Householder: a person in whose name the housing unit is rented or owned. This person must be at least 15 years old.
- Family household: a household in which there is at least 1 person present who is related to the householder by birth, marriage or adoption.
- Family: in table titles, this term is used to refer to a family household. In general, family consists of those related to each other by birth, marriage or adoption.

- Family group: in CPS tables labeled as family groups, each married couple or parent/child group is counted separately, even if they reside in the same household. (Example: if a household consists of a married couple, one of whom is the householder, and their adult daughter and her child, the married couple will be one family group, and the adult daughter and her child will be a second family group.)

- Subfamily: a married couple or parent/child group that does not include the householder. Subfamilies may be related (meaning they are related to the householder) or unrelated (meaning they are unrelated to the householder).

- Unmarried partners: a couple who shares an intimate relationship. In decennial and ACS data, these couples always include the householder, since only relationship to the householder is collected. In CPS, and in some cases, SIPP data, these couples include those where neither partner is the householder. (*Source:* United States Census Bureau (2016). *Families and Living Arrangements.* Washington, DC. Retrieved from https://www.census.gov/hhes/families/about/ on December 1, 2016.)

TRADITIONAL FAMILY AND RACE

A family is traditionally defined as a basic social unit consisting of one or more parent or guardian adult(s) and their children, which is considered a collective group whether the unit dwells together or not. Most families exist by relationships established through *consanguinity*, in which all members have a kinship from being descendants of the same ancestors. However, others exist because of close affiliations or simply because of established cohabitation. This latter description is officially used to define households, but people in these households often consider themselves as part of a family.

The traditional or "nuclear" American family consists of a mother and a father who are married and living in the same house with their children (two to three children on average). With increasing numbers of single-parent households, children being raised by older siblings, adoptions, and children being raised by same-sex couples, the concept of "family" in the 21st century has expanded from its traditional meaning. For example, Census data has revealed 55.2% of households in 1990 were headed by both a husband and wife. By 2010, this rate had reduced to 48.4%. Conversely, the families with female householders increased from 11.6% to 13.1%, and those with single-male householders from 3.4% to 5% (Lofquist et al. 2012).

The concept of the traditional family does not adequately reflect the various forms for families and households discussed previously. It particularly does not reflect the various family arrangements of minorities. Studies show approximately 40% of adult blacks, compared to fewer than 20% of whites, share households with relatives other than partners or young children. This may include grandparents, uncles, aunts, and cousins living as a family unit. Even when not actually living with extended family members, African Americans are likely to live close to relatives. Over 50% of blacks, compared to roughly 33% of whites, live within two miles of relatives (Gerstel 2011). Therefore, blacks are more likely to rely on relatives for practical assistance.

Table 6.1 shows the living situations for American children under 18 years of age, by race and Hispanic origin, from 2008 through 2015. For all races, approximately 70% of children lived in families with two parents. Of the 30.5% that lived in single-parent homes, the majority lived in homes headed by the mother. For whites, approximately 70% lived in two-parent homes. However, the rates were much lower for blacks. For example, in 2015, only 40% lived in two-parent family homes, and 34% lived in two-parent family homes where the parents were not married. The majority of black children lived in single-parent homes (approximately 59%); 91% of these single-parent families were headed by the mother. In comparison, 67% of Hispanic children lived in two-parent homes.

MARRIAGE

Table 6.2 shows the marital status of Americans 15 years and older between the years 2008 and 2015. The majority of Americans were married in 2015; 53.7% of men and 51.2% of women. However, the number of married adults slightly decreased over that period, falling from 55.6% of men and 52.8% of women in 2008. By race, 56.1% of white men (not in combination with any other race) and 54% of women were married in 2015. However, the percentages are much smaller for blacks. In 2015, only 37.8% of black men and 32% of black women were married. The majority (49.9% of black men and 47.4% of black women) had never been married, rather than being divorced or widowed. The percentage of married blacks was also much lower than the percentage of married Hispanics. In 2015, 48.1% of Hispanic males and 36.1% of Hispanic females were married.

Reid, Golub, and Vazan (2014, p. 471) outlined the concern with the black cohabitation rate versus marriage by pointing out:

> Scholars and policy makers are concerned with the low marriage rate corresponding high single mothering rate in the low-income Black population. Marriage rates decline with income, and low-income blacks have the lowest rates; 42% of Black adults are married, and 62% of Black families are headed by a single parent. Though marriage rates are low in this population, cohabitation and increasing serial cohabitation are common. The Black population has higher rates of serial cohabitation than any other racial or ethnic group. Serial cohabitation is commonly viewed as an adaptation to economic hardship, especially for single mothers, who may cycle between partners in response to economic circumstances. Dissolution rates among low-income cohabiting couples are exceptionally high, which sets the stage for the formation of new relationships, including new cohabiting relationships.

Table 6.1 All Parent/Child Situations by Type, Race, and Hispanic Origin of the Householder or Reference Person, 1970–Present

Year	Total Families with Children under 18[1] Total	Two-Parent Families						One-Parent Families					
		Total	% Total Families	Married	% Total Families	Not Married	% Total Families	Total	% Total Families	Mother Only	% Total Families	Father Only	% Total Families
All races													
2015[2]	38,642	26,862	69.5	24,857	64.3	2,005	5.2	11,780	30.5	9,891	25.6	1,889	4.9
2014[2,3]	38,586	26,712	69.2	24,775	64.2	1,937	5.0	11,874	30.8	9,929	25.7	1,945	5.0
2013[2]	38,576	26,569	68.9	24,677	64.0	1,892	4.9	12,007	31.1	10,007	25.9	2,000	5.2
2012[2]	38,582	26,304	68.2	24,445	63.4	1,859	4.8	12,278	31.8	10,322	26.8	1,956	5.1
2011[2,4]	38,690	26,823	69.3	24,936	64.5	1,887	4.9	11,867	30.7	10,144	26.2	1,723	4.5
2011[2]	38,350	26,590	69.3	24,739	64.5	1,851	4.8	11,760	30.7	10,025	26.1	1,735	4.5
2010[2]	38,768	27,082	69.9	25,317	65.3	1,765	4.6	11,686	30.1	9,924	25.6	1,762	4.5
2009[2]	38,943	27,321	70.2	25,799	66.2	1,522	3.9	11,622	29.8	9,880	25.4	1,742	4.5
2008[2]	38,938	27,344	70.2	25,778	66.2	1,566	4.0	11,594	29.8	9,753	25.0	1,841	4.7
White													
2015[2,5]	29,303	21,664	73.9	20,188	68.9	1,476	5.0	7,639	26.1	6,177	21.1	1,462	5.0
2015[2,6]	29,919	22,058	73.7	20,510	68.6	1,548	5.2	7,861	26.3	6,362	21.3	1,499	5.0
2014[2,3,5]	29,370	21,591	73.5	20,162	68.6	1,429	4.9	7,779	26.5	6,298	21.4	1,481	5.0
2014[2,3,6]	30,054	22,036	73.3	20,515	68.3	1,521	5.1	8,018	26.7	6,490	21.6	1,528	5.1
2013[2,5]	29,359	21,625	73.7	20,200	68.8	1,425	4.9	7,734	26.3	6,230	21.2	1,504	5.1
2013[2,6]	29,964	21,988	73.4	20,501	68.4	1,487	5.0%	7,976	26.6	6,427	21.4	1,550	5.2
2012[2,5]	29,492	21,437	72.7	20,035	67.9	1,402	4.8	8,055	27.3	6,566	22.3	1,489	5.0
2012[2,6]	30,122	21,815	72.4	20,372	67.6	1,443	4.8	8,307	27.6	6,789	22.5	1,518	5.0
2011[2,4,5]	29,759	22,004	73.9	20,610	69.3	1,394	4.7	7,755	26.1	6,446	21.7	1,309	4.4
2011[2,5]	29,921	22,126	73.9	20,728	69.3	1,398	4.7	7,795	26.1	6,460	21.6	1,335	4.5
2011[2,4,6]	30,424	22,416	73.7	20,959	68.9	1,457	4.8	8,008	26.3	6,648	21.9	1,360	4.5
2011[2,6]	30,474	22,475	73.8	21,026	69.0	1,449	4.8	7,999	26.2	6,622	21.7	1,377	4.5
2010[2,5]	30,186	22,457	74.4	21,106	69.9	1,351	4.5	7,729	25.6	6,396	21.2	1,333	4.4

(Continued)

Table 6.1 (Continued)

Year	Total Families with Children under 18[1]	Two-Parent Families						Total	% Total Families	One-Parent Families			
		Total	% Total Families	Married	% Total Families	Not Married	% Total Families			Mother Only	% Total Families	Father Only	% Total Families
All races													
2010[2,6]	30,659	22,746	74.2	21,375	69.7	1,371	4.5	7,913	25.8	6,545	21.3	1,368	4.5
2009[2,5]	30,292	22,735	75.1	21,574	71.2	1,161	3.8	7,557	24.9	6,232	20.6	1,325	4.4
2009[2,6]	30,802	23,060	74.9	21,877	71.0	1,183	3.8	7,742	25.1	6,382	20.7	1,360	4.4
2008[2,5]	30,451	22,857	75.1	21,625	71.0	1,232	4.0	7,594	24.9	6,138	20.2	1,456	4.8
2008[2,6]	30,950	23,183	74.9	21,915	70.8	1,268	4.1	7,767	25.1	6,286	20.3	1,481	4.8
Black													
2015[2,5]	5,471	2,209	40.4	1,894	34.6	315	5.8	3,262	59.6	2,971	54.3	291	5.3
2015[2,6]	5,798	2,395	41.3	2,049	35.3	346	6.0	3,403	58.7	3,096	53.4	308	5.3
2014[2,3,5]	5,609	2,300	41.0	1,992	35.5%	308	5.5	3,309	59.0	2,967	52.9	341	6.1
2014[2,3,6]	5,973	2,518	42.2	2,151	36.0	367	6.1	3,455	57.8	3,102	51.9	353	5.9
2013[2,5]	5,664	2,316	40.9	2,024	35.7	292	5.2	3,348	59.1	2,998	52.9	350	6.2
2013[2,6]	6,001	2,485	41.4	2,151	35.8	334	5.6	3,516	58.6	3,154	52.6	362	6.0
2012[2,5]	5,621	2,262	40.2	1,961	34.9	301	5.4	3,359	59.8	3,035	54.0	324	5.8
2012[2,6]	5,887	2,398	40.7	2,078	35.3	320	5.4	3,489	59.3	3,150	53.5	339	5.8
2011[2,4,5]	5,488	2,208	40.2	1,891	34.5	317	5.8	3,280	59.8	3,011	54.9	269	4.%
2011[2,5]	5,424	2,159	39.8	1,849	34.1	310	5.7	3,265	60.2	2,991	55.1	274	5.1
2011[2,4,6]	5,793	2,378	41.0	2,027	35.0	351	6.1	3,415	59.0	3,113	53.7	302	5.2
2011[2,6]	5,673	2,298	40.5	1,959	34.5	339	6.0	3,375	59.5	3,074	54.2	301	5.3
2010[2,5]	5,555	2,275	41.0	1,964	35.4	311	5.6	3,280	59.0	2,977	53.6	303	5.5
2010[2,6]	5,768	2,387	41.4	2,065	35.8	322	5.6	3,381	58.6	3,062	53.1	319	5.5
2009[2,5]	5,683	2,296	40.4	2,043	35.9	253	4.5	3,387	59.6	3,093	54.4	294	5.2
2009[2,6]	5,862	2,395	40.9	2,135	36.4	260	4.4	3,467	59.1	3,162	53.9	305	5.2
2008[2,5]	5,603	2,256	40.3	2,032	36.3	224	4.0	3,347	59.7	3,080	55.0	267	4.8
2008[2,6]	5,772	2,353	40.8	2,115	36.6	238	4.1	3,419	59.2	3,145	54.5	275	4.8

Hispanic origin[7]

Year													
2015[2]	8,095	5,407	66.8	4,783	59.1	624	7.7	2,688	33.2	2,338	28.9	350	4.3
2014[2,3]	7,996	5,230	65.4	4,596	57.5	634	7.9	2,766	34.6	2,429	30.4	337	4.2
2013[2]	7,999	5,246	65.6	4,658	58.2	588	7.4	2,753	34.4	2,409	30.1	344	4.3
2012[2]	7,990	5,264	65.9	4,655	58.3	609	7.6	2,726	34.1	2,381	29.8	345	4.3
2011[2,4]	7,939	5,289	66.6	4,655	58.6	634	8.0	2,650	33.4	2,363	29.8	287	3.6
2011[2]	7,437	4,977	66.9	4,393	59.1	584	7.9	2,460	33.1	2,177	29.3	283	3.8
2010[2]	7,355	4,856	66.0	4,348	59.1	508	6.9	2,499	34.0	2,186	29.7	313	4.3
2009[2]	7,337	5,013	68.3	4,572	62.3	441	6.0	2,324	31.7	2,041	27.8	283	3.9
2008[2]	7,213	5,072	70.3	4,626	64.1	446	6.2	2,141	29.7	1,903	26.4	238	3.3

Note: Numbers in thousands. Family groups with children[8] include all parent/child situations (two-parent and one-parent): those that maintain their own household (family households with children); those that live in the home of a relative (related subfamilies); and those that live in the home of a nonrelative (unrelated subfamilies).

[1] In 2007, the total of family groups with children under 18 does not match the total on table FG7 because of weighting.

[2] Estimates produced using PELNMOM and PELNDAD, the new parent pointer variables introduced in 2007.

[3] The 2014 CPS ASEC included redesigned questions for income and health insurance coverage. All of the approximately 98,000 addresses were selected to receive the improved set of health insurance coverage items. The improved income questions were implemented using a split panel design. Approximately 68,000 addresses were selected to receive a set of income questions similar to those used in the 2013 CPS ASEC. The remaining 30,000 addresses were selected to receive the redesigned income questions. The source of data for this table is the CPS ASEC sample of 98,000 addresses.

For more information about ASEC, including the source and accuracy statement, see the technical documentation accessible at: http://www.census.gov/cps/methodology/tech docs.html.

[4] Revised based on population from the most recent decennial census.

[5] Householder whose race was reported as only one race.

[6] Householder whose race was reported as only a single race or in combination with one or more other races. Includes unrelated subfamilies.

[7] Persons of Hispanic origin may be of any race.

[8] Family groups prior to 2007 were restricted to married couple and single-parent families and their "own" children. In 2007, unmarried two-parent families were added to the table. Unmarried two-parent family groups are opposite sex partners who have at least one joint child under 18.

Source: U.S. Census Bureau. *Current Population Survey, March and Annual Social and Economic Supplements, 2015 and Earlier*. Retrieved from http://www.census.gov/hhes/families/data/families.html on March 6, 2016.

Table 6.2 Marital Status of the Population 15 Years Old and over by Sex, Race, and Hispanic Origin, 2008–2015

Year	Total Men	Married[1]	% of Total Men	Unmarried Total	Never Married	% of Total Men	Widowed	Divorced	Total Women	Married[1]	% of Total Women	Unmarried Total	Never Married	% of Total Women	Widowed	Divorced
All Races																
2015	123,621	66,347	53.7	57,274	43,052	34.8	3,270	10,952	131,395	67,217	51.2	64,179	37,974	28.9	11,331	14,874
2014[2]	122,353	65,853	53.8	56,499	42,711	34.9	3,059	10,729	129,871	66,732	51.4	63,139	37,311	28.7	11,214	14,614
2013	121,067	65,369	54.0	55,698	41,620	34.4	3,124	10,954	128,826	66,287	51.5	62,538	36,879	28.6	11,225	14,434
2012	119,877	65,281	54.5	54,595	41,035	34.2	2,864	10,696	127,695	66,049	51.7	61,646	36,238	28.4	11,193	14,215
2011	118,670	64,995	54.8	53,675	40,128	33.8	2,969	10,578	126,605	65,772	52.0	60,834	35,456	28.0	11,454	13,924
2011	118,828	64,381	54.2	54,446	40,847	34.4	2,929	10,670	125,030	65,000	52.0	60,031	34,963	28.0	11,306	13,762
2010	117,686	64,525	54.8	53,161	40,206	34.2	2,974	9,981	124,361	65,197	52.4	59,165	34,037	27.4	11,368	13,760
2009	116,666	64,842	55.6	51,823	39,052	33.5	2,813	9,958	123,366	65,604	53.2	57,762	33,013	26.8	11,441	13,308
2008	115,599	64,217	55.6	51,383	38,685	33.5	2,916	9,782	122,394	64,638	52.8	57,756	32,794	26.8	11,398	13,564
White																
2015[3]	98,077	55,025	56.1	43,053	31,369	32.0	2,673	9,011	102,056	55,075	54.0	46,981	25,916	25.4	9,256	11,809
2015[4]	99,944	55,658	55.7	44,286	32,422	32.4	2,706	9,158	104,112	55,880	53.7	48,233	26,873	25.8	9,341	12,019
2014[2,3]	97,605	54,682	56.0	42,923	31,452	32.2	2,522	8,949	101,303	54,748	54.0	46,555	25,838	25.5	9,056	11,661
2014[2,4]	99,581	55,356	55.6	44,226	32,580	32.7	2,557	9,089	103,341	55,492	53.7	47,848	26,828	26.0	9,156	11,864
2013[3]	96,957	54,454	56.2	42,503	30,780	31.7	2,592	9,131	100,802	54,678	54.2	46,123	25,453	25.3	9,172	11,498
2013[4]	98,819	55,096	55.8	43,721	31,825	32.2	2,621	9,275	102,773	55,422	53.9	47,351	26,365	25.7	9,269	11,717
2012[3]	96,372	54,612	56.7	41,760	30,486	31.6	2,437	8,837	100,293	54,680	54.5	45,613	25,106	25.0	9,104	11,403
2012[4]	98,158	55,266	56.3	42,892	31,450	32.0	2,464	8,978	102,274	55,418	54.2	46,856	25,991	25.4	9,233	11,632
2011[3]	95,576	54,566	57.1	41,008	29,807	31.2	2,464	8,737	99,659	54,599	54.8	45,060	24,603	24.7	9,398	11,059
2011[4]	97,348	55,266	56.8	42,082	30,690	31.5	2,509	8,883	101,597	55,354	54.5	46,243	25,478	25.1	9,493	11,272
2011[3]	96,895	54,516	56.3	42,380	31,028	32.0	2,444	8,908	99,625	54,546	54.8	45,078	24,764	24.9	9,288	11,026
2011[4]	98,441	55,149	56.0	43,293	31,768	32.3	2,486	9,039	101,240	55,184	54.5	46,056	25,467	25.2	9,378	11,211

2010[3]	96,159	54,742	56.9	41,417	30,592	31.8	2,483	8,342	99,309	54,823	55.2	44,486	24,126	24.3	9,276	11,084
2010[4]	97,650	55,370	56.7	42,280	31,291	32.0	2,512	8,477	100,831	55,447	55.0	45,384	24,746	24.5	9,358	11,280
2009[3]	95,494	55,023	57.6	40,472	29,801	31.2	2,359	8,312	98,794	55,110	55.8	43,684	23,494	23.8	9,436	10,754
2009[4]	96,988	55,637	57.4	41,352	30,509	31.5	2,383	8,460	100,265	55,714	55.6	44,552	24,082	24.0	9,519	10,951
2008[3]	94,707	54,546	57.6	40,160	29,517	31.2	2,450	8,193	98,134	54,392	55.4	43,741	23,399	23.8	9,419	10,923
2008[4]	96,157	55,142	57.3	41,015	30,214	31.4	2,474	8,327	99,580	54,995	55.2	44,585	23,991	24.1	9,495	11,099
Black																
2015[3]	14,627	5,536	37.8	9,090	7,297	49.9	422	1,371	17,381	5,560	32.0	11,822	8,234	47.4	1,390	2,198
2015[4]	15,470	5,795	37.5	9,675	7,833	50.6	425	1,417	18,394	5,873	31.9	12,521	8,830	48.0	1,424	2,267
2014[2,3]	14,354	5,660	39.4	8,693	7,014	48.9	374	1,305	17,090	5,681	33.2	11,409	7,863	46.0	1,463	2,083
2014[2,4]	15,177	5,938	39.1	9,239	7,513	49.5	382	1,344	18,074	5,941	32.9	12,133	8,452	46.8	1,512	2,169
2013[3]	14,114	5,637	39.9	8,478	6,776	48.0	370	1,332	16,879	5,603	33.2	11,277	7,808	46.3	1,403	2,066
2013[4]	14,892	5,892	39.6	9,000	7,265	48.8	375	1,360	17,815	5,865	32.9	11,951	8,364	46.9	1,439	2,148
2012[3]	13,829	5,477	39.6	8,353	6,686	48.3	309	1,358	16,655	5,522	33.2	11,133	7,668	46.0	1,426	2,039
2012[4]	14,486	5,669	39.1	8,816	7,106	49.1	310	1,400	17,419	5,708	32.8	11,711	8,140	46.7	1,455	2,116
2011[3]	13,671	5,373	39.	8,300	6,626	48.5	335	1,339	16,474	5,466	33.2	11,008	7,536	45.7	1,392	2,080
2011[4]	14,340	5,588	39.0	8,753	7,010	48.9	347	1,396	17,273	5,718	33.1	11,554	7,975	46.2	1,417	2,162
2011[3]	13,529	5,252	38.8	8,276	6,651	49.2	324	1,301	16,223	5,356	33.0	10,868	7,454	45.9	1,381	2,033
2011[4]	14,096	5,440	38.6	8,656	6,970	49.4	334	1,352	16,875	5,560	32.9	11,314	7,803	46.2	1,406	2,105
2010[3]	13,304	5,241	39.4	8,063	6,490	48.8	357	1,216	16,046	5,352	33.4	10,694	7,245	45.2	1,465	1,984
2010[4]	13,820	5,422	39.2	8,397	6,761	48.9	365	1,271	16,630	5,524	33.2	11,106	7,564	45.5	1,488	2,054
2009[3]	13,095	5,299	40.5	7,795	6,262	47.8	330	1,203	15,811	5,506	34.8	10,306	7,040	44.5	1,400	1,866
2009[4]	13,604	5,454	40.1	8,151	6,581	48.4	337	1,233	16,362	5,671	34.7	10,692	7,330	44.8	1,430	1,932
2008[3]	12,878	5,234	40.6	7,643	6,121	47.5	332	1,190	15,615	5,376	34.4	10,240	6,872	44.0	1,378	1,990
2008[4]	13,360	5,394	40.4	7,966	6,412	48.0	335	1,219	16,094	5,520	34.3	10,574	7,136	44.3	1,404	2,034
Asian[5]																
2015[3]	6,928	4,207	60.7	2,721	2,409	34.8	102	210	7,719	4,752	61.6	2,967	2,051	26.6	474	442
2015[4]	7,419	4,351	58.6	3,067	2,716	36.6	106	245	8,210	4,936	60.1	3,274	2,330	28.4	483	461
2014[2,3]	6,564	3,997	60.9	2,567	2,290	34.9	88	189	7,386	4,629	62.7	2,757	1,862	25.2	453	442

(Continued)

Table 6.2 (Continued)

	Men								Women							
			% of Total Men	Unmarried		% of Total Men					% of Total Women	Unmarried		% of Total Women		
Year	Total Men	Married[1]		Total	Never Married		Widowed	Divorced	Total Women	Married[1]		Total	Never Married		Widowed	Divorced
Asian[5]																
2014[2,4]	7,050	4,131	58.6	2,919	2,621	37.2	89	209	7,904	4,818	61.0	3,086	2,149	27.2	467	470
2013[3]	6,273	3,797	60.5	2,476	2,204	35.1	87	185	7,147	4,429	62.0	2,719	1,887	26.4	426	406
2013[4]	6,720	3,933	58.5	2,787	2,500	37.2	87	200	7,638	4,614	60.4	3,023	2,160	28.3	433	430
2012[3]	6,102	3,751	61.5	2,351	2,105	34.5	63	183	6,924	4,322	62.4	2,601	1,829	26.4	425	347
2012[4]	6,573	3,883	59.1	2,690	2,412	36.7	64	214	7,389	4,486	60.7	2,902	2,077	28.1	430	395
2011[3]	5,985	3,628	60.6	2,357	2,082	34.8	86	189	6,758	4,123	61.0	2,634	1,807	26.7	464	363
2011[4]	6,399	3,754	58.7	2,645	2,337	36.5	92	216	7,219	4,272	59.2	2,948	2,069	28.7	480	399
2011[3]	5,423	3,343	61.6	2,080	1,812	33.4	84	184	6,076	3,764	61.9	2,312	1,527	25.1	450	335
2011[4]	5,786	3,458	59.8	2,328	2,031	35.1	89	208	6,460	3,889	60.2	2,571	1,742	27.0	464	365
2010[3]	5,285	3,310	62.6	1,975	1,736	32.8	67	172	5,916	3,720	62.9	2,196	1,433	24.2	457	306
2010[4]	5,612	3,419	60.9	2,193	1,931	34.4	70	192	6,260	3,848	61.5	2,413	1,622	25.9	463	328
2009[3]	5,077	3,214	63.3	1,863	1,619	31.9	77	167	5,695	3,667	64.4	2,028	1,325	23.3	413	290
2009[4]	5,400	3,326	61.6	2,074	1,812	33.6	81	181	6,010	3,789	63.0	2,221	1,491	24.8	422	308
2008[3]	5,106	3,137	61.4	1,968	1,751	34.3	79	138	5,670	3,545	62.5	2,125	1,400	24.7	419	306
2008[4]	5,408	3,249	60.1	2,159	1,922	35.5	83	154	6,022	3,677	61.1	2,345	1,596	26.5	424	325
Hispanic																
2015	20,190	9,711	48.1	10,479	8,829	43.7	310	1,340	20,170	10,097	50.1	10,072	7,284	36.1	1,000	1,788
2014[2]	19,682	9,243	47.0	10,439	8,880	45.1	268	1,291	19,473	9,666	49.6	9,808	6,995	35.9	976	1,837
2013	19,178	9,254	48.3	9,925	8,447	44.0	266	1,212	19,029	9,590	50.4	9,439	6,730	35.4	962	1,747
2012	18,858	9,092	48.2	9,766	8,366	44.4	253	1,147	18,627	9,349	50.2	9,278	6,597	35.4	972	1,709
2011	18,272	8,874	48.6	9,398	8,024	43.9	287	1,087	18,145	9,138	50.4	9,008	6,454	35.6	962	1,592

2011	18,097	8,587	47.4	9,510	44.9	302	1,090	16,954	8,608	50.8	8,346	5,909	34.9	942	1,495
2010	17,673	8,601	48.7	9,072	43.4	297	1,100	16,599	8,576	51.7	8,023	5,601	33.7	898	1,524
2009	17,210	8,720	50.7	8,490	41.8	203	1,087	16,229	8,726	53.8	7,503	5,235	32.3	861	1,407
2008	16,832	8,704	51.7	8,128	41.3	228	945	15,845	8,555	54.0	7,290	5,066	32.0	839	1,385

Note: Numbers in thousands.

[1] Includes married spouse present, married spouse absent, and separated.

[2] The 2014 CPS ASEC included redesigned questions for income and health insurance coverage. All of the approximately 98,000 addresses were selected to receive the improved set of health insurance coverage items. The improved income questions were implemented using a split panel design. Approximately 68,000 addresses were selected to receive a set of income questions similar to those used in the 2013 CPS ASEC. The remaining 30,000 addresses were selected to receive the redesigned income questions. The source of data for this table is the CPS ASEC sample of 98,000 addresses.

[3] Householder whose race was reported as only one race.

[4] Householder whose race was reported as only a single race or in combination with one or more other races.

[5] Before 2003, Asian includes Asians and Pacific Islanders. In 2003 and later Asian includes only Asian alone.

Source: U.S. Census Bureau, Current Population Survey, March and Annual Social and Economic Supplements, 2015 and earlier. For more information about ASEC, including the source and accuracy statement, see the technical documentation accessible at: http://www.census.gov/cps/methodology/techdocs.html.

The highest divorce rates ever recorded were in the 1970s and early 1980s. Since then, the divorce rate has decreased, but has remained high. Divorce has become a part of American life. Those who marry between ages 20 and 24 have the highest divorce rates and most couples are in their mid-30s when they divorce. Twenty-five percent of adults in the United States have had at least one divorce during their lifetime. Statistic show that 41% of first marriages in the United States end in divorce. Remarrying does not improve a couple's chances of a successful marriage; 60% of second marriages and 73% of third marriages end in divorce (Divorce Statistics 2016). Even with these high rates, 81% of men and 86% of women marry by the age of 40.

Table 6.3 shows divorce rates by race and age groups for the years 1996 through 2009. As shown, divorce rates have decreased across ages, except for the age group of 50 and older. This group also has the highest divorce rates. The rates for each race generally follow the same trend. By race, the highest divorce rates have been for blacks. For example, in 2009, blacks had the highest divorce rates for every age group except those between 25 and 29. Non-Hispanic whites had the second highest rates, followed by Hispanics, and then Asians.

The high rate of divorce for blacks is especially troublesome for women. African American woman have the highest chance (47%) of their first marriage ending within 10 years. For other groups, divorce is mitigated by such conditions as earning higher incomes and having higher levels of education. This does not apply to black women. For example, a study in the journal *Family Relations* found that overall divorce rates have "(leveled) off since the 1980s after more than a century-long rise but the rate has increasingly diverged by race and socioeconomic class, when educational attainment is factored in. While married couples who have attained higher levels of education are less likely to divorce than less-educated couples, African-American women don't enjoy the same degree of protection that education confers on marriage" (Grohol 2013).

According to Jeounghee Kim, assistant professor at Rutgers University, the divorce rate for whites has remained steady since 1980 and this protective effect of education on marriage increased consistently among the recent generations. However, for African American women having college educations it did not translate into the higher earnings that would help protect marriage. She analyzed white and African American women in five-year marriage cohorts starting from 1975–1979 and ending in 1995–1999, taking into account demographic characteristics including age, motherhood status, and postsecondary education (associate degree at minimum) when married, and participants' geographic region. She also factored in marital dissolution (within nine years of first marriage) rather than by legal divorce, which many African American women eschew in favor of a permanent separation.

College degree attainment made it much more likely for black women to get married, but education was insufficient in addressing the high levels of economic inequality that even well-educated African Americans experience. Many black women are the first in their families to have attained a postsecondary education

Table 6.3 Percentage Ever Divorced for Ever-Married Women by Age, Race, and Hispanic Origin, for Selected Years, 1996–2009

Year	25–29 Years	30–34 Years	35–39 Years	40–49 Years	50–59 Years	60–69 Years	70 and over
Total							
1996	18.8	25.6	32.4	40.5	36.4	27.1	17.5
2001	18.9	23.7	33.3	39.6	41.5	29.6	18.3
2004	11.9	22.0	30.6	38.5	44.1	33.7	18.7
2009	13.8	21.3	27.4	35.6	41.1	36.7	22.3
White, non-Hispanic							
1996	20.5	27.4	33.2	41.6	36.6	26.8	17.0
2001	22.1	26.4	34.7	42.3	42.5	29.9	17.9
2004	13.9	24.9	32.1	41.0	45.6	34.7	18.0
2009	15.2	23.5	30.3	38.6	42.4	38.1	21.7
Black							
1996	14.7	28.0	40.7	44.5	42.0	35.6	21.9
2001	20.6	24.5	37.3	42.2	44.7	33.8	25.4
2004	11.0	20.1	37.1	39.0	47.8	37.2	26.7
2009	14.6	23.9	32.7	35.0	48.2	40.3	27.8
Asian							
1996	9.3	12.0	14.3	22.8	23.2	4.9	8.5
2001	4.1	10.7	18.1	17.5	22.7	9.9	5.0
2004	1.9	6.1	11.4	20.1	19.9	9.6	9.1
2009	1.3	7.8	13.2	20.6	18.5	16.0	11.3
Hispanic							
1996	15.5	17.4	24.0	33.2	31.7	25.6	20.3
2001	12.5	15.5	26.5	28.5	34.0	26.5	21.5
2004	8.8	16.3	24.7	24.4	33.1	23.9	19.5
2009	10.5	16.3	18.1	23.7	30.2	25.0	24.2

Source: Kreider, Rose M. and Ellis, Renee (2011). *Number, Timing, and Divorce of Marriages and Divorces: 2009 (Household Economic Studies).* Washington, DC: U.S. Census Bureau.

and did not benefit from intergenerational wealth possessed by some white families. There was also a gap in educational attainment in the black community, with
nearly twice as many African American women college graduates as there were
men. Thus, black women had greater difficulty selecting a spouse that was educa-
tionally equal and less like to marry outside of their race. All of this contributed to
higher divorce rates (Black Voices 2013).

Gibson-Davis (2011) also outlined the concern by stating:

> Data emerging from several qualitative and quantitative studies has
> suggested, though, that temporal changes in unwed mothers' marital
> behavior are likely to be profound. Recent analyses of family-formation
> behaviors have indicated that marriage and childbearing have become
> increasingly disconnected, both temporally and theoretically. In part
> because of the emergence of norms that sanction sexual intimacy and
> childbearing out-side of marriage, the once-strong connection between
> marriage and fertility has weakened considerably. Couples who desire to
> have children or who face an unplanned pregnancy they do not wish to
> abort no longer face a strong normative deadline for legally marrying.
> Attitudes affirming the decoupling of marriage from childbearing have
> been found in several qualitative studies, which reported that low-income
> and working-class individuals view marriage and fertility as distinct pro-
> cesses, with different motivations and expectations. (p. 264)

Table 6.4 shows the reasons why so many children are being raised in
single-parent homes. Coupled with the high numbers of blacks who aren't mar-
ried, the birth rates for black mothers is higher than those of almost all other races.
For example, in 2014, birth rates for black mothers was 14.5 per 1,000 people,
compared to 12.5 for all races combined, 12 for whites, and 9.9 for American
Indians or Alaska Natives. The only race with a higher rate was Asian or Pacific
Islanders at 14.6. These higher rates for blacks over whites date back to the 1980s.
As shown in the table, in the 1980s and 1990s there were over 20 per 1,000.

Data about black families is also changing because of an increase in interracial
marriages. According to a report from the Pew Research Center (2013), the percentage of all marriages between multiracial couples increased from 3.2% in 1980
to 8.4% in 2013. The number of new interracial marriages increased from 6.7%
in 1980 to 15.1%. The report shows that in 2013, of the 3.6 million adults who
were married, "58% of American Indians, 28% of Asians, 19% of blacks and 7%
of whites (had) a spouse whose race was different from their own." For whites,
both white men and white women were likely to marry someone of a different
race. However, for blacks, men (25%) were more likely to marry someone of a
different race than black women (12%). The opposite is true for Asians, where
37% of women married outside their race, compared to 16% of men, and American Indians, where 61% of women married outside their race, compared to the
54% of men (Wang 2015).

Table 6.4 Births and Birth Rates, by Race, United States, 2008–2014

| | Race of Mother | | | | | Race of Mother | | | | |
| | Registered Births | | | | | Birth Rate | | | | |
Year	All Races	White	Black	American Indian or Alaska Native	Asian or Pacific Islander	All Races	White	Black	American Indian or Alaska Native	Asian or Pacific Islander
2014	3,988,076	3,019,863	640,562	44,928	282,723	12.5	12.0	14.5	9.9	14.6
2013	3,932,181	2,985,757	634,760	45,991	265,673	12.4	12.0	14.5	10.3	14.3
2012	3,952,841	2,999,820	634,126	46,093	272,802	12.6	12.1	14.7	10.5	15.1
2011	3,953,590	3,020,355	632,901	46,419	253,915	12.7	12.2	14.8	10.7	14.5
2010	3,999,386	3,069,315	636,425	47,760	246,886	13.0	12.5	15.1	11.0	14.5
2009	4,130,665	3,173,293	657,618	48,665	251,089	13.5	13.0	15.8	11.8	15.1
2008	4,247,694	3,274,163	670,809	49,537	253,185	14.0	13.5	16.3	12.4	15.7
2000	4,058,814	3,194,005	622,598	41,668	200,543	14.4	13.9	17.0	14.0	17.1
1990	4,158,212	3,290,273	684,336	39,051	141,635	16.7	15.8	22.4	18.9	19.0
1980	3,612,258	2,936,351	568,080	29,389	74,355	15.9	15.1	21.3	20.7	19.9

Note: Birth rates are births per 1,000 population in specified group. Populations based on counts enumerated as of April 1 for census years and estimated as of July 1 for all other years. Excludes births to nonresidents of the United States.

Source: Hamilton, Brady E., Joyce A. Martin, Michelle J. K. Osterman, Sally C. Curtin, and T. J. Mathews (2015). *Births: Final Data for 2014 (National Vital Statistics Report).* Volume 64, Number 12, Hyattsville, MD: National Center for Health Statistics. Retrieved from http://www.cdc.gov/nchs/data/nvsr/nvsr64/nvsr64_12.pdf on February 25, 2016.

The number of interracial marriages increased after the Supreme Court ruled in *Loving v. Virginia*, 388 U.S. 1 (1967) that laws prohibiting interracial marriage were unconstitutional. With this ruling, antimiscegenation laws that existed in 16 states at the time were struck down. Laws that passed as a result of the Civil Rights Movement also ushered in a sociocultural change that increased interracial relations. Beyond the legal changes, American approval of interracial marriages has increased. For example, a Gallup poll found that Americans' approval of marriages between blacks and whites increased from 4% in 1959 to 87% in 2013. In 1969, only 17% of whites approved of these marriages, but this increased to 84% in 2013, compared to 56% and 96% of blacks, respectively. The highest approval ratings were among those 18–29 years old (96%), and the lowest approval ratings were attributed to those 65 years and older (70%). It is interesting that the lowest approval ratings, while still very high, were in the Southern states (83%), and the highest were in the western states (93%) (Newport 2013).

Among whites, studies have shown that demographic and socioeconomic differences indicate the likelihood of who will be most accepting of interracial marriages. For example, Perry (2013) reports that more progressive whites support interracial marriage. This includes those that are "younger, female, politically liberal, less religious, live out of the American South, live in urban areas, have racially diverse backgrounds, racially tolerant families, higher incomes, and tend to be more educated and come from more educated families" (p. 426).

The true number of interracial relationships is not known because more young adults are seeking cohabitation rather than marriage. This was also found by Qian and Litcher (2011), especially for interracial couples as they may find family opposition to being married. They found this particularly the case for blacks, who face the greatest stigmatization from relatives and their communities.

Families are also being redefined by the drastic increase in same-sex couples. Census data shows the number of same-sex partners increased from 358,390 in 2000 to 646,464 in 2010. Although these households comprised less than 1% of all households in both 2000 and 2010, the number in 2010 represents an 80% increase (Lofquist et al. 2012). Table 6.5 shows the raw numbers of same-sex unmarried couples in 2010 by race and ethnicity, based on the householder and their partner. Note that while approximately 60% of whites were coupled with other whites, the majority of blacks (approximately 63%) were coupled with partners from different races.

Even with increases in same-sex couples, many members of the black community still oppose gay and lesbian partnerships. While African American and Latino media outlets appear supportive of gay and lesbian issues in their coverage, many African Americans feel unfavorably about homosexuality, and believe individuals can choose to not be homosexuals. This view is contrary to the view of the majority of the United States, shown in a new report by The Opportunity Agenda (2012). According to a report called the *Public Opinion and Discourse on the Intersection of Lesbian, Gay, Bi-sexual, and Transgender (LGBT) Issues and Race*, there is tension in the African American and Latino communities between

Table 6.5 Hispanic Origin and Race of Same-Sex Unmarried-Partner Households for the United States: 2010 Summary File Counts

Hispanic Origin and Race of Householder	Total	Hispanic or Latino							Not Hispanic or Latino						
		White Alone	Black or African American Alone	American Indian/ Alaska Native Alone	Asian Alone	Native Hawaiian/ Other Pacific Islander Alone	Some Other Race Alone	Two or More Races	White alone	Black Or African American Alone	American Indian/ Alaska Native alone	Asian alone	Native Hawaiian/ Other Pacific Islander Alone	Some Other Race Alone	Two or More Races
Total	901,997	67,910	3,277	2,001	723	224	44,065	7,115	638,030	84,200	7,070	29,001	1,792	1,749	14,840
Hispanic or Latino															
White alone	60,562	**37,480**	406	156	86	24	1,179	554	18,268	913	221	574	63	45	593
Black alone[1]	2,898	326	**1,060**	16	9	5	116	59	426	753	10	25	10	9	74
AIAN alone[1]	1,798	179	21	**687**	7	3	165	64	483	49	73	15	7	2	43
Asian alone	540	48	6	9	**111**	3	35	19	197	21	1	54	2	0	34
NHPI alone[1]	191	12	8	2	0	**67**	8	6	46	8	4	5	15	1	9
Some other race alone	38,727	1,190	113	99	34	10	**29,658**	649	5,233	817	169	312	47	95	301
Two or more races	6,930	780	83	70	30	14	906	**2,387**	1,768	313	34	120	17	11	397
Not Hispanic or Latino															
White alone	661,927	25,567	667	737	345	70	9,709	2,504	**586,278**	12,096	3,423	11,097	716	674	8,044
Black alone[1]	80,459	954	773	55	20	8	1,081	325	7,972	**67,195**	221	471	72	94	1,218
AIAN alone[1]	6,832	216	15	84	2	0	222	35	3,116	203	**2,668**	69	17	12	173
Asian alone	23,490	435	23	22	49	3	355	95	6,111	292	47	**15,520**	67	29	442
NHPI alone[1]	1,404	40	4	3	3	6	51	10	436	46	15	73	**652**	2	63
Some other race alone	1,442	46	3	2	0	0	99	13	396	82	8	30	4	**728**	31
Two or more races	14,797	637	95	59	27	11	481	395	7,300	1,412	176	636	103	47	3,418

Note: Numbers in bold represent unmarried partners where both partners are of the same ethnicity (either both Hispanic origin or not of Hispanic origin) and single race alone.

[1]Black—Black or African American; AIAN—American Indian and Alaska Native; NHPI—Native Hawaiian and Other Pacific Islander.

Source: U.S. Census Bureau. *2010 Census.* Retrieved from https://www.census.gov/population/www/cen2010/briefs/cph-t-4.html on April 25, 2012.

supporters for LGBTQ equality and those who see homosexuality as a violation of moral and religious principles.

The Opportunity Agenda has studied public opinion research to get an overall view of opinions in the African American and Latino communities on issues regarding homosexuality. This group notes that views of homosexuality have been evolving over time. The report points out that while there is tension within the African American community over the morality of homosexuality, there does not appear to be this sentiment in the black media. The report noted that most of the stories pertaining to homosexuality in the black media have focused on HIV, bullying, homophobia, and discrimination, and advocates or civil rights leaders often provide commentary on the stories or events. The report also found that African American ministers tended to be overwhelmingly against homosexuality.

In general, people who go to church weekly are statistically unlikely to be proponents of same-sex marriages. This is evident by the Opportunity Agenda's findings that only 24% of weekly church attendees support marriage equality, compared with 57% of people who rarely or never attend worship services. Gay marriage is incompatible with the beliefs, sacred texts, and traditions of many religious groups. The Catholic Church, Presbyterian Church, Islam, United Methodist Church, Southern Baptist Convention, Church of Jesus Christ of Latter-day Saints, National Association of Evangelicals, and American Baptist Churches USA all oppose same-sex marriage.

Same-sex couples face obstacles in states that do not recognize same-sex marriages. The biological parent of a child born to a same-sex union has custody. Unless the spouse who is the nonbiological parent has legally adopted the child, he or she has no legal rights to custody or visitation. If the same-sex couple adopted the children jointly, the parent who is not the adoptive parent of record generally will have no rights. In regard to divorce, a same-sex married couple can relocate to the state where they got married to get a divorce. This can be problematic because all states have residency requirements. The spouse filing for divorce has to live in the state in which they're filing for divorce for a period of time (depending on individual state laws) before filing and being granted a divorce. However, this can be unrealistic when employment and other factors are involved. To combat some of these legal impediments, same-sex spouses can also create prenuptial agreements, postnuptial agreements, cohabitation agreements, and estate planning documents to deal with the possibility of divorce. These are legal contracts, and therefore these are not under the jurisdiction of a family court. They are also enforceable in those states that do not recognize same-sex marriages or same-sex divorce.

DIVORCE

Divorce is the legal termination of a marriage or marital union that formally dissolves the bonds of matrimony under law in a court of law. Divorces are different than separations, which may be legal but do not terminate or cancel legal duties and responsibilities of a couple. Data on separations, even legal separations, is very difficult to obtain because some couples live apart but haven't formally dissolved their marriage via legal actions.

Currently, there are over two million marriages in the United States each year (6.8 per 1,000 population) and over 800,000 divorces (3.6 per 1,000 population) according to the Centers for Disease Control and Prevention (2016). Data shows that African Americans have a higher rate of divorce than their white counterparts. Data on this topic is still emerging as the increased propensity for divorce among blacks is an issue that has taken place in recent decades. Analyzing marital separations and divorces (also called marital interruptions), Sweeney and Phillips (2004, p. 643) wrote, "our results suggest that the increase in rates of marital disruption since the mid-1970s has been steeper among blacks than among whites. Although the disruption rate appeared to level off for whites in the post-1980 period, it began to rise for blacks beginning in the mid-1980s."

New studies are finding conclusive results about divorce rates by race and ethnicity. For example, Raley, Sweeney, and Wondra (2015, p. 91) compiled the data in Table 6.6 from 2008 through 2012 ACS, Integrated Public Use Microdata Series. They organized this data on divorce by race, ethnicity, and nativity. Notice that American Indian and Native Alaskan women had the highest rates of divorce across all age groups. The second highest rate was blacks (both men and women), except those 20 through 24 years old, a category in which whites had the second highest rate. It is also interesting to note that Asian and Pacific Islanders had the lowest divorce rates, three times lower than the divorce rates of blacks. While U.S.-born Hispanics' rates were higher than whites', and only slightly lower than blacks', their rates were substantially higher than foreign-born Hispanics for all age groups. Another interesting point is that divorce rates declined for all races and ethnic groups after the age of 40, except for American Indians and Native Alaskans.

Table 6.6   Women's Age-Specific Rates of Divorce by Race, Ethnicity, and Nativity

Age	White (%)	Black (%)	Asian/ Pacific Islander (%)	American Indian/ Native Alaskan (%)	Hispanic, Total (%)	Hispanic, U.S. Born (%)	Hispanic, Foreign Born (%)
20–24	48.44	40.13	12.23	63.61	26.79	36.74	16.13
25–29	38.80	44.29	13.23	52.02	26.71	40.43	15.31
30–34	31.60	44.43	15.95	40.15	25.03	37.09	16.83
35–39	29.66	41.20	12.98	41.58	23.70	36.31	16.43
40–44	26.33	38.86	13.07	48.60	21.47	30.15	16.78

Note: Rates are calculated as the number of marriages per 1,000 unmarried women and number of divorces per 1,000 married women.

Source: Raley, R. Kelly, Megan M. Sweeney, and Danielle Wondra (2015). "The Growing Racial and Ethnic Divide in U.S. Marriage Patterns." *Future Of Children*, 25, 2, Fall, pp. 89–109. From *The Future of Children*, a collaboration of The Woodrow Wilson School of Public and International Affairs at Princeton University and the Brookings Institution.

The increase in divorce rates has been contributed to a number of factors. Per the Bureau of Labor Statistics (2013):

> Many changes in the last half century have affected marriage and divorce rates. The rise of the women's liberation movement, the advent of the sexual revolution, and an increase in women's labor force participation altered perceptions of gender roles within marriage during the last 50 years. Cultural norms changed in ways that decreased the aversion to being single and increased the probability of cohabitation. In addition, a decrease in the stigma attached to divorce and the appearance of no-fault divorce laws in many states contributed to an increase in divorce rates.

Table 6.7 shows extensive data on divorce rates in the United States from the Bureau of Labor Statistics as of 2013. The data is sorted by age, gender, race/ethnicity, and educational attainment. This data is based on the National Longitudinal Survey of Youth 1979 (NLSY79) which consists of men and women who were born in the years 1957–1964 and were ages 14–22 when first interviewed in 1979. These individuals were ages 45–52 in 2010–2011. The following are some notable points from the Bureau of Labor Statistics:

- Both men and women delayed first marriage, with the age of first marriage rising to ages 25.6 and 23.4 for men and women, respectively, compared with ages 24.7 and 22.6 in the 1950–1955 cohort. In addition, a larger proportion of marriages ended in divorce, approximately 44.2% of first marriages, compared with the earlier birth cohorts (32.7% and 40.8% of first marriages end in divorce among the 1940–1945 and 1950–1955 cohorts).
- Three out of ten Black non-Hispanics born during 1957–1964 did not marry by the age of 46, while the same statistic for Whites remained close to the 1-in-10 ratio seen in the earlier cohorts. That is, the proportion ever married among Blacks decreased from 77.6% for the 1950–1955 cohort to 68.3% in the NLSY79 cohort. The age of Black non-Hispanics who have ever divorced is lower than that of Whites or of Hispanics, reflecting the smaller percentage of Black non-Hispanics who marry.
- Hispanics marry at a younger age. Hispanics who divorced have first marriages that tend to last longer than other racial/ethnic groups.

The "divorce gap" between college graduates and those with less education was larger in the NLSY79 cohort than it was for the 1950–1955 birth cohort. In the NLSY79 cohort, the divorce rate for first marriages is nearly 20 percentage points lower for those who have completed their bachelor's degree compared with those who have completed high school, regardless of whether they have some college or not. The gap is even greater, approaching 30 percentage points, when comparing those with a college degree to those with less than a high school diploma.

Table 6.7 Marriage Outcomes by Age 46 by Gender, Race/Ethnicity, and Educational Attainment: Based on the National Longitudinal Survey of Youth 1979 (NLSY79)

Characteristic	Full Sample	Men	Women	Blacks Non-Hispanics	Nonblack Non-Hispanics	Hispanics	Less than High School Diploma	High School Graduate, No College	Some College or Associate's Degree	Bachelor's Degree or Higher
Percent ever married	86.8	84.3	89.5	68.3	90.4	84.6	81.3	87.0	87.1	89.0
Percent ever divorced	38.9	36.0	42.0	33.1	40.0	39.3	47.8	42.8	42.3	26.5
Among those ever married, percent ever divorced	44.8	42.7	46.9	48.4	44.2	46.5	58.8	49.1	48.5	29.8
Among those ever married										
Average age at first marriage	24.4	25.6	23.4	26.2	24.2	23.8	22.7	23.6	24.2	26.5
Percent still in first marriage	53.0	56.1	49.9	47.0	53.9	51.4	37.6	48.6	48.9	69.0
Percent of first marriages ending in divorce	44.2	42.4	46.0	47.9	43.7	45.5	58.2	48.2	47.9	29.7
Among those who divorced										
Average duration of marriage (in years)	9.2	8.9	9.5	9.3	9.1	10.9	10.1	9.0	9.0	9.5
Percent remarrying	65.7	65.3	66.1	52.4	68.6	54.8	60.8	68.0	64.8	66.3
Among those who remarried after divorce										
Average time to remarriage (in years)	4.3	4.2	4.4	4.6	4.3	4.2	4.5	4.3	4.4	3.9

(Continued)

Table 6.7 (Continued)

Characteristic	Full Sample	Men	Women	Blacks Non-Hispanics	Nonblack Non-Hispanics	Hispanics	Less than High School Diploma	High School Graduate, No College	Some College or Associate's Degree	Bachelor's Degree or Higher
Percent still in second marriage	62.0	63.9	60.2	63.7	61.8	61.0	57.1	60.0	59.4	73.6
Percent of second marriage ending in divorce	36.4	35.2	37.4	33.2	36.6	37.7	40.8	38.8	37.4	26.1
Among those whose second marriage ended in divorce										
Average duration of second marriage (years)	6.6	6.8	6.5	6.0	6.6	8.0	6.0	6.7	6.8	6.6
Percent remarrying NLSY79 (N=7357)	54.0	50.4	56.8	45.3	55.2	48.7	62.0	53.8	51.1	50.1

Note: The National Longitudinal Survey of Youth 1979 (NLSY79) consists of men and women who were born in the years 1957–1964 and were ages 14–22 when first interviewed in 1979. These individuals were ages 45–52 in 2010–2011. Race and Hispanic or Latino ethnicity groups are mutually exclusive. Educational attainment is as of the most recent survey. The data used in this study are weighted such that the sample employed is representative of those born in the years 1957–1964 and living in the United States in 1978.

Source: Bureau of Labor Statistics (2013). *Marriage and Divorce: Patterns by Gender, Race, and Educational Attainment*. Washington, DC, October. Retrieved from http:// www.bls.gov/opub/mlr/2013/article/marriage-and-divorce-patterns-by-gender-race-and-educational-attainment.htm on May 16, 2016.

Just as with first marriages, college graduates were more likely to stay in a second marriage when compared with groups that have less education (2013).

TEEN PREGNANCY

The teenage birth rate in the United States is one of the highest of all Western nations. Per data from the Centers for Disease Control and Prevention (Martin et al. 2012), of the 3.9 million reported births to U.S. residents in 2010, 9.3% (372,175) were to mothers under the age of 20. For non-Hispanic whites, 6.7% of births were to those under 20. The rates were 15.2% for non-Hispanic blacks, and 13.1% for Hispanics. The birth rate for all unmarried women between the age of 15 and 19 was 31.1 per 1,000. For non-Hispanic whites in the same age range, it was 20.3, but 50.8 per 1,000 for blacks. However, all of the rates declined in 2010 from previous years. For example, in 1991, the rate for black youths was 107.8 per 1,000 compared to 32.7 per 1,000 white youths. In 2010, the states with the highest teenage birth rates (over 50 per 1,000) were Mississippi, New Mexico, Arkansas, Texas, and Oklahoma. The states with the lowest rates (under 20 per 1,000) were Connecticut, Vermont, Massachusetts, and New Hampshire. Regardless of the decline from prior years, if trends continue nationally, one-third of all girls will get pregnant during their teenage years.

Teenage pregnancy rates were highest in the early 1970s through the early 1990s, increasing by approximately 21% among women below 20 years of age. During the same decades, the number of abortions also increased. The overall rate of teenage pregnancy has substantially dropped since the early 1990s. According to the Office of Adolescent Health (2016), which is located within the U.S. Department of Health and Human Services:

> In 2014, there were 24.2 births for every 1,000 adolescent females ages 15–19, or 249,078 babies born to females in this age group. Nearly eighty-nine percent of these births occurred outside of marriage. The 2014 teen birth rate indicates a decline of nine percent from 2013 when the birth rate was 26.5 per 1,000. The teen birth rate has declined almost continuously over the past 20 years. In 1991, the U.S. teen birth rate was 61.8 births for every 1,000 adolescent females, compared with 24.2 births for every 1,000 adolescent females in 2014. Still, the U.S. teen birth rate is higher than that of many other developed countries, including Canada and the United Kingdom.

As outlined in Table 6.8, the birth rate for Hispanic teenagers in 2014 was 38 per 1,000, compared to 34.9 for blacks, and 17.3 for whites. All three show decreases from 1990, when the rates per 1,000 were 100.3, 116.2 and 42.5, respectively.

Based on data from The World Bank, Table 6.9 shows the pregnancy rates of all high-income countries that are members of the Organisation of Economic Co-operation and Development (OECD). Chile and the United States lead in

Table 6.8   Birth Rates per 1,000 Females Ages 15–19, by Race/Ethnicity, 1990–2014

Year Collected	Total	White	Black	Hispanic
1990	59.9	42.5	116.2	100.3
1991	61.8	43.4	118.2	104.6
1992	60.3	41.7	114.7	103.3
1993	59.0	40.7	110.5	101.8
1994	58.2	40.4	105.7	101.3
1995	56.0	39.3	97.2	99.3
1996	53.5	37.6	91.9	94.6
1997	51.3	36.0	88.3	89.6
1998	50.3	35.3	85.7	87.9
1999	48.8	34.1	81.0	86.8
2000	47.7	32.6	79.2	87.3
2001	45.0	30.3	73.1	84.4
2002	42.6	28.6	67.7	80.6
2003	41.1	27.4	63.7	78.4
2004	40.5	26.7	61.8	78.1
2005	39.7	26.0	59.4	76.5
2006	41.1	26.7	61.9	77.4
2007	41.5	27.2	62.0	75.3
2008	40.2	26.7	60.4	70.3
2009	37.9	25.7	56.7	63.6
2010	34.3	23.5	51.5	55.7
2011	31.3	21.7	47.3	49.6
2012	29.4	20.5	43.9	46.3
2013	26.5	18.6	39.0	41.7
2014	24.2	17.3	34.9	38.0

Source: Hamilton, Brady E., Joyce A. Martin, Michelle J.K. Osterman, Sally C. Curtin, and T.J. Mathews (2015). *Births: Final Data for 2014 (National Vital Statistics Report)*. Volume 64, Number 12, Hyattsville, MD: National Center for Health Statistics. Retrieved from http://www.cdc.gov/nchs/data/nvsr/nvsr64/nvsr64_12.pdf on February 25, 2016.

teenage pregnancy rates for all high-income OECD countries. Both have seen drastic decreases since the early 1960s when both countries had rates over 80 per 1,000 females between the ages of 15 and 19. Notice the other top countries include New Zealand, Slovak Republic, Hungary, the United Kingdom, Australia, Estonia, Poland, and Ireland. The OECD high-income countries with the lowest rates are South Korea, Switzerland, Slovenia, Netherlands, Denmark, Japan, Sweden, Norway, and Italy.

High rates of teenage pregnancy in the United States are a result of a generally more relaxed attitude toward unmarried sex than other nations are known for. As a result, teenagers are more prone to experimenting with sex at earlier ages than prior generations, and also generally don't face as much family or social scrutiny for their actions as earlier generations did. According to studies (Martinez et al.

Table 6.9 Adolescent Fertility Rates (Births per 1,000 Women Ages 15–19), Selected Years 1960–2014, for OECD High-Income Member Countries

Country	1960	1970	1980	1990	2000	2007	2008	2009	2010	2011	2012	2013	2014
Chile	88.7	87.9	69.0	64.4	57.0	52.7	52.0	51.3	50.7	50.0	49.3	48.7	48.1
United States	85.0	63.7	52.0	57.1	46.5	39.7	37.7	35.8	33.9	32.0	30.0	27.1	24.1
New Zealand	61.0	65.8	37.3	32.8	28.0	30.1	29.1	28.2	27.2	26.3	25.3	24.6	23.9
Slovak Republic	49.6	41.8	48.2	47.6	23.3	20.7	20.8	20.9	21.1	21.2	21.3	20.9	20.4
Hungary	50.2	54.2	63.4	40.6	22.8	19.6	19.5	19.4	19.4	19.3	19.2	18.7	18.2
United Kingdom	84.7	52.4	28.8	31.0	28.1	25.6	24.1	22.6	21.1	19.6	18.1	16.7	15.3
Australia	44.8	48.6	28.4	21.0	17.9	17.1	16.8	16.5	16.2	15.8	15.5	15.0	14.4
Estonia	21.4	30.7	40.8	46.1	26.3	22.6	21.3	20.0	18.7	17.4	16.1	14.9	13.7
Poland	39.9	28.3	33.9	30.6	16.9	15.9	15.7	15.5	15.2	15.0	14.7	14.2	13.7
Ireland	10.4	18.8	20.2	15.6	19.0	16.3	15.4	14.6	13.8	13.0	12.1	11.5	10.8
Portugal	26.9	31.1	38.1	24.3	20.3	16.2	15.4	14.5	13.7	12.8	12.0	11.1	10.3
Czech Republic	48.0	48.9	55.3	44.9	13.4	11.1	11.1	11.1	11.1	11.0	11.0	10.6	10.1
Canada	55.6	40.3	27.0	24.4	16.7	13.9	13.4	12.9	12.4	11.9	11.3	10.7	10.1
Israel	52.3	40.8	34.9	20.4	16.7	14.0	13.5	13.0	12.5	12.0	11.6	10.8	10.1
France	33.9	37.4	23.5	12.1	10.4	10.0	9.9	9.8	9.7	9.6	9.5	9.3	9.0
Spain	10.1	15.3	23.0	11.9	9.4	12.2	11.5	10.9	10.2	9.6	8.9	8.7	8.5
Belgium	27.1	31.1	19.4	11.0	10.6	10.4	10.1	9.8	9.6	9.3	9.0	8.7	8.4
Greece	17.3	35.2	46.7	22.0	10.9	11.7	11.0	10.4	9.8	9.2	8.5	8.1	7.7
Austria	48.4	57.3	33.4	20.8	13.9	11.1	10.6	10.1	9.6	9.1	8.6	8.0	7.4
Germany	38.0	45.0	25.3	16.3	12.7	9.8	9.4	9.1	8.7	8.4	8.0	7.5	7.0
Finland	29.0	30.5	19.4	11.9	10.1	9.2	8.8	8.4	8.0	7.6	7.3	7.0	6.7
Iceland	84.1	75.5	49.6	27.7	19.8	14.3	13.1	11.8	10.6	9.4	8.1	7.3	6.5
Luxembourg	25.9	27.7	16.2	12.1	11.1	9.6	9.1	8.6	8.0	7.5	7.0	6.6	6.1
Italy	19.2	28.0	20.0	8.6	6.8	6.9	6.8	6.7	6.6	6.5	6.4	6.2	6.1
Norway	28.0	31.4	19.9	16.6	11.1	8.9	8.4	7.8	7.2	6.7	6.1	6.0	5.9
Sweden	39.7	36.8	16.1	11.5	6.7	6.0	5.9	5.8	5.7	5.6	5.5	5.5	5.6
Japan	4.1	4.4	4.0	4.0	5.2	5.1	5.0	4.9	4.8	4.7	4.5	4.3	4.2

(Continued)

Table 6.9 (Continued)

Country	1960	1970	1980	1990	2000	2007	2008	2009	2010	2011	2012	2013	2014
Denmark	44.2	34.1	15.7	9.0	7.2	5.9	5.6	5.3	5.0	4.7	4.4	4.3	4.1
The Netherlands	17.9	19.8	8.9	7.0	6.7	5.3	5.1	5.0	4.8	4.7	4.5	4.3	4.1
Slovenia	30.6	50.8	51.3	25.6	7.2	4.9	4.8	4.8	4.7	4.6	4.5	4.2	3.9
Switzerland	18.0	20.6	9.8	6.4	5.5	4.5	4.3	4.1	3.9	3.7	3.5	3.3	3.1
Korea, Republic	32.6	16.0	13.3	5.1	2.5	2.1	2.0	2.0	1.9	1.9	1.8	1.7	1.7

Source: The World Bank (2016). *Adolescent Fertility Rate (Births per 1,000 Women Ages 15–19)*. Washington, DC. Retrieved from http://data.worldbank.org/indicator/SP.ADO.TFRT/countries?display=default on February 24, 2016.

2011), between 2006 and 2010, approximately 43% of never-married female teen-agers (4.4 million) and 42% of never-married male teenagers (4.5 million) had engaged in sexual intercourse at least once. For females, the rates for non-Hispanic whites were 41.9%, 42.1% for Hispanics, and 46.4% for non-Hispanic blacks. For males, the rates were 36.7% for non-Hispanic whites, 46% for Hispanics, and 58.4% for non-Hispanic blacks. Based on more recent data from the Office of Adolescent Health (2016):

> Birth rates are also higher among Hispanic and black adolescents than among their white counterparts. In 2014, Hispanic adolescent females ages 15–19 had the highest birth rate (38 births per 1,000 adolescent females), followed by black adolescent females (34.9 births per 1,000 adolescent females) and white adolescent females (17.3 births per 1,000 adolescent females). Estimates from 2013 data show that 11% of adolescent females in the United States will give birth by her 20th birthday, with substantial differences by race/ethnicity: 8% of white adolescent females, 16% of black adolescent females, and 17% of Hispanic adolescent females.

Higher rates of teenage pregnancy in the United States are a result of a more generally relaxed attitude toward unmarried sex than other nations. As a result, teenagers are more prone to experiment with sex at earlier ages and also not face family or social scrutiny for their actions. According to studies (Martinez et al. 2011), between 2006 and 2010 approximately 43% of never-married female teenagers (4.4 million) and 42% of never-married male teenagers (4.5 million) had engaged in sexual intercourse at least once. The rate for non-Hispanic white females was 41.9%, 42.1% for Hispanics, and 46.4% for non-Hispanic blacks. For males, the rates were 36.7% for non-Hispanic whites, 46% for Hispanics, and 58.4% for non-Hispanic blacks.

Many youth in the United States do actually use some form of birth control. Between 2006 and 2010, 78% of females and 85% of males used a method of contraception during their first sexual experience. The most commonly used form of contraception among teenagers was condoms. Ninety percent of sexually active females who don't use birth control will become pregnant within a year. The rate of contraception use is lower among minorities than whites. While 89% of non-Hispanic white males used contraception during their first sexual experience, the rate was 84% for Hispanic males and 82% for non-Hispanic black males (Martinez et al. 2011).

The internet and media play a large role in the rate of teenage pregnancy in the United States. Much of today's media promotes sex as part of entertainment. Per Somers and Tynan (2006, p. 18), "Adolescents who are sexually active are also more likely to seek out the sexually laden television programming. Similarly, as children and adolescents construct expectations for male and female sexual roles, as proposed in a symbolic interactionism perspective on sexual development, media are likely to be involved in this development and sexual socialization." Gruber and Grube (2000) also discuss the influence of media on teen sexual practices in finding that:

> Although sexual content in the media can affect any age group, adolescents may be particularly vulnerable. Adolescents may be exposed to sexual content in the media during a developmental period when gender roles, sexual attitudes, and sexual behaviors are being shaped. This group may be particularly at risk because the cognitive skills that allow them to critically analyze messages from the media and to make decisions based on possible future outcomes are not fully developed.

The increased propensity for teenage sex and pregnancy is driven by poverty, education, and parental situations. Between 60% and 80% of teenage mothers live in poverty and come from low-income families. Their children often suffer from socioeconomic depression, and are at higher-than-average risk for low birth weights, poor health, poor performance when they enter school, neglect, abuse, and behavior problems. Per studies by the CDC (Martinez et al. 2011, p. 15), 50.5% of never-married, sexually active female teenagers were raised by mothers who did not have a high school diploma, and 40.2% had mothers who had some college or higher. Many sexually active females (29.5%) were also from single parent homes. The rate was 17.1% for two-parent homes. Because African Americans have the lowest rates of educational achievement, on average, black teenage mothers are at the highest risk of issues like poverty and abuse.

Sexual abuse and violence are also factors that contribute to increased rates of teenage pregnancy. This is outlined by the following points published by the National Campaign to Prevent Teen Pregnancy (2011) about teens that have experienced dating violence or sexual abuse:

- Girls who experienced dating violence were four to six times more likely to get pregnant than girls who had not.
- Both teenage boys and girls who had experienced physical dating violence in the past year were almost three times more likely to be sexually active than those who had not experienced such violence.
- Sexually active teens with a reported history of sexual abuse were more likely to have never or rarely used birth control or condoms.
- Approximately 50% to 60% of teenage girls who became pregnant had previously been the victims of sexual or physical abuse.
- In addition to physical abuse, teens who had witnessed intimate partner violence during childhood and had been verbally abused were also linked with being sexually active at an early age.

TEEN DRUG USE

As shown in Table 6.10, 8.8% of youths ages 12–17 used an illicit drug in 2013. This marked a three-year reduction, and the lowest rate between 2002 and 2013. Also in 2013, 7.1% of youth were "using marijuana, 2.2% were using psychotherapeutic drugs for nonmedical reasons (including 1.7% who were also using pain reliever drugs for nonmedical reasons), 0.6% were using hallucinogens, 0.5% were using inhalants for nonmedical reasons, 0.2% were using cocaine, and 0.1% were using heroin." The following are other key points from the Substance Abuse and Mental Health Services Administration (2014):

> Marijuana use among teens declined from 8.2% in 2002 to 6.8% in 2005, remained similar through 2008, then increased to 7.9% in 2011 before decreasing again to 7.2% in 2012 and 7.1% in 2013. Current nonmedical use of psychotherapeutic drugs declined from 4.0% in 2002 and 2003 to 2.2% in 2013. This includes a decrease in the prevalence of current nonmedical use of pain relievers from 3.2% in 2002 and 2003 to 1.7% in 2013.

Studies show that black teens are less likely to use drugs than whites and Hispanics. A study reported in the Archives of General Psychiatry (Wu et al. 2011) found substance use and substance-related disorders commonly reported for Native American, white, and Hispanic adolescents, as well of those of multiple

Table 6.10   Past Month Use of Selected Illicit Drugs among Youths Aged 12–17, 2002–2013

Year	Illicit Drugs	Marijuana	Psychotherapeutics	Inhalants	Hallucinogens
2002	11.6	8.2	4.0	1.2	1.0
2003	11.2	7.9	4.0	1.3	1.0
2004	10.6	7.6	3.6	1.2	0.8
2005	9.9	6.8	3.3	1.2	0.8
2006	9.8	6.7	3.3	1.3	0.7
2007	9.6	6.7	3.3	1.2	0.7
2008	9.3	6.7	2.9	1.1	1.0
2009	10.1	7.4	3.1	1.0	0.9
2010	10.1	7.4	3.0	1.1	0.9
2011	10.1	7.9	2.8	0.9	0.9
2012	9.5	7.2	2.8	0.8	0.6
2013	8.8	7.1	2.2	0.6	0.5

Source: Substance Abuse and Mental Health Services Administration (2014). *Results from the 2013 National Survey on Drug Use and Health: Summary of National Findings, NSDUH Series H-48, HHS Publication No. (SMA) 14-4863.* Rockville, MD: Substance Abuse and Mental Health Services Administration. Retrieved from http://www.samhsa.gov/data/sites/default/files/NSDUHresultsPDF WHTML2013/Web/NSDUHresults2013.pdf on February 26, 2016.

races/ethnicities. However, substance use was low among black and Asian youth. The study specific found that:

> After controlling for adolescents' age, socioeconomic variables, population density of residence, self-rated health, and survey year, adjusted analyses of adolescent substance users indicated elevated odds of substance-related disorders among Native Americans, adolescents of multiple race/ethnicity, adolescents of white race/ethnicity, and Hispanics compared with African Americans; African Americans did not differ from Asians or Pacific Islanders. (p. 1176)

Other studies have shown the same findings, dispelling a popular myth that black youths engage in alcohol and illegal drug use more than whites. However, findings also show that white adolescents may contribute to black teens' substance use. Stock et al. (2013, p. 237) explain that white youth smoke, drink, and use drugs more because on average, they have greater access to these substances due to their increased wealth. Black youth, on the other hand, have deterrents associated with their ethnicity such as parents, family, and community members not condoning substance abuse and taking actions to correct the behavior of black teens. The more a black teen is exposed to white youth, the greater their chance of engaging in harmful substances and the higher their level of use.

TEEN DEPRESSION

Data shows that depression is the most common mental health disorder among both teenagers and adults. For black teens, this issue can be devastating because teen depression is prevalent in the African American community, but often is not diagnosed, especially in the low-income neighborhoods where good medical care is more difficult to obtain. Broman (2012, pp. 38–39) estimates that as many as 30% of adults and 20% of children are in need of clinical treatment for depression, such as medications, therapy, and rehabilitation. Yet, only about half of those in need receive the treatment they require. Minorities, those with low incomes, and those with the least amount of education have the greatest unmet needs, with minorities having the least access to mental health services. Broman's research revealed that black men, black women, and Latinas were only about 25–40% as likely to receive services as were non-Latino whites. This disparity exists even when controlling for health insurance coverage and socioeconomic status.

Studies show that an estimated 2.8 million adolescents aged 12–17 in the United States experienced at least one major depressive episode in the year 2014. This number represented 11.4% of the U.S. population aged 12–17. In that year, the rate of teenage depression by race and ethnicity was as follows: Hispanics—11.5%, white—12%, Asian—10.4%, black—9.1%, and those of two or more races/ethnic groups—12.5%. Further, 17.4% of females and 5.7% of males experienced a major depressive episode. By ages, 15.1% of 17-year-olds experienced a major depressive episode, compared to 14.1% of 16-year-olds, 13% of 15-year-olds, 10.7% of 14-year-olds, 8.7% of 13-year-olds, and 5.7% of 12-year-olds (Center for Behavioral Health Statistics and Quality 2015).

Living in a depressed socioeconomic condition is a major cause of depression in youth, particularly minority youth. Beyond the lack of resources is the pressure to socially conform. The fear of being different, picked on, and bullied can lead to extreme emotional distress. Studies show that those from most affluent backgrounds are more likely to have elevated moods because they are exposed to fewer social stressors and have greater access to coping resources. The data in Table 6.11 shows that black teens have the greatest percentage of those in poverty. In 2014, for example, 37.1% of black teens (not in combination with any other race) were below the poverty level, compared to 17.9% of whites, 12% of Asians, and 31.9% of Hispanics of any race. The highest rates for those 18–64 years old and over 65 years of age were also attributed to blacks.

As Miller and Taylor (2012, p. 426) explain:

> Research consistently finds that youth from socially advantaged families have the least depressive symptoms because they are exposed to fewer social stressors and have greater access to coping resources. Almost all previous investigations find that socioeconomic status (SES) and social support are both inversely associated with depressive symptoms during adolescence. There is also evidence that SES is positively related to social support, which suggests that SES may influence psychological well-being indirectly through its association with social support. Moreover, racial differences between blacks and whites across SES, depressive symptoms, and social support suggest that these mechanisms may operate differently among black and white youth.

Depression is an especially serious issue among young black men because they are less likely to be treated. This can lead to devastating consequences such as substance abuse, mental health issues that continue into adulthood, and even suicide. African American men go undiagnosed due to differences in symptoms and coping styles, poor screening and treatment, lack of access to affordable health care, stigma associated with mental illness, and the use of self-medications, such as alcohol and illicit drugs, to mask symptoms. Buzi, Weinman, and Smith (2010) report that major depressive disorder (MDD) is one of the most common and chronic conditions among teens. While rates of MDD are lower among Mexican Americans (8%) and African Americans (7.5%) compared to whites (10.41%), minorities are less likely to receive medical treatment that contributes to the condition lasting longer and possibly becoming more severe.

For teenagers, the most severe risk associated with depression is suicide attempts. Authors Buzi, Weinman, and Smith point out that "over the last fifty years the rates of suicides in teens have almost tripled, with suicide represented as the third leading cause of death among 15- to 24-year olds. Though depression

Table 6.11 Poverty Status of People by Age, Race, and Hispanic Origin, 2007–2014

Year and Characteristic	Under 18 Years — All People Total	Below Poverty Level Number	Percent	Under 18 Years — Related Children in Families Total	Below Poverty Level Number	Percent	18–64 Years Total	Below Poverty Level Number	Percent	65 Years and over Total	Below Poverty Level Number	Percent
All races												
2014	73,556	15,540	21.1	72,383	14,987	20.7	196,254	26,527	13.5	45,994	4,590	10.0
2013[1]	73,439	15,801	21.5	72,246	15,116	20.9	194,694	25,899	13.3	44,963	4,569	10.2
2013[2]	73,625	14,659	19.9	72,573	14,142	19.5	194,833	26,429	13.6	44,508	4,231	9.5
2012	73,719	16,073	21.8	72,545	15,437	21.3	193,642	26,497	13.7	43,287	3,926	9.1
2011	73,737	16,134	21.9	72,568	15,539	21.4	193,213	26,492	13.7	41,507	3,620	8.7
2010[3]	73,873	16,286	22.0	72,581	15,598	21.5	192,481	26,499	13.8	39,777	3,558	8.9
2009	74,579	15,451	20.7	73,410	14,774	20.1	190,627	24,684	12.9	38,613	3,433	8.9
2008	74,068	14,068	19.0	72,980	13,507	18.5	189,185	22,105	11.7	37,788	3,656	9.7
2007	73,996	13,324	18.0	72,792	12,802	17.6	187,913	20,396	10.9	36,790	3,556	9.7
White alone												
2014	53,637	9,602	17.9	52,732	9,172	17.4	151,562	18,086	11.9	39,054	3,400	8.7
2013[1]	53,638	10,296	19.2	52,657	9,702	18.4	151,234	17,629	11.7	38,475	3,362	8.7
2013[2]	53,846	8,808	16.4	53,074	8,428	15.9	151,334	17,931	11.8	37,905	3,197	8.4
2012	54,066	9,979	18.5	53,201	9,547	17.9	151,042	17,946	11.9	37,039	2,891	7.8
2011	54,186	10,103	18.6	53,268	9,643	18.1	151,416	18,007	11.9	35,732	2,739	7.7
2010[3]	54,490	10,092	18.5	53,573	9,590	17.9	151,218	18,353	12.1	34,274	2,638	7.7
2009	56,266	9,938	17.7	55,397	9,440	17.0	152,367	17,391	11.4	33,414	2,501	7.5
2008	56,153	8,863	15.8	55,339	8,441	15.3	151,681	15,356	10.1	32,714	2,771	8.5
2007	56,419	8,395	14.9	55,483	8,002	14.4	150,875	14,135	9.4	31,839	2,590	8.1
White alone, not Hispanic												
2014	38,057	4,679	12.3	37,457	4,440	11.9	121,424	12,173	10.0	35,727	2,801	7.8
2013[1]	38,167	5,116	13.4	37,572	4,784	12.7	121,629	11,691	9.6	35,322	2,745	7.8
2013[2]	38,395	4,094	10.7	37,849	3,833	10.1	121,991	12,133	9.9	34,781	2,569	7.4

2012	38,759	4,782	12.3	38,167	4,510	11.8	122,221	11,833	9.7	34,131	2,324	6.8
2011	38,955	4,850	12.5	38,322	4,554	11.9	123,101	12,112	9.8	32,904	2,210	6.7
2010[3]	39,437	4,866	12.3	38,823	4,544	11.7	123,731	12,230	9.9	31,616	2,155	6.8
2009	40,917	4,850	11.9	40,319	4,518	11.2	125,511	11,658	9.3	30,736	2,022	6.6
2008	41,309	4,364	10.6	40,707	4,059	10.0	125,482	10,380	8.3	30,149	2,280	7.6
2007	41,979	4,255	10.1	41,304	3,996	9.7	125,161	9,598	7.7	29,442	2,179	7.4
Black alone or in combination												
2014	12,875	4,639	36.0	12,706	4,564	35.9	27,442	6,137	22.4	4,249	805	19.0
2013[1]	13,044	4,359	33.4	12,915	4,325	33.5	27,056	6,031	22.3	4,054	772	19.0
2013[2]	13,104	4,838	36.9	12,882	4,730	36.7	26,923	6,410	23.8	4,085	712	17.4
2012	13,108	4,815	36.7	12,908	4,675	36.2	26,482	6,265	23.7	3,993	730	18.3
2011	12,968	4,849	37.4	12,815	4,762	37.2	25,962	6,241	24.0	3,718	640	17.2
2010[3]	13,015	4,923	37.8	12,759	4,814	37.7	25,815	6,031	23.4	3,555	643	18.1
2009	12,655	4,480	35.4	12,445	4,349	34.9	24,815	5,441	21.9	3,405	655	19.2
2008	12,388	4,202	33.9	12,201	4,104	33.6	24,404	5,017	20.6	3,305	663	20.0
2007	12,380	4,178	33.7	12,227	4,106	33.6	23,968	4,742	19.8	3,215	748	23.3
Black alone												
2014	11,015	4,090	37.1	10,887	4,036	37.1	25,954	5,869	22.6	4,143	796	19.2
2013[1]	11,003	3,708	33.7	10,896	3,678	33.8	25,562	5,742	22.5	3,933	736	18.7
2013[2]	11,088	4,244	38.3	10,916	4,153	38.0	25,552	6,099	23.9	3,975	698	17.6
2012	11,078	4,201	37.9	10,931	4,097	37.5	25,154	6,002	23.9	3,893	708	18.2
2011	11,138	4,320	38.8	11,005	4,247	38.6	24,831	5,980	24.1	3,640	630	17.3
2010[3]	11,173	4,355	39.0	10,953	4,271	39.0	24,667	5,775	23.4	3,443	617	17.9
2009	11,282	4,033	35.7	11,102	3,919	35.3	23,953	5,264	22.0	3,320	647	19.5
2008	11,172	3,878	34.7	10,998	3,781	34.4	23,565	4,855	20.6	3,229	646	20.0
2007	11,302	3,904	34.5	11,174	3,838	34.3	23,213	4,602	19.8	3,150	731	23.2
Asian alone or in combination												
2014	4,792	577	12.0	4,722	544	11.5	12,834	1,390	10.8	2,059	301	14.6
2013[1]	4,900	628	12.8	4,858	600	12.4	12,393	1,457	11.8	1,889	312	16.5

(Continued)

141

Table 6.11 (Continued)

Year and Characteristic	Under 18 Years						18-64 Years			65 Years and over		
	All People			Related Children in Families				Below Poverty Level			Below Poverty Level	
	Total	Below Poverty Level		Total	Below Poverty Level		Total			Total		
		Number	Percent		Number	Percent		Number	Percent		Number	Percent
2013[2]	4,740	457	9.6	4,701	442	9.4	12,374	1,258	10.2	1,910	259	13.6
2012	4,557	570	12.5	4,485	533	11.9	11,913	1,291	10.8	1,703	211	12.4
2011	4,572	607	13.3	4,495	566	12.6	11,660	1,397	12.0	1,581	185	11.7
2010[3]	4,308	586	13.6	4,256	560	13.2	11,414	1,265	11.1	1,515	214	14.1
2009	3,996	531	13.3	3,946	507	12.9	9,898	1,154	11.7	1,378	216	15.7
2008	3,717	494	13.3	3,678	476	12.9	9,507	1,031	10.8	1,319	162	12.3
2007	3,606	431	11.9	3,558	402	11.3	9,531	892	9.4	1,293	144	11.2
Asian alone												
2014	3,750	524	14.0	3,681	492	13.4	12,012	1,314	10.9	2,029	299	14.7
2013[1]	3,766	555	14.7	3,746	538	14.4	11,646	1,393	12.0	1,845	307	16.7
2013[2]	3,651	367	10.1	3,621	354	9.8	11,531	1,162	10.1	1,881	256	13.6
2012	3,596	497	13.8	3,542	470	13.3	11,153	1,220	10.9	1,669	205	12.3
2011	3,657	494	13.5	3,600	466	13.0	10,873	1,297	11.9	1,555	182	11.7
2010[3]	3,431	494	14.4	3,399	477	14.0	10,696	1,191	11.1	1,484	214	14.4
2009	3,311	463	14.0	3,271	444	13.6	9,344	1,069	11.4	1,350	213	15.8
2008	3,052	446	14.6	3,016	430	14.2	8,961	974	10.9	1,296	157	12.1
2007	2,980	374	12.5	2,932	345	11.8	9,012	832	9.2	1,265	143	11.3
Hispanic (of any race)												
2014	17,995	5,745	31.9	17,636	5,522	31.3	33,873	6,701	19.8	3,636	658	18.1
2013[1]	17,898	5,907	33.0	17,496	5,638	32.2	32,839	6,746	20.5	3,443	704	20.4
2013[2]	17,837	5,415	30.4	17,559	5,273	30.0	32,903	6,654	20.2	3,405	676	19.8
2012	17,664	5,976	33.8	17,341	5,773	33.3	32,228	6,977	21.6	3,213	663	20.6

Year											
2011	17,600	6,008	34.1	17,276	5,820	33.7	31,643	6,667	21.1	3,036	569	18.7
2010[3]	17,371	6,059	34.9	16,964	5,815	34.3	30,740	6,948	22.6	2,860	516	18.0
2009	16,965	5,610	33.1	16,655	5,419	32.5	29,031	6,224	21.4	2,815	516	18.3
2008	16,370	5,010	30.6	16,138	4,888	30.3	28,311	5,452	19.3	2,717	525	19.3
2007	15,647	4,482	28.6	15,375	4,348	28.3	27,731	4,970	17.9	2,555	438	17.1

Note: Numbers in thousands. People as of March of the following year.

Footnotes are available at http://census.gov/hhes/www/poverty/histpov/footnotes.html.

Source: U.S. Bureau of the Census (2015). *Current Population Survey, Annual Social and Economic Supplements.* Washington, D.C. For information on confidentiality protection, sampling error, nonsampling error, and definitions, see ftp://ftp2.census.gov/programs-surveys/cps/techdocs/cpsmar15.pdf.

rates are higher among females than males, males make up 79.4% of all suicides in the United States" (p. 92). Although more white teens commit suicide
than black teens, it is the third leading cause of death among African Americans
between the ages of 10 and 24 after homicide and unintentional injury. Allen and
Johnson (2010) further outline various stressors that increase the rate of suicide
for black youth, including such social stressors as oppression, racism, economic
disparity, and discrimination.

Depression in black youth is often tied to their self-perception. This is a direct
result of their attitude about their race in such areas as their physical features,
socioeconomic position, relationships with family and friends, and general feeling of racial pride. Their self-perception is also influenced by their social development through parental influence. Ethnic–racial socialization (being social with
those of other ethnic groups or races) results in teens' ethnic/racial identity and
adjustment, and determines whether they develop positive esteem or depressive
symptoms (Neblett et al. 2013, p. 201).

Depressed teens are at an increased risk of developing a substance abuse
problem, and are likely to have small social circles. If this pattern continues
throughout their life, they will have fewer opportunities for mobile social net-
works, higher education, or professional careers. They are also more likely to
engage in risky sexual behaviors, leading to higher rates of unplanned pregnancies and sexually transmitted diseases (STDs). When depression is not treated,
many teens struggle with their intimate relationships, and this problem can continue into adulthood.

Issues such as depression, poverty, discrimination, and being raised in single-
parent homes contribute to black teens being more prone to contract STDs and
HIV. These factors, particularly poverty, also limit access to healthcare and the
knowledge of sex safe practices. The Centers for Disease Control and Prevention
(CDC) (2012) aptly summarizes all of these challenges:

> Social and economic conditions, such as high rates of poverty, income
> inequality, unemployment, and low educational attainment, can make
> it more difficult for individuals to protect their sexual health. People
> who struggle financially are often experiencing life circumstances that
> increase their risk for STDs. Those who cannot afford basic necessities
> may have trouble accessing and affording quality sexual health services.
> As an example, in 2010, the poverty rates, unemployment rates, and high
> school drop-out rates for blacks, American Indians/Alaska Natives, and
> Hispanics were considerably higher than for whites, differences com-
> mensurate with observed disparities in STD burden. Recent data show
> that one-fifth of blacks (20.8%) do not have health insurance. Many peo-
> ple of Hispanic ethnicity face similar challenges; and for some, there
> are the additional barriers arising from immigration or undocumented
> citizenship status. Even when health care is available, fear and distrust
> of health care institutions can negatively affect the health care-seeking

experience for many racial/ethnic minorities when there is social discrimination, provider bias, or the perception that these may exist.

The following statistics from the CDC (2012) substantiate the disparities of African American teens:

- In 2011, 67% of reported gonorrhea cases with known race/ethnicity occurred among blacks (excluding cases with missing information on race or ethnicity, and cases whose reported race or ethnicity was other). The rate of gonorrhea among blacks in 2011 was 427.3 cases per 100,000 population, which was 17.0 times the rate among whites (25.2 per 100,000). This disparity has changed little in recent years. This disparity was larger for black men (19.4 times) than for black women (15.2 times).
- As in previous years, the disparity in gonorrhea rates for blacks in 2011 was larger in the Midwest and Northeast than in the West or the South.
- Considering all racial/ethnic and age categories, gonorrhea rates were highest for blacks aged 15–19 and 20–24 years in 2011. Black women aged 15–19 years had a gonorrhea rate of 1,929.6 cases per 100,000 women. This rate was 15.9 times the rate among white women in the same age group (121.2). Black women aged 20–24 had a gonorrhea rate of 2050.4 cases per 100,000 women, which was 12.1 times the rate among white women in the same age group (169.2 per 100,000).
- Black men aged 15–19 years had a gonorrhea rate of 959.9 cases per 100,000 men, which was 30.3 times the rate among white men in the same age group (31.7 per 100,000). Black men aged 20–24 years had a gonorrhea rate of 1875.1 cases per 100,000 men, which was 20.4 times the rate among white men in the same age group (91.8 per 100,000).

Teens who suffer from depression are more likely to use contraception irregularly or not at all. This potentially destructive behavior can also exacerbate their mental condition, and lead to sexual abuse and even violence by perpetrators who feel they can take advantage of the depressed victim without legal consequences. Studies have found depressive symptoms include not caring about one's well-being and feeling hopelessness, which can lead to apathy about whether contraception is used or not (Rizzo et al. 2012).

TEEN VIOLENCE

Teen violence is defined as crimes committed by those under the age of 18, including homicide, sexual violence (e.g., date rape), gang violence, school shootings, bullying, hate crimes, and other acts committed because of anger issues. Teen violence has become an issue in the African American community, and particularly in urban areas. Zimmerman and Messner (2013, p. 435) report homicide as the leading cause of death among young Americans, accounting for 14.8% of deaths among persons 10–24 years old. Between 50% and 96% of urban youth have witnessed some form of community violence such as a shooting or assault, or hearing a gunshot. As a result of such startling statistics, the U.S. Attorney General announced the Task Force on Children Exposed to Violence in 2011 as part of his Defending Childhood Initiative. The Department of Justice awards grants to cities and tribal communities to develop strategic plans for comprehensive community-based efforts to reduce youth exposure to violence. It also funds research, evaluation, public awareness, and training for professional members and affiliates of national organizations supporting the initiative.

African American youth are the most predisposed to violence. They represent the largest percentage of those in poverty, from single-parent homes, living in urban areas, and those with the least amount of education. All of these factors increase both exposure to and involvement in violent and lesser crimes. They are prone to violent crime exposure in their homes, schools, workplace, and communities (Pinckney et al. 2011; Wilson et al. 2012).

Table 6.12 shows extensive data from the National Center for Juvenile Justice (2015) on juvenile arrests from select years between 1980 and 2014. This data is based on crimes committed by those between the ages of 10 and 17 per 100,000 people. Notice that black juveniles commit more crimes overall than any other race. This particularly applies to property crimes (burglary, larceny-theft, motor vehicle theft, and arson), robbery, aggravated assault, drug abuse violations, and disorderly conduct. The only crimes that white youth commit more often than black youth are driving under the influence, liquor law violations, and drunkenness. More of these crimes are committed by American Indian youth than black youth, as well. The violent crime index is a composite, or the sum, of arrests for murder and nonnegligent manslaughter, forcible rape, robbery, and aggravated assault. By race, white juveniles have a violent crime index of 96.6, blacks 514.5, American Indians 76.8, and Asians 29.8. The positive factor from this chart is that the violent crime index has reduced for all races over the designated time period. Based on the select years shown, the average violent crime index has reduced by 7% per period for whites, 9.3% for blacks, 10.9% for American Indians, and 17.1% for Asians. It must be noted that this data is based on juvenile arrests. Studies have shown that black youth are more prone to be profiled and targeted than youth of any other race. This is a factor that contributes to the higher rates of criminal arrests for black youths.

More than 2,500 minors have been sentenced to prison or jail for life without the chance for parole (known by the abbreviation JLWOP), and most of these minors were black. The results of a survey conducted by the Sentencing Project (Nellis 2012, p. 14) of 1,579 juveniles with this sentence revealed 60% were black and the vast majority (1,534) were male. The survey also revealed the following statistics about the juvenile's socioeconomic, education, and prison conditions, supporting the theory that structural racism was a major contributor to their propensity for crime:

Table 6.12 Juvenile Arrest Rates by Offense and Race, Selected Years 1980–2014

Offense	1980	1990	2000	2007	2008	2009	2010	2011	2012	2013	2014
White juvenile arrest rates (arrests of whites ages 0–17/100,000 whites ages 10–17)											
All crimes[1]	6051.4	6567.2	5993.6	5270.3	5123.6	4644.3	4242.9	3786.9	3362.0	2790.2	2537.8
Violent Crime Index[2]	172.5	247.6	210.3	175.3	172.4	155.6	140.6	125.5	111.1	99.3	96.6
Murder and nonnegligent manslaughter	4.0	5.7	2.1	2.1	1.9	1.8	1.7	1.5	1.3	1.3	1.2
Forcible rape	7.9	14.0	10.8	8.5	8.0	7.8	7.0	7.0	6.4	6.7	8.4
Robbery	58.5	64.2	41.7	40.0	42.0	38.1	33.2	28.0	24.6	22.2	21.2
Aggravated assault	102.1	163.8	155.7	124.7	120.5	107.8	98.7	89.0	78.8	69.1	65.7
Property Crime Index[3]	2123.9	2316.7	1392.5	1042.6	1089.8	1037.1	914.0	819.0	710.5	600.6	552.3
Burglary	664.8	494.3	270.5	204.0	203.4	177.2	157.1	145.4	124.7	101.7	90.1
Larceny-theft	1251.3	1546.9	983.8	756.5	816.7	802.0	709.6	629.2	543.7	462.0	427.7
Motor vehicle theft	178.7	244.9	112.0	61.1	50.3	41.9	33.8	30.4	29.7	26.0	25.6
Arson	29.1	30.6	26.3	21.0	19.4	15.9	13.4	13.9	12.4	11.0	8.9
Other assaults	229.5	422.9	592.0	542.8	528.1	502.9	491.5	444.3	400.1	342.3	313.3
Vandalism	423.9	489.3	361.7	334.4	325.0	276.2	234.6	202.6	176.9	140.5	129.0
Weapons carrying, possessing, etc.	73.9	111.8	93.4	100.9	92.7	79.9	75.9	67.3	58.7	50.3	47.3
Drug abuse violations	368.7	187.5	539.8	517.0	492.0	479.9	492.7	433.3	408.2	348.3	329.3
Driving under the influence	123.9	88.7	77.1	64.3	56.6	48.1	42.8	36.3	34.0	27.5	24.7
Liquor laws	576.9	673.2	464.2	483.9	451.0	383.6	327.1	306.8	271.0	212.7	183.1
Drunkenness	163.6	99.2	77.1	57.8	53.3	47.6	43.9	39.1	34.2	25.9	22.1
Disorderly conduct	379.2	369.0	409.9	447.7	419.2	376.6	351.6	312.6	262.3	206.0	171.0
Curfew and loitering law violations	226.0	281.5	441.7	350.4	327.0	266.4	219.4	185.0	158.2	127.5	108.0
Runaways	507.3	644.0	430.7	280.7	280.4	237.5	n/a	n/a	n/a	n/a	n/a

(Continued)

Table 6.12 (Continued)

Offense	1980	1990	2000	2007	2008	2009	2010	2011	2012	2013	2014
Black juvenile arrest rates (arrests of blacks ages 0–17/100,000 blacks ages 10–17)											
	1980	1990	2000	2007	2008	2009	2010	2011	2012	2013	2014
All crimes[1]	9912.8	12949.5	10738.6	10920.5	10755.2	10096.3	9137.2	8374.0	7814.1	7054.5	6443.5
Violent Crime Index[2]	1040.0	1373.2	817.3	842.4	861.9	780.3	683.9	627.0	574.4	548.3	514.5
Murder and nonnegligent manslaughter	17.2	43.9	11.5	13.2	12.9	12.0	10.1	8.1	6.9	7.9	7.9
Forcible rape	56.1	64.5	30.4	22.4	20.8	18.4	18.2	17.7	15.4	16.8	19.8
Robbery	656.1	602.0	308.0	403.5	416.9	377.6	325.2	292.5	269.7	268.3	253.4
Aggravated assault	310.7	662.8	467.4	403.4	411.1	372.3	330.4	308.6	282.4	255.4	233.4
Property Crime Index[3]	4385.2	4265.3	2712.4	2279.1	2486.7	2448.9	2165.1	2088.1	1924.1	1736.1	1612.6
Burglary	1287.4	742.6	446.9	460.4	510.9	491.3	423.1	427.9	382.6	328.9	307.8
Larceny-theft	2730.1	2652.1	1854.1	1577.1	1757.9	1787.3	1605.4	1531.2	1426.8	1293.7	1181.8
Motor vehicle theft	340.1	838.4	381.5	215.8	195.5	151.0	118.7	106.2	94.2	97.2	108.7
Arson	27.6	32.2	29.9	25.9	22.4	19.3	17.9	22.8	20.6	16.4	14.2
Other assaults	615.7	1269.2	1469.4	1628.8	1578.3	1512.4	1421.3	1322.7	1233.8	1133.5	1040.8
Vandalism	332.5	532.2	346.2	361.2	347.8	305.5	270.3	262.9	248.6	212.0	208.1
Weapons carrying, possessing, etc.	158.5	347.0	222.7	282.8	263.0	223.2	201.4	189.3	167.6	149.4	150.5
Drug abuse violations	336.8	935.0	1060.9	978.5	850.7	765.2	723.7	624.2	598.7	539.4	470.3
Driving under the influence	19.5	16.5	18.8	13.7	12.1	12.1	12.2	9.9	8.7	7.4	7.5
Liquor laws	76.2	157.1	131.5	121.5	127.1	119.3	118.1	108.2	99.9	84.0	70.1
Drunkenness	41.2	54.8	29.4	22.4	22.1	21.7	19.2	19.8	16.2	13.0	11.5
Disorderly conduct	669.1	889.7	1009.2	1424.1	1341.7	1239.3	1123.3	1025.2	934.7	800.4	648.7
Curfew and loitering law violations	263.8	399.2	695.4	835.9	797.9	735.2	646.7	496.8	507.7	504.7	449.3
Runaways	467.9	661.3	461.0	481.7	509.5	443.1	n/a	n/a	n/a	n/a	n/a

American Indian juvenile arrest rates (arrests of American Indians ages 0–17/100,000 American Indians ages 10–17)

Offense	1980	1990	2000	2007	2008	2009	2010	2011	2012	2013	2014
All crimes[1]	6798.5	6576.5	5687.2	4307.4	3826.5	3677.3	3348.1	3296.7	3052.7	2714.9	2337.4
Violent Crime Index[2]	204.9	223.2	200.0	146.0	118.1	118.3	114.2	104.7	94.0	83.8	76.8
Murder and nonnegligent manslaughter	4.5	4.1	2.3	3.6	1.1	1.7	0.8	1.0	2.0	2.2	1.1
Forcible rape	16.9	13.8	9.1	5.8	4.7	3.9	4.5	2.8	5.2	4.5	4.0
Robbery	54.5	40.9	38.7	27.8	20.5	23.5	21.1	17.3	18.9	13.6	18.1
Aggravated assault	128.9	164.4	149.9	108.8	91.7	89.6	87.9	83.5	67.8	63.6	53.6
Property Crime Index[3]	2671.7	2564.3	1579.6	897.3	821.5	835.6	738.1	722.0	651.2	619.9	540.4
Burglary	685.5	507.2	235.3	147.8	120.0	110.0	85.4	86.9	77.4	71.3	61.0
Larceny-theft	1714.7	1762.2	1174.6	661.9	638.1	662.4	608.2	599.7	537.6	510.2	449.7
Motor vehicle theft	253.6	270.9	150.6	76.8	52.5	51.3	36.3	29.3	31.7	29.1	23.2
Arson	17.8	24.1	19.1	10.9	11.0	11.9	8.3	6.0	4.5	9.3	6.6
Other assaults	265.7	443.5	581.4	436.8	386.0	396.2	366.3	372.8	333.3	314.3	267.0
Vandalism	315.5	370.3	279.9	244.6	216.3	181.5	158.8	150.2	135.0	110.1	103.5
Weapons carrying, possessing, etc.	73.2	55.9	65.4	59.7	50.5	45.5	37.6	36.5	31.8	29.9	23.2
Drug abuse violations	203.0	111.2	318.8	298.9	254.9	272.7	303.3	283.9	272.0	265.9	258.3
Driving under the influence	136.2	102.7	75.8	57.4	51.1	42.8	33.8	34.5	27.1	24.1	21.7
Liquor laws	626.6	1047.0	732.8	665.8	618.7	581.4	491.8	489.4	414.0	369.1	274.7
Drunkenness	394.1	130.4	91.1	62.7	60.7	45.7	46.9	46.5	36.5	30.4	26.6
Disorderly conduct	422.5	273.3	295.6	367.7	308.8	293.7	272.2	265.6	241.0	192.6	172.2
Curfew and loitering law violations	407.5	267.8	434.3	218.3	177.9	184.2	166.9	176.9	179.0	131.4	95.7
Runaways	732.1	732.2	447.0	367.7	352.3	349.9	n/a	n/a	n/a	n/a	n/a

Asian juvenile arrest rates (arrests of Asians ages 0–17/100,000 Asians ages 10–17)

Offense	1980	1990	2000	2007	2008	2009	2010	2011	2012	2013	2014
All crimes[1]	2820.1	2977.5	2197.0	1650.7	1613.0	1459.6	1293.0	1113.7	1155.2	696.4	603.7

(Continued)

Table 6.12 (Continued)

Offense	1980	1990	2000	2007	2008	2009	2010	2011	2012	2013	2014
Violent Crime Index[2]	118.5	128.5	111.8	69.2	63.1	59.1	46.0	40.7	46.6	29.3	29.8
Murder and nonnegligent manslaughter	2.2	3.5	2.2	0.9	0.9	0.6	0.4	0.2	0.1	0.5	0.4
Forcible rape	7.2	5.3	1.9	2.2	1.1	2.1	1.1	1.3	1.6	1.3	0.8
Robbery	66.8	46.8	37.1	25.8	24.4	22.0	17.5	16.6	18.5	9.0	9.2
Aggravated assault	42.3	72.9	70.6	40.3	36.7	34.3	27.0	22.7	26.5	18.5	19.4
Property Crime Index[3]	1525.8	1215.9	712.8	430.9	423.2	427.9	369.5	316.7	325.4	207.3	169.2
Burglary	328.2	203.4	95.0	51.4	54.9	42.6	39.9	35.1	40.3	28.3	23.8
Larceny-theft	1043.0	836.1	540.1	341.0	340.0	364.3	313.7	268.8	270.7	170.4	136.8
Motor vehicle theft	146.4	168.8	71.5	31.6	22.2	16.6	12.2	9.4	11.3	6.2	6.2
Arson	8.2	7.6	6.3	6.9	6.2	4.4	3.8	3.4	3.1	2.3	2.4
Other assaults	158.6	253.9	196.5	157.5	158.8	138.9	134.6	110.9	113.4	68.4	64.4
Vandalism	103.2	151.0	95.1	92.4	84.6	61.9	48.0	43.1	36.9	21.8	21.6
Weapons carrying, possessing, etc.	43.8	60.4	42.1	33.3	27.2	24.2	22.0	19.9	23.3	18.3	15.3
Drug abuse violations	101.9	55.1	140.9	112.2	108.0	114.3	110.6	108.2	118.5	81.6	76.7
Driving under the influence	11.4	11.3	13.6	11.2	11.9	9.9	10.2	6.9	7.0	6.0	6.0
Liquor laws	73.4	102.1	65.3	98.3	91.3	84.6	77.1	62.5	66.4	41.8	34.8
Drunkenness	15.8	8.1	10.5	8.2	6.3	6.4	5.3	5.8	7.5	6.2	5.1
Disorderly conduct	45.1	84.8	92.9	91.2	87.6	80.4	68.7	56.6	53.1	37.8	29.0
Curfew and loitering law violations	85.3	181.7	213.2	107.4	102.0	79.8	72.8	63.7	65.0	44.3	35.2
Runaways	303.8	373.0	381.4	331.3	319.0	299.3	n/a	n/a	n/a	n/a	n/a

Note: Persons of Hispanic ethnicity may be of any race. Arrests of Hispanics are not reported separately.

n/a: As of 2010, the FBI no longer reports arrests for running away.

[1] "All crimes" excludes suspicion. Effective in 2010, the FBI no longer reported arrests for running away. As a result, this offense group is not included in the "All crimes" category.

[2] Violent crime index includes murder and nonnegligent manslaughter, rape, robbery, and aggravated assault.

[3] Property crime index includes burglary, larceny-theft, motor vehicle theft, and arson.

Source: National Center for Juvenile Justice (2015). *Juvenile Arrest Rates by Offense, Sex, and Race*. Retrieved from http://www.ojjdp.gov/ojstatbb/crime/excel/JAR_2014.xls on December 13, 2015. Also see http://www.ojjdp.gov/ojstatbb/crime/JAR_Display.asp?ID=qa05261.

- 79% of individuals reported witnessing violence in their homes.
- More than half (54.1%) witnessed weekly violence in their neighborhoods.
- Nearly half (46.9%) experienced physical abuse, including 79.5% of girls.
- A third (31.5%) of juvenile lifers were raised in public housing.
- Two in five respondents had been enrolled in special education classes.
- Fewer than half (46.6%) of these individuals had been attending school at the time of their offense.
- The vast majority (84.4%) of juvenile lifers had been suspended or expelled from school at some point in their academic career.
- The proportion of African Americans serving JLWOP sentences for the killing of a white person (43.4%) is nearly twice the rate at which African American juveniles are arrested for taking a white person's life (23.2%).
- Conversely, white juvenile offenders with black victims are only about half as likely (3.6%) to receive a JLWOP sentence as their proportion of arrests for killing blacks (6.4%).

FURTHER READINGS

Franklin, Nancy Boyd (2003). *Black Families in Therapy: Understanding the African American Experience, 2nd edition.* New York: Guilford Press.

Hattery, Angela J. and Earl Smith (2007). *African American Families.* Thousand Oaks, CA: Sage.

Hattery, Angela J. and Earl Smith (2012). *African American Families Today: Myths and Realities.* Lanham, MD: Rowman & Littlefield.

Males, Mike A. (2010). *Teenage Sex and Pregnancy: Modern Myths, Uneasy Realities.* Santa Barbara, CA: ABC-CLIO.

Mondimore, Francis Mark (2002). *Adolescent Depression: A Guide for Parents.* Baltimore, MD: The Johns Hopkins University Press.

Willie, Charles V. and Richard J. Reddick (2010). *A New Look at Black Families, 6th edition.* Lanham, MD: Rowman & Littlefield.

7

Religion

Data on religion is difficult to obtain from government sources. For example, the Census Bureau stopped collecting data on religious affiliation in its demographic surveys and decennial census due to Public Law 94–521, which prohibits questions being asked about religious affiliation on a mandatory basis. Some information on religious practices can be collected on a voluntary basis. Therefore, most data is available from private sources, such as surveys conducted by research organizations like the Pew Center and Gallup, Inc. Additionally, many scholars conduct surveys as part of research projects.

Researchers use survey data to aggregate findings based on religious affiliation, religious practices, race, ethnicity, and gender. However, care must be taken to review the methodology used as some surveys may only contain very small sample sizes, target specific populations, or may omit responses.

It's also important to identify what data was collected and if the findings are representative of different religions. For example, a survey may ask respondents how often they attend church. Some religions define "church" differently, not all religious practices meet at the same frequency (e.g., weekly services), and some respondents might interpret religious terminology in questions very differently. Be sure to also determine if the survey was based on a domestic or international sample of respondents, as culture plays a major role in religion. For example, some cultures place social and religious restrictions on women that directly affect how they would respond to a survey.

A final issue topic to consider is that people of the same religion, even within the United States, may have very different views and practices based on such factors as race and geographic location. A survey may outline "Christians" or "Protestants" as single religious affiliations. However, there are many subcategories of each affiliation that practice religious rituals very differently. Even within the subcategory of "Baptists" there are differences based on congregations and geographic locations (e.g., different practices between black churches in the South and in the North).

Understanding religious beliefs goes beyond an ideological analysis for the purpose of unveiling spiritual propensities. Religion has a direct impact on social interactions and civic behaviors. Read and Eagle (2011), for example, point out that religion impacts physical and mental health, wealth accumulation, forming racist beliefs, and political views:

> Understanding how religion relates to attitudes and behaviors is not merely an academic exercise: religion has been implicated in an array of consequential social outcomes, including physical and mental health, wealth accumulation, the formation of racist beliefs, and in the enduring prevalence of the culture wars in American politics, just to name a few. . . . Consequently, the picture that emerges is one of a unified, straightforward relationship between religious beliefs and outcomes. But in fact, the evidence is mixed on this point—white conservative Protestants overwhelmingly vote with the Republican Party while black conservative Protestants fall in line with Democrats; pro-feminist attitudes coexist with high levels of religiosity among blacks while the opposite is true among whites; frequent religious attendance increases the political participation of Arab-American men while dampening that of their female peers. (pp. 117–118)

The black church has and continues to serve as a cornerstone of the African American community. With that, it carries a tremendous amount of influence in all facets of black life in the United States, including politics. Traditionally, religion has been a cornerstone of the African American community. It has served as not only the center of faith and worship, but also an institution that has fostered and in many cases been the catalyst for every major social, cultural, and political change experienced by African Americans in the United States. This included helping southern slaves escape to the North, fighting against slavery in the Civil War, electing blacks and supportive whites to political offices, being at the forefront of the Civil Rights Movement, and working with public agencies for equality in hiring, education, and national politics.

Collins and Perry (2015, pp. 430–431) highlight the historical importance of black churches as the social and political center of the black community by being places where blacks could exercise autonomy and have leadership roles that were not available in hostile mainstream culture. The black church supported the financial, social justice, and mental health needs of its members. Further, "Contemporarily, many African Americans still seek consultation with the black church when faced with major decisions and difficulties related to issues involving the family. Thus, the church's current and future role as a vehicle for change is particularly salient given the concerns regarding the changing demographics of African American families."

Taylor and Chatters (2010) highlight the importance of religion in the United States and particularly for African Americans. They point out that black churches have a history of spearheading social, educational, health, youth, elderly, and educational programs for their black communities.

Littlefield (2005, p. 687) further explains the primary support of the black church has come from integrating politics into their services to foster a message of hope and liberation. Since before slavery, survival, liberation, and the value of self- help were the original doctrines of the black church. For example, the black church led the Civil Rights Movement using sit-ins, marches, and other types of protest activities. It also financed these activities.

Its appeal continues to cross education and socioeconomic boundaries in the black community.

African American scholars have noted and widely documented the significance of religion as a central part of African American culture. For example, in 1903 W. E. B. Du Bois wrote a seminal work entitled *The Negro Church* in which he discussed the importance of the Negro church. Du Bois stated:

> The Negro Church is the only social institution of the Negroes which started in the African forest and survived slavery; under the leadership of priest or medicine man, afterward of the Christian pastor, the Church preserved in itself the remnants of African tribal life and became after emancipation the center of Negro social life. So that today the Negro population of the United States is virtually divided into church congregations which are the real units of race life.

In 1974, E. Franklin Frazier in his work *The Negro Church in America* postulated that African American religion historically has functioned as a "refuge in a hostile white world." In addition to showcasing the African American experience, black religion provides significant insights into the social condition of black people in the United States. Franklin also noted that the black church has served as a form of cultural identity and resistance to a white-dominated society.

The Pew Research Center has conducted extensive analysis on religion in the United States. Their seminal research covers years of evaluation based on many levels of analysis. In particularly, they have evaluated the relationship between race and religion. Data they retrieved about religion in 2016 shows that the majority of blacks (94%) are historically Protestants, while whites traditionally identify as Jewish, mainline Protestants, Mormon, and Orthodox Christian. The majority of Asians are Hindu and Muslim, while most Latinos identify as Catholic and Jehovah's Witnesses.

Their data also shows that the majority of blacks (83%) believe in the Christian God with absolutely certainty, and another 11% express being fairly certain.

Comparatively, 61% of whites express absolute certainty, and 20% are fairly certain. The survey also found that 11% of whites don't believe in God, compared to only 2% of blacks. Asians are the least religious; 19% do not believe in the Christian God, and 44% report being absolutely certain that God exists. Based on the data, Latinos tend to be religions, with 59% expressing being absolutely certain in their belief in God and 26% being fairly certain.

A study by the Pew Center on religious service attendance outlined the percentage of sampled population that attends church. Blacks have the highest attendance; 47% reported they went to church at least once a week, and another 36% attended once or twice a month, or at least a few times a year. Asians reported attending church the least; only 26% attended once a week and 32% attended rarely or never. In comparison, 34% of whites attended church at least once a week, 32% attended once or twice a month or a few times a year, and 33% never attended. For these same categories, Latinos report 39%, 35%, and 26%, respectively.

These findings by Pew Research are consistent with other studies. Briggs (2015) reports the following data from several studies on blacks in the United States and religion from comparing the religious lives of black and white Americans:

- Seven in 10 black Americans read the Bible outside of worship; just 44% of white Americans read the Bible on their own, the Bible in American Life study showed.

- The 2012 General Social Survey found nearly half of blacks reported praying several times a day; just 27% of whites prayed with the same frequency.

- Fifty-one percent of blacks, compared to 37% of whites, strongly agree that they have a personally meaningful relationship with God, according to the Portraits of American Life Study.

- Fifty-nine percent of members of historically black churches reported attending services at least once a week; nationally 39% of Americans reported attending with similar frequency, according to the 2007 Pew U.S. Religious Landscape Survey.

- The percentage of white religious "nones"—individuals with no religious affiliation—rose from 15% in 2007 to 20% in 2012, while there was no statistically significant change among black Americans.

Another interesting survey by Gallup (Newport 2011) analyzed race, religion, and political ideology. Among its principal findings was that:

Very religious white Americans are more than twice as likely to identify with or lean toward the Republican Party, while nonreligious whites are significantly more likely to identify with the Democratic Party. This relationship between religion and partisanship is also evident to a lesser degree among Asians and Hispanics, but does not occur among blacks, who are strongly likely to identify themselves as Democrats regardless of how religious they are.

That same report found blacks to be the most religious on average, followed by Hispanics, then whites, and finally Asian Americans.

FURTHER READINGS

Davis, Reginald F. (2010). *The Black Church: Relevant or Irrelevant in the 21st Century*. Macon, GA: Smyth & Helwys.

Lincoln, C. Eric and Lawrence H. Mamiya (2001). *The Black Church in the African American Experience*. Durham, NC: Duke University Press.

Pinn, Anthony B. (2002). *The Black Church in the Post-Civil Rights Era*. Maryknoll, NY: Orbis Books.

Sernett, Milton C. (ed.) (1999). *African American Religious History: A Documentary Witness, 2nd edition*. Durham, NC: Duke University Press.

Ware, Frederick. L. (2013). *African American Theology: An Introduction*. Louisville, KY: Westminster John Knox Press.

Warnock, Raphael G. (2014). *The Divided Mind of the Black Church: Theology, Piety & Public Witness*. New York: New York University Press.

Bibliography

Aja, Alan A., William A. Darity Jr., and Darrick Hamilton (2013). "Segregated Education in Desegregated Schools: Why We Should Eliminate 'Tracking' with 'Gifted and Talented' for All." *Huffington Post*, August 17. Retrieved from http://www.huffingtonpost.com/alan-a-aja/segregated-education-in-d_b_3443865.html on March 5, 2016.

Allen, Viviette L. and Oliver J. Johnson (2010). "African American Male Stress: Best Practices for Assessment and Intervention Based on a Qualitative Analysis of Selected Survey Responses." *Journal of Best Practices in Health Professions Diversity: Education, Research & Policy*, 3, 1, March, pp. 1–19.

American Civil Liberties Union (2014). *Written Submission of the American Civil Liberties Union on Racial Disparities in Sentencing: Hearing on Reports of Racism in the Justice System of the United States*. Submitted to the Inter-American Commission of Human Rights, October 27, 2014. Retrieved from https://www.aclu.org/sites/default/files/assets/141027_iachr_racial_disparities_aclu_submission_0.pdf on December 30, 2015.

American Civil Liberties Union (2016). *Oppose Voter ID Legislation—Fact Sheet*. Retrieved from https://www.aclu.org/oppose-voter-id-legislation-fact-sheet on May 14, 2016.

American Sociological Association (2007). *Race, Ethnicity, and the Criminal Justice System*. Washington, DC. Retrieved from http://www.asanet.org/images/press/docs/pdf/ASARaceCrime.pdf on September 2, 2013.

Amurao, Carla (2013). *Fact Sheet: How Bad if the School-to-Prison Pipeline*. Retrieved from http://www.pbs.org/wnet/tavissmiley/tsr/education-under-arrest/school-to-prison-pipeline-fact-sheet/ on March 19, 2016.

Aull, Elbert H., IV (2012). "Zero Tolerance, Frivolous Juvenile Court Referrals, and the School-to-Prison Pipeline: Using Arbitration as a Screening-Out

Method to Help Plug the Pipeline." *Ohio State Journal on Dispute Resolution*, 27, 1, March, pp. 179–206.

Aura, Saku and Gregory D. Hess (2010). "What's in a Name?" *Economic Inquiry*, 48, 1, January, pp. 214–227.

Ayanian, John Z. (2015). "The Costs of Racial Disparities in Health Care." *Harvard Business Review*, October 1. Retrieved from https://hbr.org/2015/10/the-costs-of-racial-disparities-in-health-care on May 13, 2016.

Barrett, David E. and Antonis Katsiyannis (2015). "Juvenile Delinquency Recidivism: Are Black and White Youth Vulnerable to the Same Risk Factors?" *Behavioral Disorders*, 40, 3, pp. 184–195.

Bertrand, Marianne and Sendhil Mullainathan (2004). "Are Emily and Greg More Employable than Lakisha and Jamal? A Field Experiment on Labor Market Discrimination." *American Economic Review*, 94, 4, September, pp. 991–1013.

Black Voices (2013). "Divorce Rate, Education Conversely Related; Protection Varies by Race, Study Shows." *HuffingtonPost.com*, March 11. Retrieved from http://www.huffingtonpost.com/2013/03/11/divorce-rate-education-conversely-related-varies-by-race_n_2854790.html?view=print&comm_ref=false on April 7, 2015.

Braveman, Paula A., Katherine Heck, Susan Egerter, Kristin S. Marchi, Tyan Parker Dominguez, Catherine Cubbin, Kathryn Finger, Jay A. Pearson, and Michael Curtis (2015). "The Role of Socioeconomic Factors in Black-White Disparities in Preterm Birth." *American Journal of Public Health*, 105, 4, pp. 694–702.

Breslow, Jason, Evan Wexler, and Robert Collins (2014). "The Return of School Segregation in Eight Charts." *Frontline, PBS*. Retrieved from http://www.pbs.org/wgbh/frontline/article/the-return-of-school-segregation-in-eight-charts/ on March 4, 2016.

Briggs, David (2015). "Are Black Americans the Most Religious—and Virtuous—of All?" *Huffington Post*, February 27. Retrieved from http://www.huffingtonpost.com/david-briggs/are-black-americans-the-m_b_6769296.html on March 12, 2016.

Broman, Clifford L. (2012). "Race Differences in the Receipt of Mental Health Services among Young Adults." *Psychological Services*, 9, 1, February, pp. 38–48.

Brooks, Cornell Williams, Roslyn M. Brock, and Barbara Bolling-Williams (2014). *Born Suspect: Stop-and-Frisk Abuses & the Continued Fight to End Racial Profiling in America*. Baltimore, MD: National Association for the Advancement of Colored People.

Bureau of Justice Statistics (2015). *Criminal Victimization, 2014*. Office of Justice Programs, U.S. Department of Justice, September 29. Retrieved from http://www.bjs.gov/content/pub/pdf/cv14.pdf on December 19, 2015.

Bureau of Labor Statistics (2013). *Marriage and Divorce: Patterns by Gender, Race, and Educational Attainment*. Washington, DC, October. Retrieved from http://www.bls.gov/opub/mlr/2013/article/marriage-and-divorce-patterns-by-gender-race-and-educational-attainment.htm on May 16, 2016.

Bureau of Labor Statistics (2015). *Labor Force Characteristics by Race and Ethnicity, 2014 (Report 1057)*. Washington, DC, November. Retrieved from http://www.bls.gov/opub/reports/cps/labor-force-characteristics-by-race-and-ethnicity-2014.pdf on January 23, 2016.

Buzi, Ruth, Maxine L. Weinman, and Peggy B. Smith (2010). "Depression and Risk Behaviors among Males Attending Family Planning Clinics." *International Journal of Men's Health*, 9, 2, June, pp. 91–101.

Callis, Robert R. and Melissa Kresin (2016). *Residential Vacancies and Homeownership in the Fourth Quarter 2015*. Washington, DC: Social, Economic and Housing Statistics Division, U.S. Census Bureau, U.S. Department of Commerce. Retrieved from http://www.census.gov/housing/hvs/files/currenthvspress.pdf on February 24, 2016.

Caprio, Sonia, Stephen R. Daniels, Adam Drewnowski, Francine R. Kaufman, Lawrence A. Palinkas, Arlan L. Rosembloom, and Jeffrey B. Schwimmer (2008). "Influence of Race, Ethnicity, and Culture on Childhood Obesity: Implications for Prevention and Treatment." *Diabetes Case*, 31, 11, pp. 2211–2221.

Carson, E. Ann (2015). *Prisoners in 2014*. Washington, DC: Bureau of Justice Statistics, U.S. Department of Justice. Retrieved from http://www.bjs.gov/content/pub/pdf/p14.pdf on February 24, 2016.

Center for Behavioral Health Statistics and Quality (2015). *Behavioral Health Trends in the United States: Results from the 2014 National Survey on Drug Use and Health* (HHS Publication No. SMA 15–4927, NSDUH Series H-50). Retrieved from http://www.samhsa.gov/data/sites/default/files/NSDUH-FRR1-2014/NSDUH-FRR1-2014.htm on February 26, 2016.

Centers for Disease Control and Prevention (2012). *STDs in Racial and Ethnic Minorities*. Atlanta, GA. Retrieved from http://www.cdc.gov/std/stats11/minorities.htm on November 1, 2015.

Centers for Disease Control and Prevention (2015). *Heart Disease Facts*. Atlanta, GA. Retrieved from http://www.cdc.gov/heartdisease/facts.htm on March 6, 2016.

Centers for Disease Control and Prevention (2016a). *Health, United States, 2014*. Atlanta, GA. Retrieved from http://www.cdc.gov/nchs/hus/contents2014.htm#055 on March 6, 2016.

Centers for Disease Control and Prevention (2016b). *Diabetes Public Health Resource*. Atlanta, GA. Retrieved from http://www.cdc.gov/diabetes/statistics/prev/national/figraceethsex.htm on March 6, 2016.

Centers for Disease Control and Prevention (2016c). *Marriage and Divorce*. Atlanta, GA. Retrieved from http://www.cdc.gov/nchs/fastats/marriage-divorce.htm on May 21, 2016.

Centers for Disease Control and Prevention (2016d). *Adult Obesity Facts*. Atlanta, GA. Retrieved from https://www.cdc.gov/obesity/data/adult.html on February 3, 2017.

Chung, Jean (2015). *Felony Disenfranchisement: A Primer*. Washington, DC: The Sentencing Project. Retrieved from http://www.sentencingproject. org/doc/publications/fd_Felony%20Disenfranchisement%20Primer.pdf on March 2, 2016.

Collins, Wanda Lott and Armon R. Perry (2015). "Black Men's Perspectives on the Role of the Black Church in Healthy Relationship Promotion and Family Stability." *Social Work & Christianity*, 42, 4, pp. 430–448.

Cooper, Hannah L. F., Samuel R. Friedman, Barbara Tempalski, and Risa Friedman (2007). "Residential Segregation and Injection Drug Use Prevalence among Black Adults in U.S. Metropolitan Areas." *American Journal of Public Health*, 97, 2, February, pp. 344–352.

Correa, Vanesa Estrada (2014). "Blueprint for the American Dream? A Critical Discourse Analysis of Presidential Remarks on Minority Homeownership." *Social Justice*, 40, 3, pp. 16–27.

Crosby, James W. and Jorge G. Varela (2014). "Preferences for Religious Help-Seeking: Racial and Gender Differences, Interfaith Intolerance, and Defensive Theology." *Mental Health, Religion & Culture*, 17, 2, pp. 196–209.

DeNavas-Walt, Carmen and Bernadette D. Proctor (2015). *Income and Poverty in the United States: 2014*. Washington, DC: Census Bureau, U.S. Department of Commerce. Retrieved from https://www.census.gov/content/dam/Census/library/publications/2015/demo/p60-252.pdf on December 1, 2015.

Department of Health and Human Services Press Office (2016). *20 Million People Have Gained Health Insurance Coverage Because of the Affordable Care Act, New Estimates Show*. Washington, DC, March 3. Retrieved from http://www.hhs.gov/about/news/2016/03/03/20-million-people-have-gained-health-insurance-coverage-because-affordable-care-act-new-estimates on May 13, 2016.

Department of Justice (2013a). "Attorney General Eric Holder Speaks at the 15th Annual National Action Network Convention." *Justice News*, April 4. Retrieved from http://www.justice.gov/iso/opa/ag/speeches/2013/ag-speech-130404.html on January 11, 2014.

Department of Justice (2013b). "Attorney General Eric Holder Delivers Remarks at the Congressional Black Caucus Gathering on Voting Rights." *Justice News*, September 20. Retrieved from https://www.justice.gov/opa/speech/attorney-general-eric-holder-delivers-remarks-congressional-black-caucus-gathering-voting on September 15, 2016.

Department of Justice (2014). *Attorney General Holder: Justice Dept. to Collect Data on Stops, Arrests as Part of Effort to Curb Racial Bias in Criminal Justice System*. Office of Public Affairs, Department of Justice, April 28. Retrieved from http://www.justice.gov/opa/pr/attorney-general-holder-justice-dept-collect-data-stops-arrests-part-effort-curb-racial-bias on December 30, 2015.

DeSilva, Sanjaya and Yuval Elmelech (2012). "Housing Inequality in the United States: Explaining the White-Minority Disparities in Homeownership." *Housing Studies*, 27, 1, pp. 1–26.

Divorce Statistics (2016). *Marriage and Divorces*. Retrieved from http://www. divorcestatistics.org/.

Drake, Bruce (2015). "Divide between Blacks and Whites on Police Runs Deep." *Pew Research Center*, April 28. Retrieved from http://www.pewresearch. org/fact-tank/2015/04/28/blacks-whites-police/ on May 15, 2016.

Du Bois, W. E. B. (1903). *The Negro Church in America*. Atlanta, GA: Atlanta University Press.

The Economist (2014). "Don't Shoot: America's Police Kill Too Many People. But Some Forces Are Showing How Smarter, Less Aggressive Policing Gets Results." December 13. Retrieved from http://www.economist. com/news/united-states/21636044-americas-police-kill-too-many-people-some-forces-are-showing-how-smarter-less on May 15, 2016.

Epperly, Jessica (2014). *UCLA Report Finds Changing U.S. Demographics Transform School Segregation Landscape 60 Years after Brown v Board of Education*. Los Angeles, CA: The Civil Rights Project. Retrieved from http://civilrightsproject. ucla.edu/news/press-releases/2014-press-releases/ucla-report-finds-changing-u.s.-demographics-transform-school-segregation-landscape-60-years-after-brown-v-board-of-education on March 4, 2016.

Federal Bureau of Investigation (2015a). *Crime in the United States, 2014*. Washington, DC: Department of Justice. Retrieved from https://www.fbi. gov/about-us/cjis/ucr/crime-in-the-u.s/2014/crime-in-the-u.s.-2014/tables/table-43 on December 3, 2015.

Federal Bureau of Investigation (2015b). *2014 Hate Crime Statistics*. Washington, DC: Department of Justice. Retrieved from https://www.fbi.gov/about-us/cjis/ucr/hate-crime/2014/tables/table-1 on January 23, 2016.

Federal Bureau of Investigation (2016). *Crime Statistics in the United States, 2011*. Retrieved from https://www.fbi.gov/about-us/cjis/ucr/crime-in-the-u.s/2011/crime-in-the-u.s.-2011/tables/expanded-homicide-data-table-6 on February 5, 2016.

Federico, Christopher M. and Samantha Luks (2005). "The Political Psychology of Race." *Political Psychology*, 26, 5, pp. 661–666.

Feierman, Jessica, Marsha Levick, and Ami Mody (2009). "The School-to-Prison Pipeline . . . and Back: Obstacles and Remedies for the Re-Enrollment of Adjudicated Youth." *New York Law School Law Review*, 54, 4, December, pp. 1115–1129.

Ferré, Cynthia, Arden Handler, Jason Hsia, Wanda Barfield, and James W. Collins Jr. (2011). "Changing Trends in Low Birth Weight Rates among Non-Hispanic Black Infants in the United States, 1991–2004." *Maternal & Child Health Journal*, 15, 1, pp. 29–41.

File, Thom (2013). *The Diversifying Electorate—Voting Rates by Race and Hispanic Origin in 2012 (and Other Recent Elections)*. Washington, DC: United States Census Bureau, U.S. Department of Commerce, May. Retrieved from https://www.census.gov/prod/2013pubs/p20-568.pdf on February 5, 2016.

File, Thom and Sarah Crissey (2012). *Voting and Registration in the Election of November 2008: Population Characteristics*. Washington, DC: U.S. Census

Bureau, July. Retrieved from http://www.census.gov/prod/2010pubs/p20-562.pdf on December 1, 2015.Flannery, Mary Ellen (2015). "The School-to-Prison Pipeline: Time to Shut It Down." *neaToday*, January 5. Retrieved from http://neatoday.org/2015/01/05/school-prison-pipeline-time-shut/ on May 21, 2016.

Ford, Donna Y. and Janet E. Helms (2012) "Overview and Introduction: Testing and Assessing African Americans: 'Unbiased' Tests are Still Unfair." *Journal of Negro Education*, 81, 3, Summer, pp. 186–189.

Frazier, Edward Franklin (1974). *The Negro Church in America*. New York: Schocken Publishing.

Gamboa, Suzanne (2013). "Housing Discrimination Makes Search More Costly For Minorities: Study." *Huffington Post*, June 11. Retrieved from http://www.huffingtonpost.com/2013/06/11/housing-discrimination-minorities-race-housing-market_n_3423576.html on June 29, 2013.

Gerstel, Naomi (2011). "Rethinking Families and Community: The Color, Class, and Centrality of Extended Kim Ties." *Sociological Forum*, 26, 1, March, pp. 1–20.

Gibson-Davis, Christina (2011). "Mothers but Not Wives: The Increasing Lag between Nonmarital Births and Marriage." *Journal of Marriage & Family*, 73, 1, pp. 264–278.

Ginder, Scott A., Janice E. Kelly-Reid, and Farrah B. Mann (2014). *Enrollment in Postsecondary Institutions, Fall 2013; Financial Statistics, Fiscal Year 2013; and Employees in Postsecondary Institutions, Fall 2013*. National Center for Education Statistics, U.S. Department of Education (http://nces.ed.gov/pubs2015/2015012.pdf).

Goldstein, Joseph (2013). "Judge Rejects New York's Stop-and-Frisk Policy." *The New York Times*, August 12. Retrieved from http://www.nytimes.com/2013/08/13/nyregion/stop-and-frisk-practice-violated-rights-judge-rules.html?pagewanted=all&_r=0 on September 21, 2013.

González, Thalia (2012). "Keeping Kids in Schools: Restorative Justice, Punitive Discipline, and the School to Prison Pipeline." *Journal of Law & Education*, 41, 2, April, pp. 281–335.

Goyette, Braden and Alissa Scheller (2014). "15 Charts that Prove We're Far from Post-Racial." *Huffington Post*, July 2. Retrieved from http://www.huffingtonpost.com/2014/07/02/civil-rights-act-anniversary-racism-charts_n_5521104.html on May 20, 2016.

Graham, David A. (2015). "The Shockingly Familiar Killing of Walter Scott." *The Atlantic*, April 8. Retrieved from http://www.theatlantic.com/national/archive/2015/04/the-shockingly-familiar-killing-of-walter-scott/390006/ on May 15, 2016.

Grohol, John M. (2013). "College Fails to Protect African-American Women From Divorce." *PsychCentral*. March 10. Retrieved from http://psychcentral.com/news/2013/03/10/college-fails-to-protect-african-american-women-from-divorce/52397.html on November 16, 2015.

Gruber, Enid and Joel W. Grube (2000) "Adolescent Sexuality and the Media." *Western Journal of Medicine*, 172, 3, March, pp. 210–214.

Haimerl, Amy (2015). "The Fastest-Growing Group of Entrepreneurs in America." *Fortune*, June 29. Retrieved from http://fortune.com/2015/06/29/black-women-entrepreneurs/ on April 10, 2016.

Hamilton, Brady E., Joyce A. Martin, Michelle J. K. Osterman, Sally C. Curtin, and T. J. Mathews (2015). *Births: Final Data for 2014 (National Vital Statistics Report)*. Volume 64, Number 12, Hyattsville, MD: National Center for Health Statistics. Retrieved from http://www.cdc.gov/nchs/data/nvsr/nvsr64/nvsr64_12.pdf on February 25, 2016.

Heslin, Peter A., Myrtle P. Bell, and Pinar O. Fletcher (2012). "The Devil Without and Within: A Conceptual Model of Social Cognitive Processes Whereby Discrimination Leads Stigmatized Minorities to Become Discouraged Workers." *Journal of Organizational Behavior*, 33, 6, August, pp. 840–862.

Holley, Lynn C. and Russell K. Van Vleet (2006). "Racism and Classism in the Youth Justice System: Perspectives of Youth and Staff." *Journal of Poverty*, 10, 1, March, pp. 45–67.

Hovick, Shelly R., Vicki S. Freimuth, Ashani Johnson-Turbes, and Doryn D. Chervin (2011). "Multiple Health Risk Perception and Information Processing among African Americans and Whites Living in Poverty." *Risk Analysis: An Official Publication of the Society for Risk Analysis*, 31, 11, November, pp. 1789–1799.

Huffington Post (2013). *Stop and Frisk Leads to Mistrust of NYPD and Refusal to Cooperate with Cops, According to Study*. New York. Retrieved from http://www.huffingtonpost.com/2013/09/19/stop-and-frisk-nypd-mistrust_n_3955175.html on January 1, 2016.

Iloh, Constance and Ivory A. Toldson (2013). "Black Students in 21st Century Higher Education: A Closer Look at For-Profit and Community Colleges." *The Journal of Negro Education*, 82, 3, pp. 205–212.

Ingraham, Christopher (2015). "The Ugly Truth about Hate Crimes—in 5 Charts and Maps." *The Washington Post*, June 18. Retrieved from https://www.washingtonpost.com/news/wonk/wp/2015/06/18/5-charts-show-the-stubborn-persistence-of-american-hate-crime/ on May 21, 2016.

Johnson, Deborah J. (2000). "Disentangling Poverty and Race." *Applied Developmental Science*, 4, 1, September, pp. 455–467.

Jones, Jeffrey M. (2015). "In U.S., Confidence in Police Lowest in 22 Years." *Gallup,* June 19. Retrieved from http://www.gallup.com/poll/183704/confidence-police-lowest-years.aspx on May 15, 2016.

Kaeble, Danielle, Lauren Glaze, Anastasios Tsoutis, and Todd Minton (2016). *Correctional Populations in the United States, 2014*. Washington, DC: Bureau of Justice Statistics, U.S. Department of Justice. Retrieved from http://www.bjs.gov/content/pub/pdf/cpus14.pdf on February 24, 2016.

Kena, Grace, Lauren Musu-Gillette, Xiaolei Wang, Amy Rathbun, Jijun Zhang, Sidney Wilkinson-Flicker, Amy Barmer, and Erin Dunlop Velez (2015).

The Condition of Education 2015. Washington, DC: U.S. Department of Education, National Center for Education Statistics. Retrieved from http://nces.ed.gov/pubs2015/2015144.pdf on April 24, 2016.

Kidd, Quentin, Herman Diggs, Mehreen Farooq, and Megan Murray (2007). "Black Voters, Black Candidates, and Social Issues: Does Party Identification Matter?" *Social Science Quarterly (Wiley-Blackwell)*, 88, 1, pp. 165–176.

Kirby, James B. and Toshiko Kaneda (2010). "Unhealthy and Uninsured: Exploring Racial Differences in Health and Health Insurance Coverage Using a Life Table Approach." *Demography*, 47, 4, November, pp. 1035–1051.

Kirwan Institute for the Study of Race and Ethnicity (2014). *Racial Disproportionality in School Discipline: Implicit Bias Is Heavily Implicated*. Columbus: The Ohio State University, February. Retrieved from http://kirwaninstitute.osu.edu/wp-content/uploads/2014/02/racial-disproportionality-schools-02.pdf on March 1, 2016.

Kochanek, Kenneth D., Jiaquan Xu, Sherry L. Murphy, Arialdi M. Miniño, and Hsiang-Ching Kung (2011). "Deaths: Final Data for 2009." *National Vital Statistics Reports*, 60, 3, December 29.

Kohli, Sonali (2014). "Modern-Day Segregation in Public Schools: The Department of Education Has Branded 'Tracking'—Designating Students for Separate Educational Paths Based on Their Academic Performance—as a Modern Day Form of Segregation." *The Atlantic*, November 18. Retrieved from http://www.theatlantic.com/education/archive/2014/11/modern-day-segregation-in-public-schools/382846/ on March 5, 2016.

Kosanovich, Karen and Eleni Theodossiou Sherman (2015). *Trends in Long-Term Unemployment*. Washington, DC: U.S. Bureau of Labor Statistics. Retrieved from http://www.bls.gov/spotlight/2015/long-term-unemployment/pdf/long-term-unemployment.pdf on January 2, 2016.

Krouse, William J. (2012). *Gun Control Legislation*. Washington, DC: Congressional Research Service. Retrieved from http://www.fas.org/sgp/crs/misc/RL32842.pdf on October 25, 2015.

Langton, Lynn and Michael Planty (2010). *Hate Crime, 2003–2009*. Washington, DC: Bureau of Justice Statistics.

Lee, Jolie (2014). "Still Apart: Map Shows States with Most-Segregated Schools." *USA Today*, May 15. Retrieved from http://www.usatoday.com/story/news/nation-now/2014/05/15/school-segregation-civil-rights-project/9115823/ on March 4, 2016.

Littlefield, Marci Bounds (2005). "The Black Church and Community Development and Self-Help: The Next Phase of Social Equality." *Western Journal of Black Studies*, 29, 4, December, pp. 687–693.

Lofquist, Daphne, Terry Lugaila, Martin O'Connell, and Sarah Feliz (2012). *Household and Families: 2010 (2010 Census Briefs)*. Washington, DC: U.S. Census Bureau. Retrieved from http://www.census.gov/prod/cen2010/briefs/c2010br-14.pdf on February 26, 2016.

Lopez, Mark Hugo and Richard Fry (2013). "Among Recent High School Grads, Hispanic College Enrollment Rate Surpasses That of Whites." *Pew Research Center*. Retrieved from http://www.pewresearch.org/fact-tank/2013/09/04/hispanic-college-enrollment-rate-surpasses-whites-for-the-first-time/ on February 27, 2016.

Mangum, Maurice (2013). "The Racial Underpinnings of Party Identification and Political Ideology." *Social Science Quarterly (Wiley-Blackwell)*, 94, 5, pp. 1222–1244.

Manning, Jennifer E. (2015). *Membership of the 114th Congress: A Profile*. Washington, DC: Congressional Research Service. Retrieved from https://www.fas.org/sgp/crs/misc/R43869.pdf on March 6, 2016.

Martin, Joyce, Brady E. Hamilton, Stephanie J. Ventura, Michelle J. K. Osterman, Elizabeth C. Wilson, and T. J. Mathews (2012). "Births: Final Data for 2010." *National Vital Statistics Reports*, 61, 1, August. Retrieved from http://www.cdc.gov/nchs/data/nvsr/nvsr61/nvsr61_01.pdf on October 7, 2012.

Martin, Monica J., Bill McCarthy, Rand D. Conger, Frederick X. Gibbons, Ronald Simons, Carolyn Cutrona, and Gene H. Brody (2011). "The Enduring Significance of Racism: Discrimination and Delinquency among Black American Youth." *Journal of Research On Adolescence (Wiley-Blackwell)*, 21, 3, pp. 662–676.

Martinez, Gladys M., Casey E. Copen, and Joyce C. Abma (2011). *Teenagers in the United States: Sexual Activity, Contraceptive Use, and Childbearing, 2006–2010 National Survey of Family Growth (Vital and Health Statistics, Series 23, Number 31*. Hyattsville, MD: National Center for Health Statistics.

McCallister, Doreen (2013). "North Carolina Governor Signs Controversial Voter ID Bill." *NPR*, August 13. Retrieved from http://www.npr.org/blogs/thetwo-way/2013/08/13/211537833/n-c-gop-gov-pat-mccrory-signs-voter-id-bill on September 28, 2013.

McDaniel, Anne, Thomas A. DiPrete, Claudia Buchmann, and Uri Shwed (2011). "The Black Gender Gap in Educational Attainment: Historical Trends and Racial Comparisons." *Demography*, 48, 3, pp. 889–914.

Miller, Byron and John Taylor (2012). "Racial and Socioeconomic Status Differences in Depressive Symptoms among Black and White Youth: An Examination of the Mediating Effects of Family Structure, Stress and Support." *Journal of Youth & Adolescence*, 41, 4, April, pp. 426–437.

Mozaffarian D., E. J. Benjamin, A. S. Go, D. K. Arnett, Blaha M. J. Blaha, M. Cushman, S. de Ferranti, J.-P. Després, H. J. Fullerton, V. J. Howard, M. D. Huffman, S. E. Judd, B. M. Kissela, D. T. Lackland, J. H. Lichtman, L. D. Lisabeth, S. Liu, R. H. Mackey, D. B. Matchar, D. K. McGuire, E. R. Mohler III, C. S. Moy, P. Muntner, M. E. Mussolino, K. Nasir, R. W. Neumar, G. Nichol, L. Palaniappan, D. K. Pandey, M. J. Reeves, C. J. Rodriguez, P. D. Sorlie, J. Stein, A. Towfighi, T. N. Turan, S. S. Virani, J. Z. Willey, D. Woo, R. W. Yeh, M. B. Turner; on behalf of the American

Heart Association Statistics Committee and Stroke Statistics Subcommittee. *Heart Disease and Stroke Statistics—2015 Update: A Report from the American Heart Association.* Retrieved from https://www.heart.org/idc/groups/ahamah-public/@wcm/@sop/@smd/documents/downloadable/ucm_470704.pdf on March 6, 2016.

Mozaffarian D., V. L. Roger, E. J. Benjamin, J. D. Berry, W. B. Borden, D. M. Bravata, S. Dai, E. S. Ford, C. S. Fox, S. Franco, H. J. Fullerton, C. Gillespie, S. M. Hailpern, J. A. Heit, V. J. Howard, M. D. Huffman, B. M. Kissela, S. J. Kittner, D. T. Lackland, J. H. Lichtman, L. D. Lisabeth, D. Magid, G. M. Marcus, A. Marelli, D. B. Matchar, D. K. McGuire, E. R. Mohler, C. S. Moy, M. E. Mussolino, G. Nichol, N. P. Paynter, P. J. Schreiner, P. D. Sorlie, J. Stein, T. N. Turan, S. S. Virani, N. D. Wong, D. Woo, M. B. Turner; on behalf of the American Heart Association Statistics Committee and Stroke Statistics Subcommittee (2013). "Heart Disease and Stroke Statistics—2013 Update: A Report from the American Heart Association." *Circulation,* 127, pp. e6–e245. Retrieved from https://www.heart.org/idc/groups/heart-public/@wcm/@sop/@smd/documents/downloadable/ucm_319568.pdf on March 6, 2016.

NAACP Legal Defense Fund (2013). *Education: School to Prison Pipeline.* New York. Retrieved from http://www.naacpldf.org/case/school-prison-pipeline on August 31, 2015.

National Campaign to Prevent Teen Pregnancy (2011). *Why It Matters: Teen Pregnancy and Violence.* Washington, DC. Retrieved from http://www.thenationalcampaign.org/why-it-matters/pdf/violence.pdf on June 2, 2012.

National Center for Juvenile Justice (2015). *Juvenile Arrest Rates by Offense, Sex, and Race.* December 13. Retrieved from http://www.ojjdp.gov/ojstatbb/crime/excel/JAR_2014.xls. Also see http://www.ojjdp.gov/ojstatbb/crime/JAR_Display.asp?ID=qa05261.

National Conference of State Legislatures (2016a). *Felon Voting Rights.* Washington, DC. Retrieved from http://www.ncsl.org/research/elections-and-campaigns/felon-voting-rights.aspx on February 28, 2016.

National Conference of State Legislatures (2016b). *Voter Identification Requirements/Voter ID Laws.* Retrieved from http://www.ncsl.org/research/elections-and-campaigns/voter-id.aspx on April 30, 2016.National Center for Education Statistics (2016). *IPEDS Data Collection System 2016–2017 Survey Materials: Glossary.* Retrieved from https://surveys.nces.ed.gov/ipeds/Downloads/Forms/IPEDSGlossary.pdf on December 1, 2016.

National Diabetes Education Program (2011). *The Diabetes Epidemic among African Americans.* January. Atlanta, GA: Centers for Disease Control and Prevention. Retrieved from http://ndep.nih.gov/media/fs_africanam.pdf on July 4, 2012.

National Institute of Diabetes and Digestive and Kidney Diseases (2016). *Risk Factors for Type 2 Diabetes.* Retrieved from https://www.niddk.nih.gov/health-information/health-communication-programs/ndep/am-i-at-risk/diabetes-risk-factors/Pages/diabetesriskfactors.aspx on February 6, 2017.

Neblett, Enrique W., Jr., Kira Hudson Banks, Shauna M. Cooper, and Ciara Smalls-Glover (2013). "Racial identity mediates the association between ethnic-racial socialization and depressive symptoms." *Cultural Diversity and Ethnic Minority Psychology*, 19, 2, April, pp. 200–207.

Nellis, Ashley (2012). *The Lives of Juvenile Lifers: Findings from a National Survey*. Washington, DC: The Sentencing Project.

Neubert, Amy Patterson (2012). "Study: Unkindness linked to alcohol, drug abuse in black populations." *Purdue News*, November 14. Retrieved from http://www.purdue.edu/newsroom/releases/2012/Q4/study-unkindness-linked-to-alcohol,-drug-abuse-in-black-populations.html on October 20, 2015.

Newport, Frank (2011). "Religion and Party ID Strongly Linked among Whites, Not Blacks." *Gallup*. Retrieved from http://www.gallup.com/poll/148361/Religion-Party-Strongly-Linked-Among-Whites-Not-Blacks.aspx on March 12, 2016.

Newport, Frank (2013a). "Democrats Racially Diverse: Republicans Mostly White." *Gallup,* February 8. Retrieved from http://www.gallup.com/poll/160373/democrats-racially-diverse-republicans-mostly-white.aspx on February 6, 2016.

Newport, Frank (2013b). "In U.S., 87% Approve of Black-White Marriage, vs. 4% in 1958." *Gallup*. Retrieved from http://www.gallup.com/poll/163697/approve-marriage-blacks-whites.aspx on February 26, 2016.

Newport, Frank (2014). "Three-Quarters of American Identify as Christian." *Gallup*. Retrieved from http://www.gallup.com/poll/180347/three-quarters-americans-identify-christian.aspx on March 12, 2016.

Nicholson-Crotty, Sean, Zachary Birchmeier, and David Valentine (2009). "Exploring the Impact of School Discipline on Racial Disproportion in the Juvenile Justice System." *Social Science Quarterly*, 90, 4, December, pp. 1003–1018.

Obama, Barack (2015). *Remarks by the President on Community Policing: Salvation Army Ray and Joan Kroc Corps Community Center, Camden, New Jersey*. Washington, DC: The White House, Office of the Press Secretary, May 18. Retrieved from https://www.whitehouse.gov/the-press-office/2015/05/18/remarks-president-community-policing on May 15, 2016.

Ochs, Holona Leanne (2006). " 'Colorblind' Policy in Black and White: Racial Consequences of Disenfranchisement Policy." *Policy Studies Journal*, 34, 1, pp. 81–93.

Office of Adolescent Health (2016). *Trends in Teen Pregnancy and Childbearing*. Rockville, MD: U.S. Department of Health and Human Services.

Office of the Deputy Assistant Secretary of Defense (Military Community and Family Policy) (2015). *2014 Demographics Profile of the Military Community*. Washington, DC: Department of Defense. Retrieved from http://download.militaryonesource.mil/12038/MOS/Reports/2014-Demographics-Report.pdf on February 23, 2016.

Ogden, Cynthia L., Margaret D. Carroll, Brian K. Kit, and Katherine M. Flegal (2014). "Prevalence of Childhood and Adult Obesity in the United States,

2011–2012." *The Journal of the American Medical Association,* 311, 8, February, pp. 806–814.

The Opportunity Agenda (2012). *Public Opinion and Discourse on the Intersection of Lesbian, Gay, Bi-sexual, and Transgender (LGBT) Issues and Race.* New York: The Opportunity Agenda.

Orfield, Gary, Erica Frankenberg, Jongyeon Ee, and John Kuscera (2014). *Brown at 60: Great Progress, a Long Retreat and an Uncertain Future.* Los Angeles, CA: The Civil Rights Project.

Pearl, Robert (2015). "Why Health Care Is Different If You're Black, Latino or Poor." *Forbes,* March 5. Retrieved from http://www.forbes.com/sites/robertpearl/2015/03/05/healthcare-black-latino-poor/#6ee52cdc1ca7 on June 1, 2016.

Perry, Armon R. and Mikia Bright (2012). "African American Fathers and Incarceration: Paternal Involvement and Child Outcomes." *Social Work in Public Health,* 27, pp. 187–203.

Perry, Samuel L. (2013). "Religion and Whites' Attitudes toward Interracial Marriage with African Americans, Asians, and Latinos." *Journal for the Scientific Study of Religion,* 52, 2, pp. 425–442.

Pew Research Center (2013). *Intermarriage on the Rise in the U.S.* Washington, DC. Retrieved from http://www.pewresearch.org/daily-number/intermarriage-on-the-rise-in-the-u-s/ on March 1, 2016.

Pew Research Center 2014 Surveys: A Deep Dive into Party Affiliation (Sharp Differences by Race, Gender, Generation and Education). Washington, DC: Pew Research Center. Retrieved from http://www.people-press.org/2015/04/07/a-deep-dive-into-party-affiliation/ and http://www.people-press.org/2015/04/07/2014-party-identification-detailed-tables/ on February 7, 2016.

Pinckney, Harrison P., IV, Corlis Outley, Jamilia J. Blake, and Brandy Kelly (2011). "Promoting Positive Youth Development of Black Youth: A Rites of Passage Framework." *Journal of Park and Recreation Administration,* 29, 1, March, pp. 98–112.

Press Office (2014). *U.S. Department of Education Announces Resolution of South Orange-Maplewood, N.J., School District Civil Rights Investigation: Black Students to Be Afforded Equal Access to Advanced, Higher-Level Learning Opportunities.* Washington, DC: U.S. Department of Education Office of Civil Rights, October 28. Retrieved from https://www.ed.gov/news/press-releases/us-department-education-announces-resolution-south-orange-maplewood-nj-school-di on March 5, 2016.

Press Office (2014a). *Expansive Survey of America's Public Schools Reveals Troubling Racial Disparities: Lack of Access to Pre-School, Greater Suspensions Cited.* Washington, DC: U.S. Department of Education Office of Civil Rights, March 21. Retrieved from http://www.ed.gov/news/press-releases/expansive-survey-americas-public-schools-reveals-troubling-racial-disparities on March 5, 2016.

Qian, Zhenchao and Daniel T. Lichter (2011). "Changing Patterns of Interracial Marriage in a Multiracial Society." *Journal of Marriage & Family*, 73, 5, pp. 1065–1084.

Quigley, Bill (2010). *Fourteen Examples of Racism in the Criminal Justice System*. July 26. Retrieved from http://www.huffingtonpost.com/bill-quigley/fourteen-examples-of-raci_b_658947.html on September 2, 2013.

Raley, R. Kelly, Megan M. Sweeney, and Danielle Wondra (2015). "The Growing Racial and Ethnic Divide in U.S. Marriage Patterns." *Future of Children*, 25, 2, Fall, pp. 89–109.

Read, Jen'nan G. and David E. Eagle (2011). "Intersecting Identities as a Source of Religious Incongruence." *Journal for the Scientific Study of Religion*, 50, 1, pp. 116–132.

Redfield, Sarah E. and Jason P. Nance (2016). *School-to-Prison Pipeline: Preliminary Report*. The School-to-Prison Pipeline Task Force (Coalition on Racial and Ethnic Justice, Criminal Justice Section and Council for Racial & Ethnic Diversity in the Educational Pipeline). Retrieved from http://jjie.org/files/2016/02/School-to-Prison-Pipeline-Preliminary-Report-Complete-Final.pdf on May 20, 2016.

Reid, Karl W. (2013). "Understanding the Relationships among Racial Identity, Self-Efficacy, Institutional Integration and Academic Achievement of Black Males Attending Research Universities." *Journal of Negro Education*, 82, 1, pp. 75–93.

Reid, Megan, Andrew Golub, and Peter Vazan (2014). "Cohabitating Partners and Domestic Labor in Low-Income Black Families." *Journal of African American Studies*, 18, 4, pp. 470–484.

Rizzo, Christie J., Heather L. Hunter, Delia L. Lang, Cassandra Oliveira, Geri Donenberg, Ralph J. DiClemente, and Larry K. Brown (2012). "Dating Violence Victimization and Unprotected Sex Acts among Adolescents in Mental Health Treatment." *Journal of Child & Family Studies*, 21, 5, October, pp. 825–832.

Ross Cody T. (2015). "A Multi-Level Bayesian Analysis of Racial Bias in Police Shootings at the County-Level in the United States, 2011–2014." *PLoS ONE*, 10, 11, pp. 1–34.

Rothstein, Richard (2013). *For Public Schools, Segregation Then, Segregation Since: Education and the Unfinished March*. Washington, DC: Economic Policy Institute, August 27.

Sauter, Michael B., Douglas A. McIntyre, Ashley C. Allen, Alexander E. M. Hess, Lisa Nelson, and Samuel Wigley (2012). "The Most Dangerous Cities in America." *24/7 Wall St.*, June 11. Retrieved from http://247wallst.com/2012/06/11/the-most-dangerous-cities-in-america-2/#ixzz2ALnGcAV6 on October 25, 2015.

Schorling, John B. and J. Terry Saunders (2000). "Is 'Sugar" the Same as Diabetes?: A Community-Based Study among Rural African-Americans." *Diabetes Care*, 23, 2, March, pp. 330–334.

Scott, Stanley (2010). "The School-to-Prison Pipeline Is One of the Most Important Civil Rights Challenges Facing Our Nation Today." *The Florida
Times-Union Jacksonville.com*, February 4. Retrieved from http://jackson
ville.com/interact/blog/stanley_scott/2010-02-04/the_school_to_prison_
pipeline_is_one_of_the_most_important_ci?page=1# on June 1, 2015.

Sealey-Ruiz, Yolanda (2011). "Dismantling the School-to-Prison Pipeline
Through Racial Literacy Development in Teacher Education." *Journal of
Curriculum & Pedagogy*, 8, 2, December, pp. 116–120.

The Sentencing Project (2013). *Report of The Sentencing Project to the United
Nations Human Rights Committee Regarding Racial Disparities in the United
States Criminal Justice System*. Washington, DC, August. Retrieved from
http://sentencingproject.org/doc/publications/rd_ICCPR%20Race%20
and%20Justice%20Shadow%20Report.pdf on December 30, 2015.

The Sentencing Project (2016). *Felony Disenfranchisement*. Washington, DC.
Retrieved from http://www.sentencingproject.org/template/page.cfm?id=133
on February 28, 2016.

Smith, Jessica C. and Carla Medalia (2015). *Health Insurance Coverage in the
United States: 2014*. Washington, DC: U.S. Bureau of Census, September.
Retrieved from https://www.census.gov/content/dam/Census/library/publi
cations/2015/demo/p60-253.pdf on May 13, 2016.

Smith, Peter and Leslie Parrish (2014). *Do Students of Color Profit from For-Profit
College? Poor Outcomes and High Debt Hamper Attendees' Futures*. Washington, DC: Center for Responsible Lending.

Somers, Cheryl L. and Joshua J. Tynan (2006). "Consumption of Sexual Dialogue
and Content on Television and Adolescent Sexual Outcomes: Multiethnic
Findings." *Adolescence*, 41, 161, Spring, pp. 15–38.

Starkey, Brando Simeo (2012). "A Failure of the Fourth Amendment & Equal
Protection's Promise: How the Equal Protection Clause Can Change Discriminatory Stop and Frisk Policies." *Michigan Journal of Race & Law*, 18,
1, September, pp. 131–187.

Stock, M. L., F. X. Gibbons, M. Gerrard, A. E. Houlihan, C. Weng, F. O. Lorenz,
and R. L. Simons (2013). "Racial Identification, Racial Composition, and
Substance Use Vulnerability among African American Adolescents and
Young Adults." *Health Psychology*, 32, pp. 237–247.

Stossel, John and Kristina Kendall (2006). "The Impact of Your Name." *ABC
News*, September 20. Retrieved from http://abcnews.go.com/2020/story?
id=2463266 on December 14, 2016.

Substance Abuse and Mental Health Services Administration (2014). *Results
from the 2013 National Survey on Drug Use and Health: Summary of
National Findings, NSDUH Series H-48, HHS Publication No. (SMA)
14–4863*. Rockville, MD: Substance Abuse and Mental Health Services
Administration. Retrieved from http://www.samhsa.gov/data/sites/default/
files/NSDUHresultsPDFWHTML2013/Web/NSDUHresults2013.pdf   on
February 26, 2016.

Sweeney, Megan M. and Julie A. Phillips (2004). "Understanding Racial Differences in Marital Disruption: Recent Trends and Explanations." *Journal of Marriage & Family*, 66, 3, pp. 639–650.

Taylor, Robert J. and Linda M. Chatters (2010). "Importance of Religion and Spirituality in the Lives of African Americans, Caribbean Blacks and Non-Hispanic Whites." *Journal of Negro Education*, 79, 3, pp. 280–294.

Uggen, Christopher, Sarah Shannon, and Jeff Manza (2012). *State-Level Estimates of Felon Disenfranchisement in the United States, 2010*. Washington, DC: The Sentencing Project.

U.S. Bureau of the Census (2011). *Census Bureau Reports the Number of Black-Owned Businesses Increased at Triple the National Rate*. Washington, DC. Retrieved from https://www.census.gov/newsroom/releases/archives/business_ownership/cb11-24.html on April 10, 2016.

U.S. Bureau of the Census (2015a). *Current Population Survey, Annual Social and Economic Supplements*. Washington, DC.

U.S. Bureau of the Census (2015b). *Los Angeles County a Microcosm of Nation's Diverse Collection of Business Owners, Census Bureau Reports*. Washington, DC. Retrieved from https://www.census.gov/newsroom/press-releases/2015/cb15-209.html on February 6, 2017.

U.S. Department of Justice, Civil Rights Division (2017). *Recent Accomplishments of the Housing and Civil Enforcement Section*. Retrieved from https://www.justice.gov/crt/recent-accomplishments-housing-and-civil-enforcement-section on February 6, 2017.

Wang, Wendy (2015). *Interracial Marriage: Who Is "Marrying Out"?* Washington, DC: Pew Research Center. Retrieved from http://www.pewresearch.org/fact-tank/2015/06/12/interracial-marriage-who-is-marrying-out/ on March 1, 2016.

Walsenmann, Katrina and Bethany A. Bell (2010). "Integrated Schools, Segregated Curriculum: Effects of Within-School Segregation on Adolescent Health Behaviors and Educational Aspirations." *American Journal of Public Health*, 100, 9, pp. 1687–1695.

Wentling, Rose Mary and Consuelo Luisa Waight (1999). "Barriers that Hinder the Successful Transition of Minority Youth into the Workplace." *Journal of Vocational Education Research*, 24, 4, 1999, pp. 165–183.

Whitaker, Morgan (2013). "Obama Admin. 'Deeply Disappointed' by Voting Rights Ruling, but not Backing Down." *MSNBC*, June 25. Retrieved from http://tv.msnbc.com/2013/06/25/obama-admin-deeply-disappointed-by-voting-rights-ruling-but-not-backing-down/ on June 27, 2013.

The White House (2013). *Statement by the President on the Supreme Court Ruling on Shelby County v. Holder*. Washington, DC. Retrieved from https://obamawhitehouse.archives.gov/the-press-office/2013/06/25/statement-president-supreme-court-ruling-shelby-county-v-holder on September 1, 2016.

The White House (2015a). *President Obama: "Our Criminal Justice System Isn't as Smart as It Should Be."* Washington, DC. Retrieved from https://

www.whitehouse.gov/blog/2015/07/15/president-obama-our-crimina
l-justice-system-isnt-smart-it-should-be on May 21, 2016.

The White House (2015b). *Remarks by the President on Community Policing*. Washington, DC. Retrieved from https://obamawhitehouse.archives.gov/the-press-office/2015/05/18/remarks-president-community-policing on May 22, 2016.

Wilson, Helen W., Briana A. Woods, and Erin Emerson, and Geri R. Donenberg (2012). "Patterns of Violence Exposure and Sexual Risk in Low-Income, Urban African American Girls." *Psychology of Violence*, 2, 2, April, pp. 194–207.

Wing, Nick (2015). "Black America Is Just 72 % Equal to White America. In Some Areas, the Inequality Is Worse than That." *Huffington Post*, March 25. Retrieved from http://www.huffingtonpost.com/2015/03/25/state-of-black-america-infographic_n_6905594.html on May 15, 2016.

Wodtke, Geoffrey T. (2012). "The Impact of Education on Intergroup Attitudes: A Multiracial Analysis." *Social Psychology Quarterly*, 75, 1, pp. 80–106.

Workneh, Lilly (2016). "Black Women-Owned Businesses Skyrocket by 322 % in Less than 20 Years." *Huffington Post*, February 1. Retrieved from http://www.huffingtonpost.com/2015/07/02/black-women-fastest-growi_n_7711078.html on April 10, 2016.

The World Bank (2016). *Adolescent Fertility Rate (Births per 1,000 Women Ages 15–19)*. Washington, DC. Retrieved from http://data.worldbank.org/indicator/SP.ADO.TFRT/countries?display=default.

Wu, Li-Tzy, George E. Woody, Chongming Yang, Jeng-Jong Pan, and Dan G. Blazer (2011). "Racial/Ethnic Variations in Substance-Related Disorders among Adolescents in the United States." *Archives of General Psychiatry*, 68, 11, pp. 1176–1185.

Zanskas, Stephen A., Daniel C. Lustig, and Terry T. Ishitani (2011). "Perceived Barriers to Employment Success: Are There Differences between European American and African American VR Consumers?" *Rehabilitation Research, Policy & Education*, 25, 3/4, pp. 127–134.

Zimmerman, Gregory M. and Steven F. Messner (2013). "Individual, Family Background, and Contextual Explanations of Racial and Ethnic Disparities in Youths' Exposure to Violence." *American Journal of Public Health*, 103, 3, pp. 435–442.

Index

Note: Page numbers in *italics* followed by *t* indicate tables.

Achievement in education, 2–6, *3t, 5t*
Achievement tests, 12
Adoption, 126
Advancement Project report, 19
Affordable Care Act (2010), 39
Alcohol abuse. *See* Substance abuse
Allen, Viviette L., 144
American Civil Liberties Union, 17, 59
American Community Survey (ACS), 109–10
American Fact Finder (AFF), 109–10
American Sociological Association, 64
Amurao, Carla, 16
Arizona v. Johnson (2009), 65
Arrest-related deaths, 76–77, *77t*
Arrests and referral to law enforcement, 21
Aull, Elbert, 23
Ayanian, John Z., 39

Bell, Bethany, 10
Bell, Myrtle P., 85
Bertrand, Marianne, 84–85
Bias crimes. *See* Hate crimes
Birchmeier, Zachary, 68
Birth control, 135
Birthrates, 122, *123t*, 131–36, *132t, 133t*
Black media, homosexuality and, 126

Black-on-black crime, 70
Bloomberg, Michael R., 67
Board of Education of Oklahoma City Public Schools v. Dowell (1991), 9–10
Body cameras, 65–66
Body mass index (BMI), 42
Breslow, Jason, 9
Bright, Mikia, 19
Brown at 60: Great Progress, a Long Retreat and an Uncertain Future (Civil Rights Project), 8
Brown v. Board of Education of Topeka, Kansas (1954), 6, 11
Bureau of Justice Statistics reports, 76–77
Bureau of Labor Statistics, 81
Burge, Jon, 76
Busing programs, 6–7, 10
Buzi, Ruth, 139

Cardiovascular disease (CVD). *See* Heart disease
Carrington v. Rash (1965), 101–2
Case law: *Arizona v. Johnson* (2009), 65; *Board of Education of Oklahoma City Public Schools v. Dowell* (1991), 9–10; *Brown v. Board of Education of Topeka, Kansas* (1954), 6, 11; *Carrington v. Rash*

(1965), 101–2; *Loving v. Virginia* (1967), 124; *Milliken v. Bradley* (1974), 7; *Shelby County, Alabama v. Holder* (2013), 104, 105; *Terry v. Ohio* (1968), 65
Causes of death, 37, *38t*, 48
Center for Responsible Lending report, 29
Chatters, Linda M., 155
Childbearing, marriage and, 122
Child custody, 126
Church attendance, 156
Civic behaviors, religion and, 154
Civil Rights Act (1964), 6, 88, 98, 124
Civil Rights Project, 8
Cohabitation agreements, 126
Cohabitation rates, 112
College degree attainment, marriage and, 120–22
College enrollment, 24–33, 30, *31t*
Collins, Robert, 9
Collins, Wanda Lott, 154
Congress, minority representation in, 95
Consanguinity, defined, 111
Contraception use, 135, 145
Cooper, Hannah L. F., 54
Correa, Vanesa Estrada, 86
Court oversight, school segregation and, 9–10, 11
Crime and criminal justice: data variables overview, 57–58; hate crimes, 72–74, *73t*, *75t*; police shootings, 74–78, *77t*; racial profiling, 61–69, *62t*; U.S. prison population and arrests, 58–61, *60t*; violent crimes, 69–72, *70t*, *71t*
Criminal justice system. *See* School-to-prison pipeline
Current Population Survey (CPS), 81, 91, 110

"Dark (or hidden) figure of crime," 57
Dating violence, 136
Death in Custody Reporting Act (2000, 2014), 76, 77
Death sentences, 59–60
Decennial Census, 110
Defending Childhood Initiative, 146
Democratic Party, 98–99
Department of Education, Office of Civil Rights, 22

Department of Housing and Urban Development (HUD), 88
Department of Justice, Civil Rights Division, 88
Depression, 138–45
DeSilva, Sanjaya, 86
Diabetes, 43–48, *47t*
Disability status, 21, 22
Disciplinary actions in education, 2, 20–23
Discriminatory housing practices, 6–7
"Dissimilarity index," 9
Divorce, 120, *121t*, 126–31, *127t*, *129t*
Dropout rates, 23–24, *25t*
Drug abuse, *51t*. *See also* Substance abuse; Teen drug use
Drug arrests, 68, 69
Drug crimes, 64–65
Drug possession, 19
Du Bois, W. E. B., 155

Eagle, David E., 154
Earning potential, 2, 4–5, *5t*
Economic Policy Institute study, 9
Education: achievement, 2–6, *3t*, *5t*; college degree attainment, 120–22; college enrollment, 24–33; data variables overview, 1–2; disciplinary actions, 20–23; divorce and, 128; dropout rates, 23–24; employment and, 82, *83t*; expulsions from school, 16–20; for-profit colleges, 29–30; high school graduation rates, 30, *31t*; learning disabilities and school suspensions, 18; literacy tests and voting, 104; marriage and, 120; parental education, dropout rates and, 24; school segregation, 2, 6–12, *7t*; school-to-prison pipeline, 13–20; segregated schools, 6–12, *7t*; standardized testing, 12–13; suspensions from school, 16–20; voter participation and, 94
Elmelech, Yuval, 86
Employment: data variables overview, 81–82; defined, 81; earning potential, 2, 4–5, *5t*; home ownership and, 85–88; income and voter participation, 94–95; insurance coverage, 37–42, *40t*; job

discrimination, 84–85; unemployment and, 82–85, *83t*, *84t*. *See also* Unemployment
Enlightenment theory, 6
Equal Credit Opportunity Act, 88
Estate planning, 126
Ethnic–racial socialization, 144
Expulsions from school, 16–20, 20, *21t*

Fair Housing Act (FHA), 88
Family: changing definition of, 111, 141; childbearing, marriage and, 122; child custody, 126; cohabitation agreements, 126; cohabitation rates, 112; consanguinity, 111; contraception use, 135, 145; data variables overview, 109–11; defined, 110; divorce, 126–31; gay partnerships, 124–26; interracial marriage, 122, *123t*, 124; legal separations, 126–27; lesbian partnerships, 124–26; marital separations, 126–27; marriage, 112–26, *116t*; marriage–fertility connection, 122; media, influence on teen pregnancy, 135–36; multiracial couples, 122, *123t*; nuclear family defined, 111; prenuptial/postnuptial agreements, 126; same-sex couples/households, 124–25, *125t*; serial cohabitation, 112; single mothering rates, 112; single-parent homes, 122, *123t*; teen depression, 138–45, *140t*, *142t*; teen drug use, 137–38, *137t*; teen pregnancy, 131–36, *132t*, *133t*; teen violence, 145–51, *147t*, *149t*; traditional family and race, 111–12, *113t*; unmarried partners, defined, 111
Family-formation behaviors, 122
Family group, defined, 111
Family household, defined, 110
Federal Bureau of Investigation (FBI), 57
Felony disenfranchisement, 99–106, *100t*, *102t*
Fifteenth Amendment, 105–6
Firearms use, 72
Fletcher, Pinar O., 85
For-profit colleges, 29–30
Fourth Amendment, 65

Frazier, E. Franklin, 155
Friedman, Risa, 54
Friedman, Samuel R., 54

Gay partnerships, 124–26
Gender disparity, 2, 4, 24, *28t*
Generational poverty, 6–7, 9
Gibson-Davis, Christina, 122
Golub, Andrew, 112
Gonorrhea rates, 145
González, Thalia, 19
Grube, Joel W., 136
Gruber, Enid, 136
Gun-Free School Zones Act (1990), 18
Gun laws, 72

Hate crimes, 72–74, *73t*, *75t*
Health: causes of death, 37, *38t*; data variables overview, 35–36; depression, 138–45, *140t*, *142t*; diabetes, 43–48, *47t*; heart disease, *38t*, 48–50; insurance coverage, 37–42, *40t*; life expectancy, 37, *38t*; major depressive disorder (MDD), 139; mental health, 154; obesity, 42–43, *44t*; primary issues, 36–37; self-perception, suicide and, 144; substance abuse, 50–55
Heart disease, *38t*, 48–50
Heslin, Peter A., 85
High blood pressure (HBP). *See* Heart disease
High cholesterol. *See* Heart disease
High school graduation rates, 30, *31t*
Holder, Eric, 61, 67–68, 106
Home ownership, 2, 85–88, *87t*
Homicide rates, 72
Homosexuality, 124–26
Household, defined, 110
Householder, defined, 110
Housing Discrimination Survey, 86

Illegal drugs, 137–38. *See also* Substance abuse
Iloh, Constance, 29
Income, voter participation and, 94–95
Ingraham, Christopher, 74
Insurance coverage, 37–42, *40t*
Integration, measure of, 9

Interracial marriage, 122, *123t*, 124
Ishitani, Terry T., 5–6

Jail for life without parole (JLWOP), 146, *147t*
Job discrimination, 84–85
Job participation, 4, *5t*, 11. *See also* Employment
Johnson, Deborah J., 4
Johnson, Oliver J., 144
Jury selection, 68–69
Juvenile arrests, 69, 146, *147t*, *149t*

Kennedy, John F., 98
Kennedy, Robert, 98
Kim, Jeounghee, 120
King, Martin Luther, Jr., 98
Kirwan Institute for the Study of Race and Ethnicity, 22
Kohli, Sonali, 10

Labor market participation, 4–6, *5t*. *See also* Employment
Learning disabilities, school suspensions and, 18
Legal separations, 126–27
Legislation: Affordable Care Act (2010), 39; Civil Rights Act (1964), 6, 88, 98, 124; Death in Custody Reporting Act (2000, 2014), 76, 77; Fair Housing Act (FHA), 88; Gun-Free School Zones Act (1990), 18; gun laws, 72; National Defense Authorization Act (1997), 78; Omnibus Consolidated Appropriation Act (1997), 18; Patient Protection and Affordable Care Act (2010), 39; Religious Land Use and Institutionalized Persons Act (RLUIPA), 88; Servicemembers Civil Relief Act (SCRA), 88; Voting Rights Act (1965), 98, 104
Lesbian partnerships, 124–26
LGBT students (lesbian, gay, bisexual, transgender), 16
Life expectancy, 37, *38t*
Life without parole (LWOP), 59, 146
Lincoln, Abraham, 98
Litcher, Daniel T., 124

Literacy tests, voting and, 104
Littlefield, Marci Bounds, 155
Loan delinquency and default, 29
Long-term unemployment, 84, *84t*
Loving v. Virginia (1967), 124
Lustig, Daniel C., 5–6

Major depressive disorder (MDD), 139
Marijuana use, 137. *See also* Drug abuse
Marriage, 112–26, *116t*
Marriage–fertility connection, 122
Mauer, Marc, 69
McDaniel, Anne, 2, 4
Media, influence on teen pregnancy, 135–36
Median income, homicide rates and, 72
Mental health, religion and, 154
Messner, Steven F., 145–46
Military weapons, 78
Miller, Byron, 139
Milliken v. Bradley (1974), 7
Mullainathan, Sendhil, 84–85
Multiracial couples, 122, *123t*
Murder rates, 72

Names, ethnic-sounding, 84–85
National Advancement of Colored People (NAACP) Legal Defense Fund, 17–18
National Campaign to Prevent Teen Pregnancy, 136
National Crime Victimization Survey (NCVS), 57
National Defense Authorization Act (1997), 78
National Education Association report, 16
National Incident-Based Reporting System (NIBRS), 58
National Longitudinal Survey of Youth, 128
The Negro Church (Du Bois), 155
The Negro Church in America (Frazier), 155
Neighborhood segregation, 9
Nicholson-Crotty, Sean, 68
"NIMBY (not-in-my-backyard) syndrome," 10
Nixon, Richard, 98

"No Child Left Behind," 11, 17
Nuclear family, defined, 111

Obama, Barack, 11, 58, 78, 105
Obamacare, 39
Obesity, 42–43, *44t*, *45t*
Ochs, Holona Leanne, 101
Omnibus Consolidated Appropriation Act
    (1997), 18
Opportunity Agenda (2012), 124–25

Pager, Devah, 69
Parental education, dropout rates and, 24
Patient Protection and Affordable Care Act
    (2010), 39
Perry, Armon R., 19, 124, 154
Physical health, religion and, 154
Plea bargains, 69
Police shootings, 74–78, 77–78, *77t*
Political disenfranchisement, 10
Political views, religion and, 154, 156–57
Poll taxes, 104
Poverty: disposition for violence and, 146;
    dropout rates and, 24; education gap
    and, 9; school segregation and, 6–7;
    teen pregnancy and, 136; violent crime
    and, 72
Prenuptial/postnuptial agreements, 126
Primary health issues, 36–37
Prison population and arrests, 58–61, *60t*,
    146
Probable cause, 65
Property crime, defined, 57
*Public Opinion and Discourse on the
    Intersection of Lesbian, Gay, Bi-sexual,
    and Transgender (LGBT) Issues and
    Race,* 124–25
"Punishment gap," 17
Punishment *vs.* rehabilitation, 23

Qian, Zhenchao, 124

Race–religion relationship, 155–57
"Race to the Top," 17
Racial disparities, causes of death and, 37,
    38t
Racial isolation, 9
Racial profiling, 19, 61–69, *62t*

Racist beliefs, religion and, 154
Raley, R. Kelly, 127
Read, Jen'nan G., 154
Readiness tests. *See* Standardized testing
Reid, Karl, 4, 112
Religion: black church as community
    cornerstone, 154–55; church attendance,
    156; civic behaviors and, 154; data
    variables overview, 153–54; Du Bois
    on, 155; Frazier on, 155; impacts on
    social interactions and civic behaviors,
    154; race–religion relationship, 155–57
Religious Land Use and Institutionalized
    Persons Act (RLUIPA), 88
Republican Party, 98–99
Residential isolation, 9
"Restorative justice" practices, 19
Ross, Cody, 76

Same-sex couples/households, 124–25,
    124–26, *125t*
SAT scores, 13, *14t*
Saunders, Mark, 48
Scheindlin, Shira A., 65–66
Scholastic aptitude tests, 12
School segregation, 2, 6–12, *7t*
School-to-prison pipeline, 2, 13–20
Schorling, John B., 48
Seasonal workers. *See* Employment
Self-perception, suicide and, 144
Sentencing disparities, 19, 59, *60t*, 69
Sentencing Project: felony
    disenfranchisement, 101; incarceration
    rates, 59–60; JLWOP and, 146;
    mandatory minimum sentences, 69;
    racial profiling, 64–65
Separations, marital, 126–27
Serial cohabitation, 112
Servicemembers Civil Relief Act (SCRA),
    88
Sex as entertainment, 135–36
Sexual abuse and violence, 136
Sexually transmitted diseases (STDs),
    144–45
Shelby County, Alabama v. Holder (2013),
    104, 105
Single mothering rates, 112
Single-parent homes, 122, *123t*

Smith, Peggy B., 139
Social interactions, religion and, 154
Socioeconomic status and depression, 138–45, *140t, 142t*
Somers, Cheryl L., 135
Specific aptitude tests, 12
Standardized testing, 2, 12–13, *14t*
Stanford University Center for Education Policy Analysis, 9
Status dropout rate, 24, *25t*
"Stop and frisk" tactics, 65–67
Stroke. *See* Heart disease
Structural racism, 146, 151
Subfamily, defined, 111
Substance abuse, 50–55, *52t*, 138–45
"Sugar." *See* Diabetes
Suicide, 139–40, 144
Survey of Income and Program Participation (SIPP), 110
Suspensions from school, 16–20, *21t*
Sweeney, Megan M., 127

Task Force on Children Exposed to Violence, 146
Taylor, John, 139
Taylor, Robert J., 155
Teen depression, 138–45, *140t, 142t*
Teen drug use, 137–38, *137t*
Teen pregnancy, 131–36, *132t, 133t*
Teen violence, 145–51, *147t, 149t*
Tempalski, Barbara, 54
Temporary workers. *See* Employment
Terry v. Ohio (1968), 65
Test, Punish and Push Out: How Zero Tolerance and High-Stakes Testing Funnel Youth Into The School, 19
Toldson, Ivory, 29
Tracking (educational process), 10, 11
Traditional family and race, 111–12, *113t*
20/20 (news program), 85
Tynan, Joshua J., 135

Unemployment, *83t, 84t*; defined, 81, 82; education achievement and, 4–5, *5t*;

for-profit colleges and, 30; homicide rates and, 72; long-term, 84, *84t*. *See also* Employment
Uniform Crime Reporting (UCR) program, 57
United Nations Committee Against Torture, 76
United States v. Alfonso Lopez, Jr. (1995), 18
Unmarried partners, defined, 111
Unmarried sex, 132–36
Unreasonable searches and seizures, 65
U.S. Department of Labor, 81
U.S. prison population and arrests, 58–61, *60t*

Valentine, David, 68
Vazan, Peter, 112
Vera Institute of Justice, 67
Victimization rates, 70, *71t*
Violent crimes, 57, 69–72, *70t, 71t*
Voting: data variables overview, 91–92; education and, 94; political party identification, 98–99; rates, 92–98, *93t, 96t*; voter disenfranchisement, 99–106, *100t*; voter I.D. requirements, 104–6
Voting Rights Act (1965), 98, 104

Waight, Consuelo Luisa, 11
Walsenmann, Katrina, 10
War on Drugs, 19, 61
Wealth accumulation, religion and, 154
Weinman, Maxine L., 139
Wentling, Rose Mary, 11
Wexler, Evan, 9
White House Initiative on Educational Excellence for African Americans (Obama), 11–12
Wodtke, Geoffrey T., 6
Wondra, Danielle, 127

Zanskas, Stephen, 5–6
Zero-tolerance policies, 13, 16, 18–19, 22
Zimmerman, Gregory M., 145–46
Zimroth, Peter L., 66

About the Author

Glenn L. Starks holds a doctorate in public policy and administration from Virginia Commonwealth University's L. Douglas Wilder School of Government and Public Affairs. He has 25 years of experience working for the U.S. government and has written extensively on public administration and American politics, including two recent books on the history of the U.S. government. He has also taught graduate courses in public administration and policy at several universities. He currently teaches graduate-level courses for Walden University.